Romania

WORLD BIBLIOGRAPHICAL SERIES

General Editors:
Robert L. Collison (Editor-in-chief)
Sheila R. Herstein
Louis J. Reith
Hans H. Wellisch

VOLUMES IN THE SERIES

VOLUME 59

Romania

Andrea Deletant
Dennis Deletant
compilers

CLIO PRESS

OXFORD, ENGLAND · SANTA BARBARA, CALIFORNIA
DENVER, COLORADO

British Library Cataloguing in Publication Data

Deletant, Andrea
Romania. – (World bibliographical series; 59)
1. Romania – Bibliography
I. Title II. Deletant, Dennis III. Series
016.9498   Z2921

ISBN 1-85109-002-9

Clio Press Ltd.,
55 St. Thomas' Street,
Oxford OX1 1JG, England.

ABC-Clio Information Services,
Riviera Campus, 2040 Alameda Padre Serra,
Santa Barbara, Ca. 93103, USA

Designed by Bernard Crossland
Typeset by Columns Design and Production Services, Reading, England
Printed and bound in Great Britain by
Billing and Sons Ltd., Worcester

THE WORLD BIBLIOGRAPHICAL SERIES

This series will eventually cover every country in the world, each in a separate volume comprising annotated entries on works dealing with its history, geography, economy and politics; and with its people, their culture, customs, religion and social organization. Attention will also be paid to current living conditions – housing, education, newspapers, clothing, etc. – that are all too often ignored in standard bibliographies; and to those particular aspects relevant to individual countries. Each volume seeks to achieve, by use of careful selectivity and critical assessment of the literature, an expression of the country and an appreciation of its nature and national aspirations, to guide the reader towards an understanding of its importance. The keynote of the series is to provide, in a uniform format, an interpretation of each country that will express its culture, its place in the world, and the qualities and background that make it unique.

SERIES EDITORS

Robert L. Collison (Editor-in-chief) is Professor Emeritus, Library and Information Studies, University of California, Los Angeles, and is currently the President of the Society of Indexers. Following the war, he served as Reference Librarian for the City of Westminster and later became Librarian to the BBC. During his fifty years as a professional librarian in England and the USA, he has written more than twenty works on bibliography, librarianship, indexing and related subjects.

Sheila R. Herstein is Reference Librarian and Library Instruction Coordinator at the City College of the City University of New York. She has extensive bibliographic experience and has described her innovations in the field of bibliographic instruction in 'Team teaching and bibliographic instruction', *The Bookmark*, Autumn 1979. In addition, Doctor Herstein coauthored a basic annotated bibliography in history for Funk & Wagnalls *New encyclopedia*, and for several years reviewed books for *Library Journal*.

Louis J. Reith is librarian with the Franciscan Institute, St. Bonaventure University, New York. He received his PhD from Stanford University, California, and later studied at Eberhard-Karls-Universität, Tübingen. In addition to his activities as a librarian, Dr. Reith is a specialist on 16th century German history and the Reformation and has published many articles and papers in both German and English. He was also editor of the *American Society for Reformation Research Newsletter*.

Hans H. Wellisch is a Professor at the College of Library and Information Services, University of Maryland, and a member of the American Society of Indexers and the International Federation for Documentation. He is the author of numerous articles and several books on indexing and abstracting, and has also published *Indexing and abstracting: an international bibliography*. He also contributes frequently to *Journal of the American Society for Information Science*, *Library Quarterly*, and *The Indexer*.

Contents

Contents

Contents

Contents

Introduction

Romania is a country of paradox. Although it is a member of the Warsaw Pact, it does not participate in joint military exercises nor, until recently, did it allow troops of the Pact on its territory. Despite being a socialist republic, the state supports the Romanian Orthodox Church and pays a stipend to its clergy. Romania was the first country in the Eastern bloc to establish diplomatic relations with West Germany (in 1967), and is the only country from the group to have diplomatic ties with Israel. In 1971 she adhered to GATT (General Agreement on Trade and Tariffs) and in the following year joined the International Monetary Fund and the World Bank. Romania's commercial position was further enhanced when she acquired preferential trading status with the Common Market in 1973, while remaining a member of the CMEA (Council for Mutual Economic Assistance), popularly known as Comecon.

Romania's pilot on this devious course has been Nicolae Ceauşescu, whose political agility has ensured him undisputed leadership of the Romanian Communist Party since 1965. The direction of his apparently independent foreign policy has intrigued Western political commentators since his condemnation in 1968 of the Warsaw Pact intervention in Czechoslovakia. In 1979 Ceauşescu attacked the Soviet invasion of Afghanistan; in 1982 he opposed Warsaw Pact plans to increase defence spending and in fact reduced Romania's defence budget. In the following year he repeated his call for a halt to the arms race and advocated multilateral nuclear disarmament in Europe. In 1984 he proposed a moratorium on the deployment of new nuclear weapons in Europe and at the same time refused to join the Soviet-led boycott of the Olympic Games in Los Angeles.

Ceauşescu has used the unique position that Romania has won for itself to act as a broker between East and West, thereby hoping to acquire international stature as a world statesman. Yet

Introduction

to most English-speaking people Romania is only a name on the map; confusion reigns in the minds of many as to whether Budapest or Bucharest is the country's capital. This ignorance of Romania is startling in view of the size of her population, 22 millions, and is indicative of an isolation from the West that has been abetted by the régime's restrictions on travel abroad for Romanian tourists and professional persons alike. The imbalance between the numbers of foreign tourists to Romania (5 millions in 1978 of whom 4.2 millions were from Eastern bloc countries including Yugoslavia) and of Romanian tourists abroad (estimated at less than 75,000 in 1978) partly explains why Romania has not made the imprint on the collective Western consciousness that is sought by the forces of light in the country.

Without doubt Romania's geographical position has contributed to her predicament. Situated at the crossroads of Europe, Romania has since early times been prey to successive waves of invaders. Her fertile soil and deposits of gold attracted a motley collection of early peoples, among them the Scythians and Thracians. It was a branch of the latter, the Dacians, that the Romans conquered between AD 101 and 106 during the reign of Trajan. The new province of Dacia was colonized by settlers from various parts of the Empire who, according to most Romanian historians, came in sufficient numbers to romanize the local population by implanting the Latin language and civilization. The resultant Daco-Roman people are said to be the forebears of the Romanians. After the withdrawal of the Roman legions between 271 and 275, Dacia became a gateway to the south for invaders from the Russian steppe and from Central Europe, the Daco-Romans retreating to the mountains and thus preserving their Latin language. It is more generally maintained, however, that the Romanians are derived from a wider group of romanized inhabitants of the Balkans known as Vlachs, who lived south of the Danube. The language of the latter, which today survives only in pockets in Istria, northern Greece, and southern Albania, shares with Romanian a similar development from Latin, but the Vlach's Roman pedigree is more established than that of the Romanians. Whereas the ancestors of the Vlachs lived under Roman rule for several centuries, the Dacians were subject to the Romans for little over one hundred and fifty years. Several historians, amongst them Romanians, have questioned whether the Romanians are descendants of romanized Dacians (Daco-Romans) and suggest instead that they derive from the Vlachs who migrated north of the Danube in the 12th and 13th centuries. The latter theory is championed in particular by Hungarian historians who argue that when the Magyars entered the central Danubian basin at the end of the 9th century, the only inhabitants of Transylvania (largely the former Dacia) were Slavonic tribes, and that the Romanians only migrated to the province at the end of the 12th century from south of the Carpathians, whence Romanian shepherds were given the right to settle in Transylvania by the Hungarian kings. Both theories are posited on mutually acceptable premises which we can reconcile by claiming that the Romanians probably derive from romanized Dacians whose numbers were strengthened by Vlach immigration from south of the Danube.

The ethnic mix in what is now Romania was enriched by the Magyar occupation of Transylvania which we have already mentioned. The Hungarian crown extended its authority over this region by encouraging Szekel and German colonists to settle during the 12th and 13th centuries. The former were a non-Magyar tribe which entered the Danubian basin with the Magyars in the 9th century; the German settlers came largely from the archbishopric of Cologne and from the bishopric of Trier. A centuries-old Hungarian link with Transylvania was thus forged and its severance, by the Treaty of Trianon (1920) when the province was awarded to Romania (on the basis that eleven of its fifteen counties had a clear Romanian majority), has left the most substantial minority in Romania, totalling almost two millions according to the 1977 census. The German minority is the second most important, numbering about 350,000, but this figure has been dwindling since emigration to West Germany was permitted in the 1960s.

The embryo of organized rule south of the Carpathians did not develop until the beginning of the 14th century. An attempt by the Hungarian king to establish his authority over the area was successfully resisted by Basarab, a prince of Cuman origin, in 1330, the date to which the emergence of the principality of Wallachia is traced. Hungarian interests also led to the creation of the sister principality to the east, Moldavia; this time, however, the Hungarian crown acted as midwife. To protect the crown's interests east of the Carpathians the noble Dragoş was granted a fiefdom circa 1347. From this, following a revolt against the Hungarian king by Dragoş's successor Bogdan, grew the principality of Moldavia.

It may be said that the history of both principalities until their union in 1859, and their final deliverance from Turkish suzerainty in 1881 when they acquired the status of a kingdom, was forged between various imperial hammers and anvils – those of Turkey, Austria, and Russia. The only Romanian figures who were masters rather than servants of events during the early part of this period were Stephen the Great, Prince of Moldavia (1457–1504), and Michael the Brave, Prince of Wallachia (1593–1601). The former successfully bore the brunt of Europe's defence against the Turks in several battles fought on his native Moldavian soil; Michael, by uniting, for a brief period in 1600, Transylvania, Moldavia, and Wallachia under his rule, ignited a fire in the imagination of Romanians which in later years acquired greater brilliance in the prevailing wind of political circumstance.

This dream of Romanian unity was realized as a result of the First World War. In return for Romania's entry into the war in 1916 on the Allied side, the Treaty of Trianon (June 1920) gave her Transylvania, and recognized Bessarabia as an integral part of the Romanian kingdom. The problems confronting the enlarged state after the war remained unsolved. Corrupt governments, subservient to sectional interests of the large landowners, the banks, or the prominent industrialists, were unable to implement the economic and social reforms sought by the bulk of the peasantry. The aftermath of the Wall Street Crash in 1929 doomed any such plans and unhinged the country, fostering an instability in which extreme right-wing movements flourished. The failure of the Western democracies to provide moral leadership in the face of Nazi Germany, their inability to come to Romania's military assistance, and the menace, even more sinister in Romanians' eyes, of the Soviet Union and of Bolshevism, finally drove Romania into the arms of Hitler. The latter was seen by Romania's dictator, General (later Marshal) Antonescu, as the only guarantor of his country's integrity against the Soviet Union which had occupied Bessarabia in June 1940, notwithstanding Hitler's own imposition some two months later of the Vienna award, by which Romania was forced to cede northern Transylvania to Hungary.

Romania's participation in the German invasion of the Soviet Union in June 1941 was characterized by Antonescu as a defensive move to pre-empt a Soviet attack on Romania and as a 'holy' crusade against Communism. The Anglo-American air raids on Romania during 1943 and, more importantly, the Soviet advance in early 1944 made Antonescu aware of the fragility of his position and led him to seek armistice terms that would guarantee Romania's independence of Soviet authority. His inability to obtain these, and his reluctance to abandon the German army which was now on the defensive, determined the opposition parties to plot his overthrow. Events, however, forced King Michael to take the initiative and he boldly arrested Antonescu on 23 August 1944. The hopes for the inauguration of democracy in Romania were short-lived for the Russians, who entered Bucharest on 31 August, employed blatant political engineering to impose their authority on the people. A puppet government under Petru Groza, appointed on 6 March 1945, supervised the first steps to communize the country which involved the arrest and imprisonment of virtually all political opponents. The complete subjugation of Romania to the Soviet Union was marked by the forced abdication of King Michael on 30 December 1947 and the proclamation of the Romanian People's Republic.

The principal political figure of the post-war period in Romania was Gheorghe Gheorghiu-Dej, General Secretary of the Romanian Communist Party (from 1947 Romanian Workers' Party) between 1945 and 1954, and First Secretary from 1955 to his death in 1965. Under his leadership Romania emerged from subservience to the Soviet Union to challenge the latter's supranational pretentions by resisting pressure to become the granary of Comecon and by developing her own industry. Dej was succeeded by Nicolae Ceauşescu as First (later General) Secretary of the RWP, which became the RCP again in June 1965. Under a new constitution, adopted in August 1965, the country's name was changed to the Socialist Republic of Romania. Ceauşescu became President of the State Council in December 1967, and President of the Republic in March 1974.

The semi-independent foreign policy inaugurated by Dej has been continued by Ceauşescu. However, the internal relaxation which took place in the late 1960s was terminated in the early 1970s when, on his return from a visit to China in 1971, Ceauşescu launched a mini cultural revolution. Ideological purity was exalted to the detriment of professional ability, nationalism was loudly trumpeted and, shortly afterwards, the rotation of cadres was introduced as a principle of party policy. The frequent changes of ministers and officials at higher levels had the dual merit of preventing any potential rival from establishing a power-base, and of making such figures dependent on the General Secretary's goodwill. In June 1973 the latter's wife, Elena, entered the Central Committee and within a few years had become the second most important figure in the party and state; in March 1980 she was appointed First Deputy Prime Minister. Ceauşescu has made his internal position impregnable by appointing other members of his family to ministerial positions, and is grooming his son Nicu for the succession by recently admitting him to the Central Committee.

Over the last two decades Romania has made impressive economic advances. Industrial expansion was the hallmark of the 1966–70, 1971–75, and 1976–80 Five-Year plans. The revolution in Iran, Romania's principal supplier of crude oil, interrupted oil imports and forced Romania to buy oil on the open market at the increased prices of the late 1970s. The country's foreign debt rose rapidly, reaching 13 billion US dollars at one stage, but it had fallen to 8.5 billion dollars by the summer of 1984. Yet it has been agriculture, largely neglected at the expense of industry during the last twenty years, that has been called upon to increase exports in order to pay off the foreign debt. In 1981 Ceauşescu announced that agriculture was to take priority over rapid industrialization, but the subsequent export of foodstuffs exacerbated an already poor food supply situation in the country. In 1982 rationing of bread, flour, sugar, and milk was introduced in some provincial towns, and in 1983 it was extended to most of the country with the exception of the capital. Further sacrifices were expected from the population with the introduction, in the autumn of 1982, of draconian energy-saving measures. These stipulated maximum temperatures in offices and private dwellings, periods for provision of hot water, and quotas of electricity and gas to be consumed in the home and in industry. In 1984 petrol for the motorist outside Bucharest was rationed to forty litres per month (when available) and there were frequent power cuts.

In spite of the affronts to human dignity represented by official attempts to limit and quantify the amount of soap to be used annually by each person, to control the diet of the individual, and to stipulate how many children each couple should have, Romanians preserve their warmth and hospitality to friends and strangers alike, and exhibit that tolerance and fatalism that has characterized the Romanian peasant throughout his history. In a society that prefers to 'interiorize' its suffering and contempt, the artist has become the repository of the collective conscience, the eyes and voice of judgement on the quality of life. In the current climate expression of that conscience may be tempered, but it cannot be stifled.

Dennis Deletant
November 1984

Introduction

The bibliography

This bibliography makes no claim to be exhaustive. In conformity with the criteria applied in the compilation of the other volumes in this series, the vast majority of the titles listed are in English. Occasionally, a book in a major Western language has been listed when it represents an outstanding contribution to studies of Romania, or when there is no comparable contribution in English. Titles in Romanian are given only where there is no equivalent work available in English, French, or German. Entries are arranged alphabetically by author or, where there is no author credited, by the institution responsible for the work; in the absence of the latter they are listed by title. Inevitably in a selective bibliography of this nature, a number of significant works, for which a case for inclusion can be made, will be absent. Their omission is due either to oversight, ignorance, or inaccessibility. For details of such lacunae we will be grateful.

Acknowledgements

The task of compiling this bibliography was facilitated by the receipt of a grant from the British Academy to enable Dennis Deletant to visit libraries in Romania. We would like to record here our appreciation to that institution. The holdings of the library of the School of Slavonic and East European Studies, University of London, are virtually unique in the English-speaking world in respect of Romania and are the source of many of the entries listed. We should like to thank its librarian, John Screen, and the assistant librarians, D. Bartkiw, John Freeman, and Diane Kemsley, for their help in tracing some of the more obscure publications. Special words of appreciation are merited by Mrs V. Gyenes, responsible for the School's Inter-Library Loans Service, who patiently processed the applications for specialist works unavailable at the School, and by Arthur Helliwell, formerly assistant librarian at SSEES, who was a constant source of advice and assistance. Amongst the several colleagues who offered orientation in those areas of Romanian studies with which we are only superficially familiar, we would like to mention Marvin R. Jackson, Professor of Economics at Arizona State University, Michael Shafir, Lecturer in Political Science at the University of Tel-Aviv, and Frank Carter, Lecturer in Geography at SSEES and at University College, London. Our hope is that the selection of titles in this volume

will not only provide a reference key to each of the areas
covered, but also direct the reader towards an understanding of
Romania's past and present.

Andrea Deletant
Dennis Deletant

The Country
and its People

Older descriptions

1 And then to Transylvania.
Henry Baerlein.   London: Harold Shaylor, 1931. 253p.
A lively travelogue that sparkles with the amusing adventures and encounters of
the author with a representative cross-section of Transylvania's variegated
population.

2 In old Romania.
Henry Baerlein.   London: Hutchinson, 1940. 287p.
Sketches of the life and background of the Romanians in the pre-First World War
Romania that comprised Moldavia and Wallachia only. A companion volume to
Henry Baerlein's *And then to Transylvania*. (q.v.)

3 United Roumania.
Charles Upson Clark.   New York: Dodd, Mead & Co., 1932. 418p.
bibliog.
This rewritten version of the author's *Greater Roumania* (1922), provides a
sympathetic picture of the country and emphasizes history, folk art and peasant
customs. The personal impressions of the author sometimes lead him into
superficiality, particularly in respect of Romania's stance during the First World
War and political developments in the country in the years that followed.

4 The Roumanian handbook.
Norman L. Forter, Demeter B. Rostovsky.   London: Simpkin
Marshall, 1931. 320p.
A mine of information on post First World War Romania with chapters on: the
constitution; legal system; national defence; geography; finance and the economy;

1

literature and art; education and social welfare; and a who's who of leading personalities.

5 Romanian furrow.
Donald J. Hall.   London: Methuen, 1933; Harrap, 1939. 224p. plates.

Described by King Carol II as the 'best book ever written about my country', this entertaining work 'captures the spirit of the Romanian peasantry as no other book by a foreigner or, for that matter, by a Romanian has ever done'. Based on the author's extensive travels and sojourns in the Romanian countryside, this is a faithful and lively account of peasant life and customs.

6 Roumanian pilgrimage.
Margaret R. Loughborough.   London: Society for Promoting Christian Knowledge; New York: Macmillan, 1939. 143p.

A delightful account of the author's visit to a number of monasteries in Romania on the eve of the Second World War. For those uninitiated in the ritual of Orthodox devotion in Romania this is a rich store of information, imparted with a series of sketches of local priests and prelates. The backwardness of village life leads the writer to reflect: 'somehow we feel sure that the sturdy, pious peasantry must win in the end; and the rich earth will turn poverty into riches and contentment, and the problems be solved in wisdom and charity'.

7 European dateline.
Patrick Maitland.   London: Quality Press, 1946. 211p.

An entertaining and informative travelogue by *The Times* correspondent in the Near East. The reader is led through the author's vivid experiences in Albania, Poland, Romania, Bulgaria, Yugoslavia and Greece between 1938 and 1941.

8 Hungary and Transylvania.
John Paget.   London: John Murray, 1855. new ed. 2 vols.

Probably the most influential and widely-read book on Hungary and Transylvania to be published in Britain during the last century. It was influential amongst politicians since it presented Hungary as a significant centre of reform in Central Europe. Volume two, which covers the author's passage down the Danube to the Banat and then across Transylvania, introduced this area to the British public and contains many pertinent observations on behaviour and custom which are not without relevance to present-day life in Transylvania.

9 Roumanian journey.
Sacheverell Sitwell.   London: B. T. Batsford, 1938. 120p.

A graphic account of the author's experiences and impressions which is notable for the splendid photographs by A. Costa and Richard Wyndham. Sitwell's eye for detail, his vivid presentation of people and places, and his comparisons with sights elsewhere in Europe and Asia, leave the reader with a memorable picture of Romania.

10 **Raggle-taggle: adventures with a fiddle in Hungary and Roumania.**
Walter Starkie. London: John Murray, Albemarle Library, 1947.
342p. bibliog.

A wonderfully evocative account of the writer's experiences with the gypsies in
Hungary and Romania during the inter-war years. Starkie's splendid accounts of
his adventures together with his observations ensure continuous enjoyment for
the reader and make this one of the first authentic books on the gypsies in Central
and Eastern Europe.

11 **Ikons and oxen.**
Philip Thornton. London: Collins, 1939. 300p.

Chapter two of this travelogue opens with the observation 'passports, visas, spy
mania, fantastic currency laws, and fanatical nationalism have made a journey
east of Budapest far from inviting'. This is not the only conclusion that Thornton
draws from his travels in Romania that still has some validity in the 1980s.

12 **An account of the principalities of Wallachia and Moldavia with
various political observations relating to them.**
William Wilkinson. London: Longman, Hurst, Rees, Orme &
Brown, 1820. 294p.

'An official residence of some years in the principalities of Moldavia and
Wallachia afforded me the most ample opportunities of observation on every
thing they contain most interesting, and I have endeavoured to make an accurate
and satisfactory description of them'. Wilkinson's balanced and judicious
assessment of the 'mores' of political life in the principalities during the final years
of Phanariot rule, coupled with his descriptions of the towns and of their
population, make this not only a fascinating record of the period, but also an
indispensable key to an understanding of the Romanian political mind.

Recent descriptions

13 **The socialist republic of Romania.**
Edited by A. Alberti. Milan: Edizioni del Calendario, 1979. 564p.

A lavishly illustrated encyclopaedic survey of contemporary Romania, produced
in collaboration with the Institute of Historical and Socio-Political Studies of the
Central Committee of the Romanian Communist Party.

14 **All about Romania in 50 questions and answers.**
Bucharest: Editura ştiinţifică şi enciclopedică, 1981. 95p.

Some of the answers to the questions asked about Romania's history, culture,
economy, political system, educational system and demography may not be
acceptable to the discerning reader but this booklet is still of informative value.

15 **Romanian invitation.**
William Forwood, foreword by C. P. Snow. London: Garnstone
Press, 1968. 128p.

A guide to, and general survey of, modern Romania which is designed for the
traveller. It is dated in some respects, but notable for some fine photographs.

16 **Romania: a developing socialist state.**
Lawrence S. Graham. Boulder, Colorado: Westview Press, 1982.
136p. bibliog.

One of a series of 'profiles' of East European states designed to introduce the
undergraduate student and general reader to Romania. The history of the
Communist Party in Romania is clearly presented but the use of ill-defined terms
such as 'democratic centralism' and 'bureaucratic authoritarianism' are likely to
cause problems for the audience to which the book is addressed. The author's
background as an expert on Latin America allows him both to provide interesting
appreciations of Romania and to make occasional perverse comparisons.

17 **Südosteuropa-Handbuch. Band II. Rumänien** (Handbook of south-
eastern Europe. Vol. II. Romania.)
Edited by K-D. Grothusen. Göttingen, GFR: Vandenhoeck und
Ruprecht, 1977. 711p.

The most comprehensive and topical area study of Romania. There are separate
sections on: political organization; the economy; society and social structure; and
cultural life. There are also documentary and bibliographical aids which include a
number of excellent survey articles in both German and English. Among the most
notable are: D. Ghermani's 'Die Rumänische Kommunistische Partei' (The
Romanian Communist Party) (p. 11-41); S. Fischer-Galaţi's 'Foreign Policy' (p.
198-231); W. Gumpel's 'Das Wirtschaftssystem' (The Economic System) (p. 259-
94); and A. U. Gabanyi's 'Literatur' (Literature) (p. 527-56).

18 **Ceauşescu's Romania: a political documentary.**
Julian Hale. London: Harrap, 1971. 208p. bibliog.

A political travelogue of use not only to students of contemporary Romania but
also to the more discerning traveller. The author describes perceptively and
authoritatively Romania's relations with her neighbours and the West; discusses
the role of the Communist Party; examines the part played by the press; and
discusses the system of education and the state of industry, as well as providing a
picture of everyday urban life.

19 **Rumanian summer: a view of the Rumanian people's republic.**
Jack Lindsay, with the collaboration of Maurice Cornforth.
London: Lawrence & Wishart, 1953. 152p.

An extremely myopic view of life in Stalinist Romania in which the authors see
only what it suits their creed to see. Much of the book reflects the literature of
official Romanian propaganda of the time. The notorious construction of the
Black Sea Canal, which cost many thousands of lives, is introduced in the
following terms: 'the token and expression of the New Rumania lies today in the

canal being cut between the Danube and the Black Sea' (p. 28). There is a tragic irony in these words.

20 **Dracula country: travels and folk beliefs in Romania.**
Andrew Mackenzie. London: Arthur Barker, 1977. 176p. bibliog.

A lively account of the author's travels in Romania in the steps of the Wallachian prince Vlad III who has been dubbed 'the historical Dracula'. Occasionally the book lapses into an apologia for the present régime but the book is very entertaining, particularly concerning folk beliefs which were once prevalent.

21 **Romanian journey.**
Andrew Mackenzie. London: Robert Hale, 1983. 240p. bibliog.

A valuable introduction to contemporary Romania for the visitor that stresses the positive aspects of the country and the life-style of the people. For a writer who is described on the cover as 'having visited Romania more times than any other writer in the West', there are some hasty and superficial conclusions drawn about religious worship and the role of the trade unions, but the historical background presented is both accurate and judicious. Contains a guide to Romanian pronunciation and a list of useful Romanian phrases.

22 **Romania: a profile.**
Ian M. Matley. New York: Praeger; London: Pall Mall Press, 1970. 292p. bibliog.

An introduction to contemporary Romania for the general reader which covers, for example, history, geography, cultural life and ethnic groups.

23 **Romania, eternal land: an ages-old civilization.**
Ion Miclea, English version by Sergiu Celac. Sibiu, Romania: Transilvania Publishing, 1982. n.p. 104 colour plates.

This is a richly illustrated homage to Romanian traditional craftsmanship. It contains sections on: agriculture; wine-making; fruit-growing; chandlery; fishing; shepherding; weaving; pottery; mining; painting; and lumbering and milling. The photographs are accompanied by explanatory notes and the volume is introduced by an historical survey of Romanian crafts by Corneliu Bucur which includes extensive bibliographical references.

24 **Romania.**
In: *The Europa yearbook 1984: a world survey.* London: Europa Publications, 1984. vol. 1, part 2, p. 753-70.

This annual survey provides statistics on population, agriculture, forestry, fishing, mining, industry, trade, transport and education followed by a directory covering the constitution, government, diplomatic representation, judicial system, religion, the press, publishers, radio and television, trade and industry, transport, tourism and atomic energy.

25 **Romania: an encyclopaedic survey.**
Bucharest: Editura ştiinţifică şi enciclopedică, 1980. 262p. map.
bibliog.

This is a compilation of contributions on the geography, history, economy and
culture of Romania which serves as a useful handbook on the country. The
contributions are unsigned and, in places, lack balance.

26 **Ceauşescu's land.**
Anthony Stuart. *Survey*, no. 76 (summer 1970), p. 112-21.

A comparison of the pessimistic moods and attitudes expressed in Romania in
1970 with the sense of optimistic expectation before, and immediately after, the
invasion of Czechoslovakia in 1968.

Geography

Maps and atlases

27 **Atlas des Donauländer** (Atlas of the Danubian countries.)
    Edited by Josef Brew.   Vienna: Österreichisches Ost-und
    Südeuropa Institut, 1970. maps in binders.

Provides maps and legends in German, English, French and Russian of the
Danubian lands including Romania. The maps are arranged under four headings:
physical features; demography; economy; and communications.

28 **Atlasul din Republica Socialistă România** (Atlas of the counties of
    the Socialist Republic of Romania.)
    Bucharest: Editura didactică şi pedagogică, 1978. 140p.

Each of Romania's thirty-eight counties, together with the municipality of
Bucharest, is represented by physical, economic and tourist maps in this finely
produced atlas. The appendix contains details of the population, the economy,
and of the principal towns of each county.

29 **Atlasul Republicii Socialiste România (Atlas of the Socialist Republic
    of Romania.)**
    Bucharest: Editura Academiei Republicii Socialiste România, 1974-
    79. 5 fascicules (1. 1974, 2. 1975, 3. 1976, 4. 1977, and 5. 1979).

This definitive atlas of Romania is divided into thirteen sections containing
seventy-six maps which present aspects of the physical, economic and social
geography of the country. The introduction is followed by sections on geology,
relief, climate, rivers, soil and vegetation, history and toponymy, population,
settlements, industry, agriculture and transport.

7

30 **Ghidul străzilor municipiului Bucureşti (Guide to the streets of the municipality of Bucharest).**
Alexandru Ionescu, Dan Emanoil. Bucharest: Editura Consiliului Naţional pentru Educaţie Fizică şi Sport, 1969. 215p. 143 maps.
An 'A to Z' of Bucharest's streets that surpasses in scope all other guides to the city's thoroughfares published before or since. Each map is divided by a grid into sections and there is an extensive street index giving the grid reference and city sector. Although new development of the city has taken place since 1969, no complementary guide has been published.

31 **International maps and atlases in print.**
Edited by Kenneth L. Winch. Essex, England: Bowker, 1976. 870p.
Section 498, p. 231-32 covers Romania and is divided as follows: A 1. General maps, Roads. C. Official surveys. D. Political and administrative. E 1. Physical: relief. F. Geology. G. Earth resources. L. Economic and O. National atlases.

32 **România: atlas rutier (Romania: road atlas.)**
Vasile Dragomir, Victor Balea, Gheorghe Mureşanu, Gheorghe Epuran. Bucharest: Editura Sport-Turism, 1982. 204p.
The most detailed road atlas of Romania published since the last war in Romania. The country is divided into seventy-three sections on a scale of 1:350.000 and each section has a separate page. These are supplemented by forty pages of town plans, a glossary of road signs, and an index of place-names.

General

33 **Eastern Europe: a geography of the Comecon countries.**
Roy E. H. Mellor. London: Macmillan; New York: Columbia University Press, 1975. 358p. bibliog.
A systematic survey of the human geography of the communist countries of Eastern Europe, in which particular attention is accorded to the impact of Comecon and to the results of a generation of Soviet-inspired economic policies. However, local variations in the application of these policies are underlined. The book is divided into three parts entitled 'Physical environment and political geography'; 'The demographic and economic framework'; and 'Comecon and the national economies'.

34 **Eastern Europe.**
Norman Pounds. London: Longman; Chicago, Illinois: Aldine, 1969. 912p. bibliog.
A lucid introduction to the major aspects of the geography of Eastern Europe. The chapter on Romania (p. 530-616) covers physical geography, population and settlement, agriculture, industrial development, trade and communications.

35 **Eastern Europe.**
David Turnock. Folkestone, England: William Dawson & Sons;
Boulder, Colorado: Westview Press, 1978. 273p. bibliog.

Notwithstanding its general title, Romania figures prominently in this survey of industrial development in Eastern Europe. Much of the data provided refers to Romanian industrial performance in the inter-war and post-war periods.

36 **An economic geography of Romania.**
David Turnock. London: G. Bell & Sons, 1974. 319p. maps.
bibliog. (Bell's Advanced Economic Geographies).

One of the first studies in English of the modern economic geography of Romania. The author examines in detail, and with an impressive knowledge of incidental information, the physical resources of the country, its agriculture and forestry, industry and power supplies, and concludes by offering an explanation of Romania's reluctance to become heavily reliant upon Comecon.

37 **Romania. Economic and social geography.**
Ion Velcea, translated from the Romanian by Carol Kormos.
Bucharest: Meridiane Publishing House, 1976. 152p. maps. bibliog.

A fine translation of a succinct textbook with chapters on: population and human settlements; industrial geography; communications and transport; and forestry. Well-illustrated with maps and photographs.

Special aspects

38 **The socialist city. Spatial structure and urban policy.**
Edited by R. A. French, Ian Hamilton. Chichester, England: John
Wiley, 1979. 541p. maps. bibliog.

The general title obscures two important contributions on Romanian cities in this collective volume: Gordon Church's, 'Bucharest: Revolution in townscape art' (p. 493-506) and Steven Sampson's, 'Urbanization – Planned and unplanned: a case study of Braşov' (p. 507-24). Significant material on Romania is also contained in Ian Hamilton's chapters 'Urbanization in socialist Eastern Europe' (p. 167-94), 'Spatial structure in East European cities' (p. 195-262) and 'Social processes of residential structure' (p. 263-304), written with A. D. Burnett.

39 **Eastern Europe: essays in geographical problems.**
Edited by George W. Hoffmann. London: Methuen, 1971. 502p.
maps.

Reference to Romania is made in several of the papers in this volume, including, for example Ian Hamilton's 'The location of industry in East and Southeast Europe'. Particular emphasis on developments there is to be found in the contribution of N. Pounds's 'The urbanization of East-Central and Southeast Europe: an historical perspective' (p. 45-82).

Geography. Special aspects

40 **Bucharest: historical perspectives of the Romanian capital.**
David Turnock. *History Today*, vol. 30 (Aug. 1980), p. 14-18.
A concise historical portrait of the Romanian capital with photographs, reproductions of engravings, and maps.

41 **Bucharest: the selection and development of the Romanian capital.**
David Turnock. *Scottish Geographic Magazine*, vol. 86 (1970), p. 53-68.
An outline history of Bucharest, from its selection as seat of the prince of Wallachia in the middle of the 17th century, its succession as capital of the united principalities of Moldavia and Wallachia in 1862 and of Greater Romania after the First World War, down to the present.

42 **The human geography of the Romanian Carpathians with fieldwork studies, 1977.**
David Turnock and members of the Geographical Field Group.
Nottingham, England: Geographical Field Group, 1980. 131p.
A notable contribution to studies of the human geography of Romania which includes chapters on: an historical approach to the pattern of settlement in the Romanian lands; aspects of economic development; and field studies in Harghita county, the Argeş valley, Buzău county, and in the towns of Curtea de Argeş and Borsec.

43 **Restructuring of rural settlement in Rumania.**
David Turnock. *Slavonic and East European Review*, vol. 54, no. 1 (Jan. 1976), p. 83-102.
A survey article of research into rural settlement in Romania and an exposition of its results. The author himself concludes: 'Not only does the unitary complex of the national economy imply certain constraints, but dangerous experiments in regionalism are unlikely in a tense international situation, and it is therefore likely that Rumania's regional planning effort will continue to concentrate for the present on the lower order units in the hierarchy and postpone the problems of higher level articulation.'

44 **Sir Charles Hartley and the development of Romania's lower Danube-Black Sea commerce in the late nineteenth century.**
David Turnock. In: *Anglo-Romanian relations after 1821.*
Anuarul Institutului de Istorie şi Arheologie 'A.D. Xenopol'
(Supplement no. 4). Iaşi, Romania: Editura Academiei Republicii Socialiste România, 1983, p. 75-98.
A fascinating study of the improvements made by a British engineer, Sir Charles Hartley, to the Danube mouth during the late 19th century. Drawing on Hartley's diaries and scrap books, the atlases produced by the European Commission of the Danube, and on an unpublished typescript outlining the technical and political considerations affecting the choice of the Sulina channel, the author ably examines Hartley's contribution to some of the largest public works ever to be carried out on Romania's territory.

Environment

45 Environmental pollution.
Anneli Maier. *Radio Free Europe Research*, vol. 8, no. 48 (Dec. 1983), p. 18-21.

Pollution in Romania, in the wake of the drive to industrialize, grew to such proportions in the early 1980s that its effects on the environment were even reported in the Bucharest journal *Flacăra* in autumn 1983. By 1982 Romania's discharge of sulphur dioxide (which combined with water in the atmosphere produces 'acid rain') had increased by 253 per cent when compared with its emission of the gas in 1972, thus pushing the country to the head of the list in this respect in Europe. This article also outlines other forms of pollution in Romania and considers projects which, if implemented, will cause environmental and ecological problems.

46 Portrait of a river.
Guy Mountfort, foreword by Peter Scott. London: Hutchinson, 1962. 207p.

A description of the wildlife of the Danube from its mouth to the city of Budapest. There are fine illustrations by Eric Hosking.

47 Flowers of Rumania.
Rodica Rarău-Bichiceanu, Mircea Bichiceanu. Bucharest: Meridiane Publishing House, 1964. 230p.

Nearly 40 per cent of plants that flower in Europe are to be found in Romania whose flora includes more than 3,500 varieties. Over 200 plates, many in colour, show the types of natural setting for the species presented.

Tourism and travel

48 Your guide to Romania.
Ted Appleton. London: Alvin Redman, 1965. 223p.

Much of the practical information in this guide is no longer valid, and therefore renders it of little use to today's holiday traveller. The historical introduction is, as far as the 20th century is concerned, largely a travesty of events.

49 Camping in Romania.
Bucharest: Ministry of Tourism, 1975. 8p.

A leaflet giving details of camp sites and a map providing their location. The tabulated key to the sites indicates the facilities available at each site. Since publication changes may have occurred in the location and facilities available at each site.

50 **Romania: a guidebook.**
Şerban Cioculescu, Ion Marin Sadoveanu, Sebastian Bonifaciu,
Mircea Grigorescu, Ioana Vasiliu, Marin Mihalache. Bucharest:
Meridiane Publishing House, 1967. 492p. map.

An excellent guide in English with a wealth of historical information for the
traveller although there is a lack of practical details such as addresses, transport
facilities and restaurants.

51 **Holidays in Romania.**
Bucharest: Romanian National Tourist Office. 1958. quarterly.

An illustrated English-language magazine devoted to tourism.

52 **Hotels, villas, motels and inns. Guide book.**
Bucharest: Ministry of Tourism, 1974. 2nd ed. 124p.

Gives details of accommodation facilities and services of most tourist hotels.
Several impressive hotels and motels have been constructed since the publication
of this guide. Tariffs listed are no longer valid.

53 **Romania: a complete guide.**
Peter Latham. London: Garnstone Press, 1967. 245p. bibliog.

Essentially a handbook of facts and figures about contemporary Romania
leavened with the author's highly subjective interpretation of recent Romanian
history. It is divided into four sections: Facts about the country; Living and
travelling; Trade and industry; and Culture and learning. Much of the practical
information for tourists is now dated, but as a reference source for scholars of
Romania the section entitled 'Trade and industry' gives some useful data.

54 **Romania.**
Geneva; Paris; Munich: Nagel Publishers, 1980. 4th ed. 396p. maps.

Presents a great deal of valid information for the traveller and the informed
tourist alike. Its thirty-six pages of town plans are particularly helpful. The
historical data is sound but the details of hotel tariffs and transport are,
inevitably, already in need of revision.

55 **Romania in one, three, seven or ten days.**
Nicolae Minei. Bucharest: Meridiane Publishing House, 1968.
199p.

Although some of the general information presented here concerning tariffs is
dated, the suggestions made for places to be visited in the periods mentioned are
admirable. There are separate sections on Bucharest, the Danube delta, the
painted monasteries, Transylvania, Maramureş and the noteworthy passes in the
Carpathians.

56 **Roumanie.**
François Monmarché. Paris: Librairie Hachette, 1966. 394p. maps. (Les guides bleus).

A splendid guide written in French combining historical information with data on such matters as hotels, garages, restaurants. Although some of this practical information is outdated, the guide is of considerable value for the detail it provides on buildings and places of interest.

57 **Romania offers you.**
Carpaţi-Bucureşti National Tourist Office. Bucharest: Publiturism, 1983. 112p.

The most complete and up-to-date guide to the tourist facilities offered in Romania by the National Tourist Office. Provides details of: organized tours; spas and medical treatment; summer and winter holidays; professional programmes and hotels.

58 **Romania by car.**
Vasile Tănăsescu, translated by Vianu Raimond. Bucharest: Publiturism, 1975. 180p.

An enthusiastic advertisement for Romania's natural and historical treasures. Some of the information for motorists now needs updating. Includes street maps of Romania's principal towns.

Prehistory, Archaeology and Ethnography

Prehistory and archaeology

59 **Continuity of the Romanian people's material and spiritual production in the territory of former Dacia.**
Ligia Bârzu.   Bucharest: Editura Academiei Republicii Socialiste România, 1980. 104p. bibliog.

In spite of its title, this is one of the more intelligible contributions in English by a Romanian to the study of Romanian continuity north of the Danube. It offers an excellent synthesis of historical and archaeological evidence of Dacian life before the Roman conquest, of the penetration of Roman civilization, of the character of the Daco-Roman symbiosis, and of the persistance of a Daco-Roman population north of the Danube.

60 **Romania before Burebista.**
Dumitru Berciu.   London: Thames & Hudson, 1967. 215p. maps. bibliog. (Ancient Peoples and Places, vol. 57).

A graphic well-presented survey of Romania's history from the early prehistorical pebble cultures to the Dacian civilization of the Iron Age. It is complemented by fine photographs and drawings in keeping with the standards of other books in this series.

61 **The Danube in prehistory.**
V. Gordon Childe.   Oxford, England: Clarendon Press, 1929. 479p. bibliog.

An impressive, scholarly, and still largely unsurpassed account of the Danube basin and its role as a highway linking Central Europe with the East.

62 **The ancient civilization of Romania.**
Emil Condurachi, Constantin Daicoviciu, translated from the
French by James Hogarth. London: Barrie & Jenkins, 1971. 250p.
maps. bibliog.
Romania offers six millennia of history, since its favourable geographical setting
encouraged man to settle there from the earliest times. This excellent book
surveys the archaeological evidence of human evolution on Romanian soil, from
the Lower and Middle Palaeolithic pottery to the artefacts of the Dacian tribe and
of the Roman conquest of Dacia.

63 **Burebista and his time.**
Ion Horaţiu Crişan. Bucharest: Editura Academiei Republicii
Socialiste România, 1978. 253p.
An attempt to inflate the importance of Burebista, a first century BC leader of the
Dacian tribe, which is based largely on unfounded supposition and is remarkable
for its hyperbole.

64 **The Dacian stones speak.**
Paul MacKendrick. Chapel Hill, North Carolina: University of
North Carolina Press, 1975. 248p. bibliog.
A finely illustrated introduction to the area that was to become the Roman
province of Dacia from the Neolithic age (3,000 BC) to the 7th century AD.
Neolithic sculptures, the citadels of the Dacian ruler Decebal, the Greek colonies
on the Black Sea, and the Roman conquest of the area are all vividly presented in
a racy style.

65 **Towards a definition of the Dacians.**
John Nandriş. *History Today*, vol. 30 (Aug. 1980), p. 53-54.
A review of an archaeological exhibition devoted to the Dacians prompts some
interesting reflections on the underestimated significance of Dacian culture.

Ethnography

66 **Folklore and ethnography in Romania.**
Octavian Buhociu. *Current Anthropology*, vol. 7, no. 3 (1966), p.
295-314.
A review article which examines the field of folklore studies in Romania. The
bibliography includes over 400 items on folk-tales and poetry.

67 **Romania: calendar of folklore events.**
Liviu Cernăianu, Lascăr Stancu. Bucharest: Publishing House of
Tourism, 1974. 326p.

This guide to cultural and artistic events reflecting Romanian folk customs is
arranged in such a way that it follows the year's cycle. It provides the name of the
event, its locality, and the date on which it is held. Each entry gives a brief
description of the event, a topographical reference for the locality, and the
address of the local tourist office. Contains a glossary of Romanian terms and an
index of persons.

68 **Coutumes rattachées à la vie humaine dans le village roumain
traditionnel** (Customs associated with the human life cycle in the
Romanian village.)
Florica Lorinţ. Brussels: Institut de Sociologie, Université Libre
de Bruxelles, 1968. 11p (Document de travail no. II/2).

A concise survey of customs related to the human life cycle. It deals first with
customs associated with birth, the new born, the many roles of the midwife and
the belief in *ursitoare* (fairies of destiny). This is followed by information about
wedding customs, including their more colourful facets, and customs regarding
death which require that the funeral take place three days after the death. A brief
analysis of two ritual ceremonies, *Bradul* (The fir tree) and *Zorile* (The dawn)
concludes the paper.

69 **Living legends in Romania.**
David Summers. *Folklore*, vol. 83 (winter 1972), p. 321-28.

This article is the result of a number of visits undertaken by the author to the
village of Breb in Maramureş, one of the most isolated regions in Romania and
one which is rich in folk traditions. He describes customs related to Christmas and
Easter, together with folk practices and spells. The most common subjects of
snoave (anecdotes) are also discussed. The author concludes with a description of
Fata pădurii (The daughter of the forest), a legendary creature believed to live in
the vicinity of the village.

70 **Funeral trees in Romanian traditional culture.**
Romulus Vulcanesco. *International Folklore Review*, vol. 1 (1981),
p. 77-79.

A brief article on the significance of Romanian funeral trees which fall into two
categories: natural trees which are planted on the deceased's land or on his
portion of village land and are looked after by a designated person; and substitute
trees, formed from branches cut off from a tree and used during the burial
ceremony when they are implanted into a large loaf of plaited bread.

History

General

71 **War, revolution and society in Romania: the road to independence.**
Edited by Ilie Ceauşescu. Boulder, Colorado: Distributed by
Columbia University Press, 1983. 298p. (East European
Monographs, no. 135).

A volume of eighteen papers by Romanian historians (and one American) which,
it is claimed, 'is designed to evaluate the political, social, and military dimensions
of war and revolution in the process of unification of all the provinces inhabited
by Romanians into the independent Greater Romania established at the end of
the First World War and, as such, it is a pioneer work in a Western language'.
The quality of these contributions is extremely uneven, several of them being
pervaded by a spirit of historical predeterminism that is conveyed in a language
full of platitudes and ill-defined concepts, notably those of justice and liberty.
Nevertheless, there is something of interest here for the student of Romanian
military history from the 14th to the 19th century.

72 **The Balkan revolutionary tradition.**
Dimitrije Djordjevic, Stephen Fischer-Galaţi. New York:
Columbia University Press, 1981. 271p. bibliog.

An examination of what the authors call the revolutionary tradition in the
Balkans, from the rising against the Turks in Wallachia under Michael the Brave
at the end of the 16th century to the insurrection in Albania in 1912. While
offering an insight into the reasons for the region's instablity over the last three
centuries, the claim that it is 'the most comprehensive study yet of the ever
evolving social and political history of the entire region' is unconvincing.

17

73 **Romania between East and West. Historical essays in memory of Constantin C. Giurescu.**
Edited by Stephen Fischer-Galaţi, Radu R. Florescu, George R. Ursul. Boulder, Colorado: Distributed by Columbia University Press, 1982. 414p.

A commemorative volume in honour of a distinguished Romanian historian that covers a wide range of topics. Five of the essays are reminiscences and appraisals of Giurescu while the remaining fifteen range from the historical Dracula (R. McNally) to the Jewish question during the 19th century (L. Cohen), Romania's oil policy (G. Buzatu), and the USA and the problem of Transylvania during the Second World War (P. Quinlan).

74 **The making of the Romanian people and language.**
Constantin C. Giurescu, translated into English by Virgiliu Ştefănescu-Drăgăneşti. Bucharest: Meridiane, 1972. 172p.

A presentation of the thesis dear to most Romanian historians concerning the origins of the Romanian people, namely that they are descended from a Daco-Roman population created from the inter-marriage of Roman colonists with the indigenous Dacians. Following the withdrawal of Roman legions from Dacia in 271-75 AD, the Daco-Romans sought refuge in the mountainous regions, thus preserving their Latin culture and language.

75 **Transylvania in the history of Romania: an historical outline.**
Constantin C. Giurescu. London: Garnstone Press, 1968. 138p.

An historical survey of Transylvania which emphasizes its importance as the cradle of the Romanian population and the role of the Transylvanian Romanians in the cultural and political life of the Romanian nation.

76 **Illustrated history of the Romanians.**
Dinu C. Giurescu, translated into English by Sonia Schlanger. Bucharest: Editura Sport-Turism, 1981. 640p. bibliog.

The most objective history of the Romanians published in Romania since 1948 and, at the same time, the only work of its kind in the Republic which does not accord the post-war period a disproportionate place in Romanian history.

77 **Rumania.**
C. Kormos. Cambridge, England: Cambridge University Press, 1944. 122p. map. (British Survey Handbooks).

Although inevitably dated in certain respects, this modest volume maintains much of its value as a generally accurate and objective account of Romania's turbulent history from the Roman invasion of Dacia in 104 AD to the Soviet invasion of 1944.

78 **Histoire de Transylvanie** (History of Transylvania.)
Ladislas Makkai. Paris: Les Presses Universitaires de France,
1946. 382p. bibliog.

This solid study of the history of Transylvania, written by a distinguished
Hungarian scholar, still throws welcome light on aspects of Transylvanian history
that are only superficially treated in other books on the subject. The author
advances the Hungarian thesis on the migration of the Romanians to Transylvania
at the end of the 12th century.

79 **Balkan background.**
Bernard Newman. London: Travel Book Club, 1945. 288p.

A reliable historical introduction to the countries of the Balkans namely:
Bulgaria, Romania, Yugoslavia, Albania, Greece and Turkey. The book was
written to dispel the British ignorance and lack of interest in the Balkans, of
which the author complains: 'We completely failed to solve their [the Balkan
countries'] problems in 1919 – not for lack of goodwill, but for sheer lack of
interest. Then we wondered why German influence became paramount in the
region – and why more than half its people are now ranged among our enemies.
If we do not take more trouble in 1945 than we did in 1919, then we head for
further disasters'.

80 **A history of Transylvania.**
Ştefan Pascu, translated by D. Robert Ladd. Detroit, Michigan:
Wayne State University Press, 1982. 318p. bibliog.

This is the first extensive history of Transylvania to be published in English and is
an abridgement of Pascu's *Voievodatul Transilvaniei* (2 vols. Cluj, 1972, 1979).
Covering the period from the early Stone Age to 1918, it is the work of a
Romanian nationalist set within a Marxist framework. Pascu's history stresses the
historical primacy and continuity of the Romanians in Transylvania and
underlines the national consciousness and unity of all Romanians there and across
the Carpathians in the principalities of Moldavia and Wallachia. The political
boundaries that divide them are regarded as artificial and will be removed in the
province's destined integration into a Greater Romania. Consequently, the author
concludes his account in the year 1918 when Transylvania's history becomes one
with that of Romania.

81 **A history of the Romanians: from Roman times to the completion of
unity.**
Robert W. Seton-Watson. Cambridge, England: Cambridge
University Press, 1934. Reprinted Hamden, Connecticut: Archon
Books, 1963. 596p. maps. bibliog.

Still the most complete history of the Romanians in English and one that is
notable both for the author's ability to see the evolution of Romanian history
within the European context, and for his insights into the problems of an ill-
starred people.

82 **Southeastern Europe under Ottoman rule, 1354-1804.**
Peter F. Sugar. Seattle, Washington; London: University of
Washington Press, 1977. 365p. maps. bibliog. (A History of East
Central Europe, vol. 5).
The history of the Romanian principalities and of Transylvania is difficult to
comprehend if not placed in the context of Balkan history. This is especially true
of the period covered by this book which has become a basic work for an
appreciation of the Ottoman impact upon the European lands that were either
directly administered, such as Serbia and Bulgaria or were vassal principalities,
such as Moldavia, Wallachia and, for a time, Transylvania. The author shows how
the Moslem and Turkish features of the Ottoman state left a permanent imprint
on these lands and principalities, and he also provides a wealth of detail on
economic and social history. The work includes an extensive bibliographical
essay, an appendix listing the reigns of the Ottoman sultans and of the princes of
Wallachia and Moldavia, and a glossary of towns and localities.

500-1750

83 **La France et les principautés danubiennes** (France and the Danubian
principalities.)
Germaine Lebel. Paris: Presses Universitaires de France, 1955.
464p. maps. bibliog.
A richly documented study of France's relations with Wallachia and Moldavia
from the 16th century until the fall of Napoleon I in 1815 based largely on the
archives of the French Foreign Ministry. The author analyses the vicissitudes of
French policy towards the principalities and shows how the establishment of
French consulates at Iaşi and Bucharest at the end of the 18th century paved the
way for a period of 'gallomania' in the first half of the 19th century.

84 **In search of Dracula: a true history of Dracula and vampire legends.**
Raymond T. McNally, Radu Florescu. New York: New York
Graphic Society; London: New English Library, 1973. 223p. bibliog.
An entertaining 'tongue-in-cheek' account of the authors' travels in Romania on
the trail of Vlad Ţepeş, Prince of Wallachia (1448, 1456-62) on whom the Dracula
legend, and Bram Stoker's *Dracula* are based. The historical authenticity of
Stoker's novel is evaluated in a lively and critical vein.

85 **The Byzantine commonwealth: Eastern Europe 500-1453.**
Dimitri Obolensky. London: Sphere Books, 1974. 552p. bibliog.
An outstanding account of the political, economic, ecclesiastical and cultural links
that the Byzantine Empire forged with the countries of the Balkans, the
Romanian principalies, and Russia during much of the Middle Ages. This
community of nations shared a common cultural tradition which included the

assimilation of Byzantine literature and art, and the adoption of Orthodox Christianity.

86 Stephen the Great, prince of Moldavia 1457-1504.

Şerban Papacostea. Bucharest: Editura ştiinţifică şi enciclopedică, 1981. 80p. bibliog.

A succinct yet penetrating account of Stephen's contribution to the defence of Christian Europe against the Ottoman invaders during the last quarter of the 15th century, and of his attempts to assert Moldavia's independence from vassalage to Poland.

87 Vlad Ţepeş: prince of Wallachia.

Nicolae Stoicescu. Bucharest: Editura Academiei Republicii Socialiste România, 1978. 194p. bibliog.

The success of Bram Stoker's *Dracula* has turned Vlad Ţepeş into a notorious figure of legend. Stoicescu's study restores fact to the life of Vlad and to the period of his reign as prince of Wallachia (1448, 1456-62). He emerges as a powerful ruler who was able to thwart the Ottoman armies on a number of occasions. To secure his rule he instilled terror into his adversaries by impaling his prisoners, hence the epithets *dracul* 'the devil' and *ţepeş* 'the impaler' that were attached to his name. However, in his desire to rehabilitate Vlad, Stoicescu attributes exaggerated aims, such as the defence of Wallachia's independence to him. Such 'independence' was extremely limited in scope and spasmodic after the Ottoman advance into the Balkans.

88 Documents concerning Rumanian history (1427-1601) collected from British archives.

Eric D. Tappe. The Hague: Mouton, 1964. 162p.

A unique collection of 218 documents, most of them previously unpublished, that have been drawn from British archives and which relate to the history of the Romanians. Many of them refer to the revolt of Michael the Brave, prince of Wallachia, against the suzerainty of the Ottoman Turks. The editor explains that 'I conceived the present collection as raw material for the historian, not as illustrations of Romanian history for the student'.

1750 to 1918

89 Austria and the emergence of Rumania, 1855-1861.

Lawrence R. Beaber. *East European Quarterly*, vol. 11, no. 1 (spring 1977), p. 65-78.

An account of Austrian attempts to block the union of the two principalities of Moldavia and Wallachia which the Austrians believed would encourage nationalist agitation amongst their Romanian subjects in Transylvania, Bukovina and the Banat, and threaten the Danube trade. The instrument of Austria's policy was Prokesch von Osten, her envoy to the Porte, who was unable to prevent the union but nevertheless had it, theoretically, restricted to the lifetime of Prince Alexandru Cuza.

90 **Habsburg und die Anfänge der Rumänischen Nationbildung** (The Habsburg Empire and the beginnings of the formation of the Romanian nation.)
Mathias Bernath. Leiden, Netherlands: Brill, 1972. 249p. bibliog.

An analysis of Habsburg policy towards the Romanians in Transylvania from the union with the Roman church in 1699 to the reign of Joseph II. It is in three parts entitled: Transylvania and Vienna's southeastern policy; Vienna's union policy and early ethnopolitical stirrings, and Vienna's policy of reform and the beginning of emancipation.

91 **The emergence of the Romanian national state.**
Gerald J. Bobango. Boulder, Colorado: Distributed by Columbia University Press, 1979. 312p. bibliog. (East European Monographs, no. 58).

On 9 May 1877 Romania, in the form of the united principalities of Moldavia and Wallachia, declared her independence of Turkish authority. This represented the climax of a development that began in earnest in 1829 with the Treaty of Adrianople. Bobango's scholarly and sympathetic study follows the course of this process from 1829 to 1859, the year of the election of Alexandru Cuza as prince in both Moldavia and Wallachia, and on to the latter's deposition in 1866.

92 **The Romanians' struggle for unification, 1834-49.**
Cornelia Bodea, translated from the Romanian by Liliana Teodoreanu. Bucharest: Publishing House of the Academy of the Socialist Republic of Romania, 1970. 295p. bibliog. (Bibliotheca Historica Romaniae, no. 25).

A laudable piece of research based on many primary sources through which the author attempts to present the common goals pursued by Romanian leaders in Transylvania, Moldavia and Wallachia.

93 **Relationship between Romanians, Czechs and Slovaks (1848-1914).**
Lucian Boia. Bucharest: Editura Academiei Republicii Socialiste România, 1977. 157p.

A unique account in English of the links established between the leading figures in the Romanian and Czech national movements on the one hand, and in the Romanian and Slovak movements on the other. One eloquent example of collaboration between the latter is the case of the Romanian journalist Ioan Poruţiu, charged in 1870 at Trnava with breaking the press laws. He was defended by the Slovak politician Pavol Mudroň and acquitted.

94   **Romania and the Balkan crisis of 1875-78.**
Richard V. Burks.   *Journal of Central European Affairs*, vol. 2, no.
2 (July 1942), p. 119-34 and no. 3 (Oct. 1942), p. 310-20.
An outline of the considerations which determined Romanian policy during the
Russo-Turkish war of 1877 and of Russia's successful steps to re-annex southern
Bessarabia.

95   **French influence and the rise of Roumanian nationalism.**
John C. Campbell.   New York: Arno Press and the New York
Times, 1971. 463p. bibliog.
The published version of the author's 1940 typescript Harvard dissertation has
retained much of its value for the anglophone scholar through its lucid
presentation of the elements responsible for the creation of a Romanian national
consciousness during the first half of the 19th century.

96   **1848 in the Rumanian principalities.**
John C. Campbell.   *Journal of Central European Affairs*, vol. 8,
no. 2 (July 1948), p. 181-90.
Some pertinent reflections on the aims of those figures involved in the events of
1848 in the Romanian principalities, prompted by the revolution in Romania
which was taking place at the same time as the article was written.

97   **The Transylvanian question in 1849.**
John C. Campbell.   *Journal of Central European Affairs*, vol. 2,
no. 1 (April 1942), p. 20-34.
An account, based on secondary sources, of the attempts to reconcile the aims of
the revolutions in Wallachia and Hungary in respect of Transylvania.

98   **Unification of the Romanian national state. The union of
Transylvania with old Romania.**
Edited by Miron Constantinescu, Ştefan Pascu.   Bucharest:
Publishing House of the Academy of the Socialist Republic of
Romania, 1971. 367p.
A translation of a collective work initially published to mark the fiftieth
anniversary of the union of Transylvania with the Romanian kingdom. The book
attempts to cover all the facets of the union but suffers, in places, from the
uneven quality of the contributions.

99   **Romanian society in the Danubian principalities in the early 19th
century.**
Dennis Deletant. In: *Balkan Society in the Age of Greek
Independence*. Edited by Richard Clogg.   London: Macmillan,
1981. p. 229-48.
A description of early 19th-century society in Moldavia and Wallachia. The
impact of Phanariot rule upon society and culture is assessed and an attempt

made to explain the development of the national regeneration of the Romanians during the period 1800-1830.

100 The union of Moldavia and Wallachia – 1859.
William G. East. Cambridge, England: Cambridge University Press, 1929. 220p. bibliog.

A well-documented account of events leading to the union of the two Romanian principalities. This work has now been superseded by Thad W. Riker's *The making of Roumania: a study of an international problem, 1856-1866.* (q.v.)

101 The great Rumanian peasant revolt of 1907. Origins of a modern jacquerie.
Philip Gabriel Eidelberg. Leiden, Netherlands: Brill, 1974. 259p. bibliog. (Studies of the Institute on East Central Europe, Columbia University).

The first dispassionate analysis of the causes of the peasant revolt of 1907 which the author attributes in part to the Liberal Party's proposals for agricultural reform during the years 1903-07. The purpose of this reform was to transfer control of the large private estates to a minority of the well-to-do peasants.

102 British reactions to the Russian régime in the Danubian principalities, 1828-34.
Radu R. Florescu. *Journal of Central European Affairs*, vol. 22, no. 1 (April 1962), p. 27-42.

An account of British reactions, based on Foreign Office papers, to the introduction by Russia of a constitution known as the *Règlement Organique* in Moldavia and Wallachia which effectively gave the tsar a form of sovereignty over the principalities.

103 Dunărea noastră. Romania, the great powers, and the Danube question 1914-1921.
Richard C. Frucht. Boulder, Colorado: Distributed by Columbia University Press, 1982. 216p. bibliog. (East European Monographs, no. 113).

This monograph reviews the measures taken by the Great Powers between the Crimean and First World Wars to maintain their influence over the regulation of the lower Danube and charts the role that Romania played in the establishment of the *Statut Définitif* in 1921 that established the administration of the Danube between Ulm and Sulina on the Black Sea.

104 Bălcescu and the national question in 1849.
Bruce C. Fryer. *East European Quarterly*, vol. 12, no. 2 (summer 1978), p. 189-208.

A lucid survey of the activities of Nicolae Bălcescu, one of the leaders of the abortive revolution of 1848 in Wallachia, during the following year. Bălcescu hoped that the revolution in Wallachia might be rekindled from the revolution in Transylvania that was still in full progress. His efforts to secure Hungarian and Romanian co-operation foundered on Kossuth's suspicions that the Romanians wished to separate Transylvania from Hungary and create an independent national Romanian state.

105 **Political ideas and the Enlightenment in the Romanian principalities (1750-1831).**
Vlad Georgescu.   Boulder, Colorado: East European Quarterly, 1971. Distributed by Columbia University Press. 232p. bibliog. (East European Monographs, no. 1).

A fundamental study of the development of political ideas in the Romanian principalities in the period of the Enlightenment.

106 **The nationality problem in Austria-Hungary. The reports of Alexander Vaida to Archduke Franz Ferdinand's chancellery.**
Keith Hitchins.   Leiden, Netherlands: Brill, 1974. 188p. (Studies in East European History, no. 18).

The correspondence of Alexander Vaida, a leading figure in the Romanian National Party, with the Archduke Franz Ferdinand between the years 1906 and 1910, provides details on the aims of that party and on Romanian discontent with the policies of the Hungarian government and their distrust of Magyar politicians.

107 **Orthodoxy and nationality. Andreiu Şaguna and the Rumanians of Transylvania, 1846-1873.**
Keith Hitchins.   Cambridge, Massachusetts; London: Harvard University Press, 1977. 325p. bibliog.

Andreiu Şaguna (1809-73), bishop and later metropolitan of the Romanian Orthodox Church, gave his people a realization of their identity. By admirably charting the course of Şaguna's career, Hitchins allows us to follow the political and cultural development of the Romanians of Transylvania during the quarter of a century that preceded the creation of the Dual Monarchy.

108 **The Rumanian national movement in Transylvania, 1780-1849.**
Keith Hitchins.   Cambridge, Massachusetts; London: Harvard University Press, 1969. 311p. bibliog.

The author combines scholarship and lucidity in this first systematic analysis in a major European language of the emergence of a Romanian national consciousness in Transylvania. The political and cultural impact of the movement in the province is admirably surveyed with the help of Hungarian and Saxon, as well as Romanian sources.

109 **Sir Stephen Lakeman (Mazar Pasha) as military governor of Bucharest at the commencement of the Austrian occupation of the Danubian principalities in 1854.**

Trevor J. Hope. *Revue Roumaine d'Histoire*, vol. 16, no. 1 (1977), p. 25-41.

The outbreak of the Russo-Turkish war in October 1853 caught the attention of British officers who had seen no major action for more than a generation. Several of them consequently made their way to Constantinople to offer their services and were warmly received by the Turkish commander of the Ottoman army on the banks of the Danube, Omer Pasha. The latter bestowed Turkish titles on a number of them, one such officer being Sir Stephen Bartlett Lakeman. Trevor Hope, an assiduous scholar of Anglo-Romanian contacts and a regular contributor to *Revue Roumaine d'Histoire*, describes Lakeman's activities as military governor of Bucharest by drawing on previously untapped primary sources both in Britain and Romania.

110 **The establishment of the Balkan national states, 1804-1920.**

Charles Jelavich, Barbara Jelavich. Seattle, Washington; London: University of Washington Press, 1977. 358p. maps. bibliog. (A History of East Central Europe, vol. 8).

The national states of the Balkans all emerged during the 19th and 20th centuries and this comprehensive account of the process has become a standard work. The formation of Greater Romania, from the creation of the United Principalities in 1859 to the integration of Transylvania after the First World War, is admirably presented, enabling this development to be appreciated in a wider Balkan context.

111 **Russia and the Rumanian national cause, 1858-1859.**

Barbara Jelavich. Bloomington, Indiana: Indiana University Publications, 1959. 169p. bibliog. (Slavic and East European Series, vol. 17).

In the union of Moldavia and Wallachia in 1859 Russia and France played the principal roles. While the accessibility of French archives has permitted research on the French contribution, Russian policy towards the principalities was obscure until the publication of this monograph, based on the private papers and official reports of Nikolai Karlovich Giers, Russian consul-general in Bucharest from 1858 to 1863, the years of the dual election of Alexandru Cuza as hospodar of Moldavia and Wallachia, and of the consequent unification of the administrative and legislative offices of the governments of the two principalities.

112 **Nationalism in the Danubian principalities: 1800-1825, a reconsideration.**

George F. Jewsbury. *East European Quarterly*, vol. 13, no. 3 (autumn 1979), p. 287-96.

An appraisal of various definitions of Romanian nationalism made by Romanian and other historians. The author concludes that none of them is valid for the period under discussion since 'a national movement, in which the nation sought political goals commonly held through an organized program that touched all of the people, did not exist'.

113 The Rumanian imbroglio.
J. Michael Kitch. In: *History of the First World War*. London: Purnell, British Publishing Corporation, vol. 7, no. 13 (1971), p. 3,029-39.

With the promise of Transylvania should the Allies be victorious, Romania declared war on the Central Powers in August 1916. Her armies were soon thrown on the defensive and the capital Bucharest was occupied by the German army. The collapse of Russia in 1917 forced Romania to conclude an armistice and in May 1918 a peace treaty was signed in Bucharest. On 10 November, with the Central Powers on their knees, Romania declared war once again, thus gaining herself a powerful position at the Paris Peace Conference. Kitch's article provides a lucid and reliable overview of Romania's participation in the war.

114 England, Russia and the Rumanian revolution of 1866.
W. E. Mosse. *Slavonic and East European Review*, vol. 39, no. 92 (Dec. 1960), p. 73-95.

'The revolution of 1866, which established on the throne of the United Principalities of Moldavia and Wallachia Prince Charles of Hohenzollern-Sigmaringen, not only marked a milestone on the road to Rumanian independence but also acquired a European significance. . . . It constituted an infringement of the treaty signed a decade before at Paris at the close of the Crimean War. The signatories of the treaty, not least England and Russia, were faced with awkward decisions'. The author shows how the establishment of a foreign prince on the throne of the principalities was accomplished and how this act struck a fatal blow to the validity of the treaty.

115 The nationality problem in the Habsburg monarchy in the nineteenth century: a critical appraisal. Part II. The national minorities.
Austrian History Yearbook, vol. 3, part 2 (1967), p. 3-531.

Two articles on the Romanians and the Habsburg monarchy by S. Fischer-Galaţi (p. 430-49) and A. Oţetea (p. 450-76), and the incisive comments of J. C. Campbell (p. 477-83), provide an illuminating discussion of this subject.

116 1859: the union of the Romanian principalities.
Gheorghe Platon, translated from the Romanian by Florin Ionescu. Bucharest: Editura ştiinţifică şi enciclopedică, 1978. 86p. bibliog.

A description of events leading up to the union of Moldavia and Wallachia through the dual election of Alexandru Cuza as prince of both principalities. As a historical narrative this is an accurate record yet it is coloured in the chapters on the 'Antecedents of union' and 'Significance and consequences of union' by a historical predeterminism into which all developments affecting the Romanian nation must fit. The union of 1859 is seen as a further step in the predestined unification of all Romanians in a Greater Romania, which was achieved at the end of the First World War.

117 **Supplex libellus valachorum, or the political struggle of the Romanians in Transylvania during the 18th century.**
David Prodan, translated by Mary Lăzărescu. Bucharest: Publishing House of the Academy of the Socialist Republic of Romania, 1971. 476p. bibliog.

An outstanding exposition of the Transylvanian Romanians' petition *Supplex libellus valachorum*, submitted to Leopold II in 1791, which sought the political emancipation of the Romanians in Transylvania.

118 **The making of Roumania: a study of an international problem, 1856-1866.**
Thad W. Riker. London: Oxford University Press, 1931. 592p. bibliog.

An exhaustive analysis, based on English, French and German primary sources, of the negotiations of the Great Powers concerning the future form of government of the Romanian principalities.

119 **The Transylvanian question: Romania and the belligerents July-October 1914.**
Zoltan Szaz. *Journal of Central European Affairs*, vol. 13, no. 4 (Jan. 1954), p. 338-51.

A brief examination of how the assassination of Archduke Franz Ferdinand affected relations between Austria-Hungary and Romania and how it determined the future of Romania's foreign policy.

120 **Rumania.**
Eric D. Tappe. In: *Contrasts in emerging societies*. Edited by Doreen Warriner. London: Athlone Press; Indiana: Indiana University Press, 1965. Reprinted New York: Indiana University Press, 1980. 402p.

Romania is well served by Eric Tappe (p. 115-203) in this collection of readings on the social and economic history of Southeastern Europe in the 19th century. The texts include extracts from works by Romanians which are translated and edited by Tappe, as well as accounts by European travellers.

121 **Enlightenment and Romanian society.**
Edited by Pompiliu Teodor. Cluj-Napoca: Editura Dacia, 1980. 280p.

A collection of articles in English, French, German and Romanian by seventeen Romanian, two East German, and one American scholar on the reception and impact of the Enlightenment upon educated Romanians. The political and cultural consequences of this contact form the subject of most of the contributions.

122 **Rumania and the belligerents 1914-1916.**
Glenn E. Torrey. *Journal of Contemporary History*, vol. 1, no. 3 (1966), p. 171-91.

The outbreak of the First World War placed Romania in a difficult position towards its neighbours and allies. King Carol's family background and secret accession to the Triple Alliance linked him to Austria and Germany. However, Austria's support of Bulgaria during the Balkan Wars alienated Romanian public opinion and prompted a rapprochement with Russia. Although Carol favoured a declaration of war on Russia, he was persuaded by his cabinet to declare neutrality on the grounds that the aggressive and unilateral nature of Austria's action relieved Romania of her treaty obligations. Prime Minister Ion Brătianu began his policy of diplomatic dissimulation with the Central Powers and the Entente in which he sought to further Romanian interests by suggestions of support for one side or the other. The article follows this duplicity up to Romania's eventual declaration of support for the Entente in 1916.

123 **The Rumanian-Italian agreement of 23 September 1914.**
Glenn E. Torrey. *Slavonic and East European Review*, vol. 44, no. 103 (July 1966), p. 403-21.

A contradiction between the obligations of Italy and Romania to the Triple Alliance and the considerations of national self-interest, and their vulnerability to retaliation from the Triple Entente led both countries to ignore the call-to-arms from Berlin and Vienna. Their common position facilitated the signing of an agreement on 23 September 1914 whereby they bound each other to give advance warning before abandoning neutrality and to communicate to each other proposals received from the Central Powers and from the Triple Entente. Torrey shows what benefit the signatories derived from the agreement in their dealings with the Entente and the Alliance.

124 **International legal aspects of the Great Powers' mediation of the Rumanian-Bulgarian territorial dispute 1912-1913.**
Idris Rhea Traylor, Jr. *East European Quarterly*, vol. 14, no. 1 (spring 1980), p. 23-37.

The purpose of the mediation of the Great Powers in the territorial dispute between Romania and Bulgaria was to prevent the two countries from going to war over the Dobrogea. The signing of the Protocol of St. Petersburg on 9 May 1913 marked the final intervention of the Great Powers in the frontier dispute and failed to solve it, for Romania declared war on Bulgaria on 10 July 1913. New frontiers which were to Romania's advantage were drawn up in the Treaty of Bucharest in August 1913.

Inter-war period (1918-1939)

125 **Behind closed doors: secret papers on the failure of Romanian-Soviet negotiations, 1931-1932.**
Translated, with an introductory essay, by Walter M. Bacon,
Jr. Stanford, California: Hoover Institution Press, 1978. 212p.
bibliog.

'This volume is composed primarily of translated documents drawn from the Nicolae Titulescu collection deposited in the archives of the Hoover Institution on War, Revolution and Peace at Stanford, California. Of the 440 documents found under the heading 'USSR Peace Negotiations 1931-1932', only the most important 103 have been translated from the original Romanian or French. Together with the introductory essay, these documents provide a detailed account of Romanian-Soviet negotiations for a pact of non-aggression in 1931 and 1932. The documents are all copies of telegrams, dispatches, and inter-departmental memos of the Royal Romanian Ministry of Foreign Affairs. They were originally used by Nicolae Titulescu, the eminent Romanian minister of foreign affairs and one of the chief protagonists of the episode, in his defense before the Romanian parliament on November 23 and 24 1932 of his decision to terminate the negotiations'.

126 **Romanian and allied involvement in the Hungarian coup d'état of 1919.**
Eva S. Balogh. *East European Quarterly*, vol. 9, no. 3 (autumn 1975), p. 297-314.

On 1 August 1919 Béla Kun the Hungarian premier, relinquished power to the Social Democrats under Gyula Peidl but five days later a counter-revolutionary group staged a coup d'état. Accusations of foreign involvement in the coup were directed principally at the Romanian government whose army had occupied half of Budapest by 6 August. This paper refutes the charge that the Romanians were instrumental in the coup and places the activities of the American, British and Italian representatives in Budapest in perspective; while not assisting in the coup, they gave it their tacit support.

127 **Psycho-historical and sociological perspectives on the Iron Guard, the fascist movement of Romania.**
Z. Barbu. In: *Who were the Fascists? Social roots of European Fascism*. Edited by S. U. Larsen, B. Hagtvet, J. P. Myklebust.
Bergen, Norway: Universitetsforlaget, 1980. p. 379-94.

A discussion of the fascist movement in Romania, generally known as the Iron Guard, with particular reference to the question 'Who joined the movement and for what reason?' In the absence of more detailed sources the author has endeavoured to form a general idea about the social composition of the Iron Guard by extrapolating from small samples extracted either from the 1937 electoral lists which contain references to 350 Iron Guard candidates, or from a few records left by the Romanian police or army. To answer the second part of the question Barbu consulted Iron Guard publications and interviewed nineteen former members.

128 **Rumania.**
Z. Barbu. In: *European Fascism*. Edited by S. J. Woolf.   London: Weidenfeld & Nicolson, 1968. p. 146-66.

A brief yet penetrating description and analysis of Romanian fascism and of the Iron Guard movement. The author discusses the national characteristics of Romanian fascism on the basis of his own personal contacts and his recollection of events concerning the movement. He also draws on the political and autobiographical works of the leader of the Iron Guard, Corneliu Codreanu. Barbu attempts to explain the ritualized violence of the movement, its political success, and the social origins of its leadership and membership. His conclusions are that 'the characteristic traits of Rumanian fascism can only be partly derived from the social class and economic conditions of its supporters. At least as, if not more, relevant, is a set of psychological factors, a state of mind, characteristic of individuals and groups suffering in various degrees and in various ways from lack of social integration and purpose'.

129 **Roumania under King Carol.**
Hector Bolitho.   London: Eyre & Spottiswoode, 1939. 175p.

An undisguised apologia for King Carol's dictatorship written by an ardent admirer. Contains several verbatim extracts from interviews given to the author by Carol and leading Romanian politicians which touch upon Romania's relations with Britain, Hungary, Bulgaria and the USSR. There is also a chapter on the position of the Jews and their treatment under the Goga government.

130 **Carol the Second and the British press.**
London, 1939. 302p.

This scrapbook of articles written on the occasion of Carol's state visit to Britain in November 1938 offers a comprehensive collage and a useful record of leader articles which reflect the contemporary British appraisal of the Romanian king.

131 **Germany, Rumania and the British guarantees of March-April 1939.**
A. Chanady, J. Jensen.   *Australian Journal of Politics and History*, vol. 6, no. 2 (Aug. 1970), p. 201-17.

German policy in Southeast Europe was to obtain a dominant share of trade with the area by adjustment of exchange controls. Romania was the key to this policy and from autumn 1938 the Office of the Four Year Plan in Germany attempted to direct the Romanian economy in Germany's interest by securing a long-term trade agreement. To this end trade negotiations took place in February and March 1939. The establishment, however, by Germany, of a protectorate over Bohemia and Moravia alerted the Romanians to the possible implications of German involvement in their economy and led the Romanian minister in London, Viorel Tilea, to report to the Foreign Secretary Lord Halifax on 17 March that the Romanian government had received 'something very much like an ultimatum' from the Germans. This paper examines in detail the background to the trade negotiations, the 'ultimatum', and the implications for Anglo-French policy.

31

132 **For my legionaries (The Iron Guard).**
Corneliu Zelea Codreanu. Madrid: Editura Libertatea, 1977.
353p.

An English translation of the political memoirs of Codreanu (1899-1938), founder
in 1927 of the right-wing Legion of the Archangel Michael, which were first
published as *Pentru legionari* at Sibiu in 1936. The militant political section of the
legion, the Iron Guard, emerged in 1930 as a powerful force in inter-war Romania
but its use of violence and the threat it posed to the established order (or rather
disorder) of political life led to Codreanu's arrest and murder in custody.

133 **The struggle for economic influence in southeastern Europe: the
French failure in Romania, 1940.**
William A. Hoisington, Jr. *Journal of Modern History*, vol. 43,
no. 3 (Sept. 1971), p. 468-82.

In spite of the fact that Anglo-French interests supplanted those of Germany in
Romania after the First World War, French economic influence declined there
throughout the inter-war period while that of Germany increased. The Anglo-
French agreement signed at San Remo in 1920 divided German petroleum
interests between the two signatories and yet French purchases of Romanian oil
had by 1939 decreased by 18 per cent over the previous year. This article follows
the attempts of Jacques Lemaigre Dubreuil, a prominent French businessman
attached to the French military mission in Bucharest, to reassert French economic
influence in Romania in 1940 by establishing a permanent economic mission and
is based largely on Dubreuil's private papers.

134 **Soviet-Romanian relations and the Bessarabian question in the early
1920s.**
Dov B. Lungu. *Southeastern Europe/L'Europe de Sud-Est*, vol. 6,
part 1 (1979), p. 29-45.

After the separation of the Ukraine from Russia in the autumn of 1917 a so-called
'national assembly' proclaimed the autonomy of Bessarabia and in March 1918
voted for its union with Romania. The Soviet government refused to recognize
the union but in 1920 invited the Romanian government to negotiate with a view
to restoring diplomatic relations and to settling their territorial differences. This
fascinating paper, based on archival material in Bucharest unavailable to western
scholars, reveals how and why, between 1920 and 1922, the Romanian
government did not take advantage of the conciliatory attitude of the USSR over
Bessarabia. Once the communist régime had consolidated itself in the USSR it
was no longer prepared to make concessions, and on 12 October 1924 the
Autonomous Moldavian Soviet Socialist Republic was proclaimed in the partly-
Romanian inhabited area of south-western Ukraine on the east bank of the
Dniester as a nucleus for a 'liberated' Moldavia which would later include
Bessarabia.

135 **The land and the peasant in Rumania: the war and agrarian reform (1917-21).**
David Mitrany. London: Oxford University Press; New Haven, Connecticut: Yale University Press, 1930. Reprinted New York: Greenwood Press, 1968. 627p. maps. bibliog.

A detailed account of the agrarian reform implemented in Romania after the First World War. The author presents a still unsurpassed analysis of Romanian peasant conditions and of the effects of the land reforms which are set against a broad historical canvas.

136 **Political life in Romania, 1918-1921.**
Mircea Muşat, Ion Ardeleanu. Bucharest: Editura Academiei Republicii Socialiste România, 1982. 259p.

'A deep-going and complex analysis – in the light of dialectical and historical materialism – of Romania's economic and socio-political evolution, of the structure and dynamics of its social classes, of the activity of the political parties working on behalf and in the interests of these classes . . .'; thus begins the sentence in the foreword describing the contents of this work. The Romanian original of this translation, published in 1976, was notable for the 4th footnote in the first chapter in which Bessarabia was described as 'this ancient Romanian territory which was occupied after the Nazi-Soviet pact of 1939'. This footnote, preserved in the English edition, was a further salvo directed at the USSR on the issue of Bessarabia which had been resurrected by the Romanian party leadership in 1964 with the publication of a manuscript by Marx entitled *Notes on the Romanians* in which he stated that Russia had unjustly acquired Bessarabia in 1812 (p. 105-06).

137 **The green shirts and the others: a history of fascism in Hungary and Rumania.**
Nicholas M. Nagy-Talavera. Stanford, California: Stanford University, Hoover Institution Press, 1970. 427p. bibliog.

A readable comparative account of the rise of fascist movements in Hungary and Romania. The emphasis is upon the former but the author, by drawing upon material published by Romanian exiles as well as upon contemporary Romanian sources, provides a useful narrative of the Iron Guard movement.

138 **Romania and the Munich crisis: August-September 1938.**
William O. Oldson. *East European Quarterly*, vol. 11, no. 2 (summer 1977), p. 177-90.

Romania has been cast in the role of a guilty party in the betrayal of Czechoslovakia for her refusal to allow Soviet troops to cross her territory in the summer of 1938. The accusation serves to make Romania a scapegoat for the policies pursued by Britain, France and the USSR towards Hitler at Munich and ignores, as this article shows, the doubtful military advantages that would have accrued to Czechoslovakia from Romania's compliance, and Romania's own fears for her territorial integrity.

139 **Nicolae Titulescu's diplomatic activity.**

I. M. Oprea. Bucharest: Publishing House of the Academy of the Socialist Republic of Romania, 1968. 188p. bibliog. (Bibliotheca Historica Romaniae, no. 22).

A reasonably balanced view of the career of Romania's most distinguished diplomat of the inter-war period. Although it admirably recounts Titulescu's efforts to create a system of collective security in Europe and his opposition to German and Italian totalitarianism, it lacks detail on the steps that he took to seek a non-aggression pact with the USSR.

140 **Sous trois dictatures (Under three dictatorships.)**

Lucreţiu Pătrăşcanu. Paris: J. Vitiano, 1946. 326p.

At the time of its publication in the original Romanian edition in 1945, this was the first Marxist interpretation of the socioeconomic evolution of Romania during the inter-war period. The author was the communist representative in the Romanian delegation at the armistice talks in Moscow in September 1944, and was Minister of Justice in the Romanian government of March 1945. He was the victim of a purge in 1948, was tried in April 1954 for 'bourgeois deviation' and executed on 17 May 1954.

141 **The Tilea affair: a further inquiry.**

Paul D. Quinlan. *Balkan Studies*, vol. 19 (1978), p. 147-57.

On 17 March 1939 the Romanian minister in London, Viorel Tilea, warned the British government that his country had received an 'ultimatum' which would bring the Romanian economy under German control. This paper examines Anglo-Romanian relations prior to March 1939, Tilea's activities, and the veracity of the 'ultimatum'. The author concludes that Tilea exaggerated because he feared that Romania would share the same fate as Czechoslovakia.

142 **Contemporary Roumania and her problems: a study in modern nationalism.**

Joseph S. Rouček. Stanford, California: Stanford University Press, 1932. Reprinted, New York: Arno Press, 1970. 422p. bibliog.

An 'overview' of Romania during the inter-war period that is divided into four principal sections: historical development; political life; the constitutional and administrative apparatus; and economic affairs. There is little critical analysis but the work contains an excellent bibliography of the period.

143 **Eastern Europe between the wars, 1918-1941.**

Hugh Seton-Watson. Cambridge, England: Cambridge University Press, 1946. 2nd ed. 445p.

One of the most accomplished treatments of Romania in the setting of Eastern Europe during the inter-war period. The author's insight into the political experience of the Romanians and his original conclusions stimulate the reader. The discussions on the impact of Trianon, the position of the national minorities,

the treatment of the Jews, and King Carol's attempts to steer a course between
Germany and the USSR are particularly illuminating.

144 **Prelude to dictatorship in Romania: the National Christian Party in
power, December 1937-February 1938.**
Paul A. Shapiro. *Canadian-American Slavic Studies*, vol. 8, no. 1
(spring 1974), p. 45-88.

The National Christian Party government of Octavian Goga and Alexandru Cuza
was the last government formed in Romania before the abrogation of the
constitution by King Carol and the institution of a royal dictatorship. This article
examines the events which brought the NCP to power and discusses the domestic
and international implications of its record in office, which was characterized by a
number of administrative measures taken against the Jews.

145 **Rumania at the Paris Peace Conference: a study of the diplomacy of
Ioan I. C. Brătianu.**
Sherman D. Spector. New York: Bookman Associates, 1962.
368p. bibliog.

The Romanian position at the Paris Peace Conferences of 1918 to 1920 is
examined through the diplomacy of Brătianu, President of the Romanian Council
of Ministers and Minister for Foreign Affairs. Spector's inability to gain access to
the Romanian archives impinges somewhat on the authority that he was able to
give to his assessment.

146 **Romania.**
Eugen Weber. In: *The European right: a historical profile*. Edited
by Hans Rogger, Eugen Weber. London: Weidenfeld &
Nicholson; Berkeley, California: University of California Press,
1965. p. 501-74. bibliog.

The most authoritative, perceptive and objective account in English of the
emergence of fascist movements in inter-war Romania with particular emphasis
on the religious accent in the creed of the Iron Guard and on the messianic role of
its leader, Codreanu.

147 **The men of the archangel.**
Eugen Weber. *Journal of Contemporary History*, vol. 1, no. 1
(1966), p. 101-26.

An analysis of the membership of the Legion of the Archangel Michael founded
in 1927, which is known in the West as the Iron Guard, and which campaigned
under the electoral label '*Totul pentru ţară* (All for the fatherland.)

The Second World War

148 Participation of the Romanian army in the anti-Hiterlite war.
Vasile Anescu, Eugen Banat, Ion Cupşa. Bucharest: Military
Publishing House, 1966. 108p.

An outline of the contributions and sacrifice made by Romanian forces to the
defeat of the German armies in Hungary and Czechoslovakia after Romania's
volte-face of 23 August 1944.

149 British policy in Southeast Europe in the Second World War.
Elisabeth Barker. London: Macmillan, 1976. 320p. bibliog.

A fascinating book, based on a detailed study of British documents and on first-
hand information from active participants in Special Operations Executive (SOE),
that casts new light on British wartime aims in Southeast Europe. The two
chapters on Romania attempt to explain British policies there, particularly in the
context of the 'percentages' agreement between Churchill and Stalin of October
1944. This developed from Churchill's desire to contain Stalin's advance into
Southeast Europe and led him to trade a 90:10 preponderance in favour of Britain
in Greece for a 90:10 Soviet preponderance in Romania.

**150 Mission de guerre. La Roumanie dans la tourmente de la seconde
guerre mondiale** (War mission. Romania in the torment of the
Second World War.)
George Béza. Paris: Editions Laumond, 1977. 176p.

Essentially a unique 'Who's who' of persons associated with the Romanian
National Committee, founded in London in November 1940, and of members of
the Special Operations Executive who saw service in Romania during the war.

151 Das Dritte Reich und die rumänische Judenpolitik (The Third
Reich and Romanian policy towards the Jews.)
Martin Broszat. Munich: Gutachten des Instituts für
Zeitgeschichte, Selbstverlag des Instituts für Zeitgeschichte, 1958.
82p.

A chronicle of German influence upon Romanian policy towards the Jews
between 1940 and 1944.

152 Speaking frankly.
James F. Byrnes. London: Heinemann, 1947. Reprinted, New
York: Greenwood Press, 1974. 324p.

As director of war mobilization in the USA from May 1943 to July 1945 and
Secretary of State from July 1945 to January 1947, the author was present at
Yalta, Potsdam and the Moscow conference of Foreign Ministers of the 19th to
the 27th of December 1945 that sealed Romania's post-war fate. Here he offers a
graphic narrative of these and other meetings based on his shorthand notes. One
cannot help feeling that the title of these memoirs is disingenuous since Byrnes

kept President Truman in the dark over the conditions of the Moscow agreement of 27 December 1945 which may be said to have marked the end of Western hopes to create a post-war democratic Romania.

153 **The lost opportunity.**
Alexandre Cretzianu. London: Cape; Toronto: Clark, Irwin, 1957. 188p

A first-hand account of the negotiations between King Michael and the Allies to extricate Romania from the war with Germany and to prevent Romania from falling under Soviet domination. The author is critical of the bland Anglo-American response towards Soviet actions in Romania between 1944 and 1947.

154 **The Rumanian armistice negotiations: Cairo 1944.**
Alexandre Cretzianu. *Journal of Central European Affairs*, vol. 11, no. 3 (Oct. 1951), p. 243-58.

An account by the Romanian minister to Ankara at the time of these negotiations which paved the way for Romania's defection from the German camp. The author, using the papers of his father-in-law Barbu Stirbey who acted as a Romanian emissary, compares the terms offered by the Allies in Cairo with the clauses of the armistice convention signed in Moscow on 12 September 1944, and berates the Americans and British for their 'naïvety' in accepting Soviet undertakings embodied in the armistice.

155 **The Soviet ultimatum to Roumania (26 June 1940).**
Alexandre Cretzianu. *Journal of Central European Affairs*, vol. 9, no. 4 (Jan. 1950), p. 396-403.

An account of the sequence of events that followed the presentation of the Soviet ultimatum demanding the return of Bessarabia and northern Bukovina.

156 **Ploieşti: the great ground-air battle of 1 August 1943.**
James Dugan, Carroll Stewart. New York: Random House, 1962; London: Cape, 1963. 309p. bibliog.

On Sunday 1 August 1943 178 B.24 Liberators of the 9th USAAF took off from Benghazi to bomb the oil refineries at Ploieşti. Unknown to Allied intelligence, the Luftwaffe had placed a signal interception group near Athens which had broken the allied code and was reading 9th USAAF transmissions. A short message to Allied forces in the Mediterranean alerting them of the mission, code name 'Tidal Wave', was intercepted. As a result German aircraft were expecting the attackers. 53 Liberators were lost (including eight interned in Turkey), 55 were damaged, and 310 American airmen killed (about one in five of the 1,620 men who reached the target area). The Luftwaffe lost four aircraft over Ploieşti and two over Greece. The Romanian air force losses were recorded as two planes. The damage inflicted at Ploieşti did not have a major effect on oil deliveries to the Reich. The courage and skill of the American aircrews is graphically recounted in this well-researched description of the operation and the excellent treatment of those taken prisoner by the Romanians is underlined.

157 **Verratene Schlachten: die tragödie der deutschen Wehrmacht in Rumänien und Ungarn** (Betrayed battles: the tragedy of the German army in Romania and Hungary.)
Hans Friessner. Hamburg, GFR: Holsten Verlag, 1956. 276p. bibliog.

A view by the commander of the German South Ukraine army group in 1944 of the consequences of Romania's entry into the war on the Allied side for Germany's military position in Central and Southeast Europe.

158 **Prelude to the Russian campaign.**
Grigore Gafencu, translated by Fletcher Allen. London: Frederick Muller, 1945. 348p.

A study of the political and diplomatic events that preceded the war between Germany and the USSR from the signing of the Moscow Pact on 21 August 1939. The author, a former Romanian Minister for Foreign Affairs and minister to Moscow, explains the Romanian view of these events, the difficult position of his country between two totalitarian powers, and Romania's decision to join Hitler in his attack on the USSR on 22 June 1941.

159 **Churchill's spheres of influence: Rumania and Bulgaria.**
Robert Garson. *Survey*, vol. 24, no. 3 (summer 1979), p. 143-58.

A discussion of Churchill's motives in making the notorious 'spheres of influence' agreement with Stalin on 9 October 1944, with particular reference to Romania and Bulgaria. The author argues that the agreement was 'an act of retrieval, not of abdication' on Churchill's part.

160 **Hitler, König Carol und Marschall Antonescu: die deutsch-rumänischen beziehungen, 1938-1944** (Hitler, King Carol and Marshal Antonescu: German-Romanian relations, 1938-1944.)
Andreas Hillgruber. Wiesbaden, GFR: F. Steiner, 1954. 382p. bibliog. (Veröffentlichungen des Instituts für europäische Geschichte, vol. 5).

An appraisal of Germany's relations with Romania over the period 1938-44 that is based on German secondary sources as well as on some unpublished despatches of the German minister in Bucharest. It casts a great deal of light on the collapse of King Carol's policy of neutrality and on Hitler's attitude towards the Iron Guard and Antonescu.

161 **Crown against sickle: the story of King Michael of Rumania.**
Arthur Gould Lee. London: Hutchinson, 1950. 199p.

This is an account of King Michael's view, as recounted to the author, of his role during Romania's subjection to German and Soviet domination between 1940 and 1947. It is illuminating for its revelations concerning the Soviet tactics of conquest by threat and perfidy, the King's clashes with Vishinsky and the Russian generals, his conflict with the Romanian communist leaders, and the events leading up to his abdication.

162   **The American non-policy towards Eastern Europe, 1943-1947.**
Geir Lundestad.   Oslo: Universitetsforlaget, 1978. 654p. bibliog.
In attempting to explain the policy of the United States towards the countries of
Eastern Europe between 1943-47, the author discusses the strategic, political and
economic interests that all played their part. American policy towards Romania is
briefly examined (p. 225-56) but it is placed in the context of three questions:
what part did the USA expect to play in Eastern Europe after the war? What kind
of régime was acceptable in each country to the US and what did Roosevelt and
Truman do to support American objectives in the area?

163   **The first Soviet double cross: a chapter in the secret history of
World War II.**
F. C. Nano.   *Journal of Central European Affairs*, vol. 12, no. 3
(Oct. 1952), p. 236-58.
The author, as Romanian minister in Stockholm from 1943 to 1944, recounts how
Soviet representatives approached him in December 1943 with a view to opening
direct armistice negotiations with Marshal Antonescu. The Soviet initiative is seen
as an attempt to short-circuit the negotiations between all three allies and the
Romanian opposition that began in April 1944 in Cairo and eventually provided a
basis for the armistice convention signed in Moscow on 12 September 1944.

164   **March 1939: the British guarantee to Poland. A study in the
continuity of British foreign policy.**
Simon Newman.   Oxford, England: Clarendon Press, 1976. 253p.
bibliog.
After Hitler's annexation of Czechoslovakia the possibility of avoiding war with
Germany became remote in the minds of most people in Britain. The British
government sought to respond to this change in opinion and on 17 March was
provided with an issue on which it could do so, the reported 'ultimatum' from
Germany to Romania that was communicated to Lord Halifax by Viorel Tilea,
Romanian minister in London. Chapter six of this study is devoted to the genesis
of the 'ultimatum', and to an examination of the resultant change in emphasis of
the British response to the German threat in Europe which led to the guarantee
to Poland given on 31 March 1939. The author's survey of the explanations given
for Tilea's report of a supposed 'ultimatum' overlooks the information presented
in A. Chanady, D. Jensen's *Germany, Rumania and the British guarantees of
March-April 1939*. (q.v.)

165   **The Nazis in the Balkans: a case study of totalitarian politics.**
Dietrich Orlow.   Pittsburgh, Pennsylvania: University of
Pittsburgh Press, 1968. 235p. bibliog.
An illuminating case-study of the Südosteuropa-Gesellschaft, created in 1940 to
formulate German wartime policy in Southeast Europe. Based largely on primary
sources, this work throws light not only on Germany's wartime exploitation of
Romania, but also on administrative procedures in the national socialist system.

166 **Yugoslavia and Rumania, 1941.**
K. St. Pavlowitch. *Journal of Central European Affairs*, vol. 23, no. 4 (Jan. 1964), p. 451-72.

An explanation of why diplomatic relations between Yugoslavia and Romania were broken off in 1941 with a vivid description of the departure of the staff of the Yugoslav embassy, amongst whom was the author.

167 **Clash over Romania. British and American policies towards Romania: 1938-1947.**
Paul D. Quinlan. Los Angeles: American Romanian Academy of Arts and Sciences, 1977. 173p. bibliog.

This is the most detailed account of British and American policy towards Romania during the Second World War and immediately afterwards. It is based on published and unpublished documents of the Foreign Office and State Department. While much of the material confirms what was already known, new information is brought to light on the part played by the American administration in the attempt to overthrow the Groza government in August 1945.

168 **Roosevelt and the Russians.**
Edward R. Stettinius Jr. Garden City, New York: Doubleday, 1949. 367p.

The belief that at Yalta the interests of the Western Allies were sacrificed to appeasement of the Soviet Union prompted the US secretary of state at the time (February 1945) to write this first hand account of the Yalta conference. The conviction that Roosevelt and Churchill awarded Eastern Europe to Stalin is still widely held, in spite of the fact that Soviet troops occupied, or were on the point of occupying, the area at the time of the conference. As Stettinius argues, the division of Europe resulted not from agreements reached at Yalta, but from the failure to honour those agreements and nowhere is this more vividly illustrated than in the case of Romania.

169 **Baker Street irregular.**
Bickham Sweet-Escott. London: Methuen, 1965. 278p.

During the Second World War the author became one of the pillars of the Special Operations Executive with special responsibility for planning and directing resistance movements in occupied territories. These memoirs are invaluable for an appreciation of SOE activities, especially in France, Greece and Yugoslavia, but they also cover operations in Romania in 1943-44.

170 **Le second diktat de Vienne: les preliminaires** (The second diktat of Vienna: the preliminaries.)
Bela Vago. *East European Quarterly*, vol. 2, no. 4 (Jan. 1969), p. 415-37.

Each of the successive inter-war Hungarian governments regarded the territorial revision of the provision of the Treaty of Trianon (1920) as a cornerstone of its foreign policy. The major 'injustice' of Trianon in Hungarian eyes was the award of Transylvania to Romania and in 1936 the Hungarian government took formal

steps in Berlin and Rome to win support for its cause. This impartial account of
the background to the Vienna diktat of 30 August 1940 examines the political and
economic considerations that led Germany and Italy to intervene in the territorial
dispute between Hungary and Romania.

171 **Le second diktat de Vienne: le partage de la Transylvanie** (The
second diktat of Vienna: the partition of Transylvania.)
Bela Vago. *East European Quarterly*, vol. 5, no. 1 (March 1971),
p. 47-73.

The failure of Hungary and Romania to resolve their differences over
Transylvania threatened to erupt into war and led Hitler to impose a solution.
The Vienna diktat of 30 August 1940 virtually partitioned Transylvania with its
award of 43,000 sq. km. containing a population of 2.6 millions (50.3 per cent
Romanians, 37.1 per cent Hungarians) to Hungary. The role played by Germany
and Italy in the adjudication, and its implications for Romania and Hungary, are
described in this paper.

172 **Romania's contribution to the defeat of Nazi Germany.**
Gheorghe Zaharia. Bucharest: Editura ştiinţifică şi enciclopedică,
1975. 53p. bibliog.

A useful pamphlet highlighting the contribution of Romania's army and air force
to the defeat of Germany following the overthrow of Marshal Antonescu by King
Michael on 23 August 1944. Over half a million Romanian troops participated in
the defeat of the Germans on Romanian territory and almost a quarter of a
million contributed to the successful campaigns in Hungary and Czechoslovakia.
By January 1945 Romania occupied fourth place in terms of the number of troops
fighting the Germans.

Post Second World War

173 **Truce in the Balkans.**
Elisabeth Barker. London: Percival Marshall, 1948. 256p.

'Based as far as possible on first-hand observation, impressions, conversations and
reading of current Balkan and Trieste newspapers', this record of political
developments in immediate post-war Bulgaria, Romania, Greece and Trieste is
one of the most dispassionate accounts in English. The author's predictions for
the régimes of the area are remarkably accurate, particularly in respect of
Romania: 'in Romania, there are too few experienced, competent and honest
men in the ranks of the Easterners to run the new political and economic machine
efficiently, or even to abolish corruption . . . Again it will take ten years or far
more probably a generation before these Balkan states can become modern
countries with balanced economies resting on a thriving industry as well as a
thriving agriculture. It will be equally long before there is any overall rise in the
average standard of living'.

41

174 **Russia astride the Balkans.**
Robert Bishop, E. S. Crayfield. London: Evans Brothers; New
York: Robert M. Mcbride, 1949. 287p.

The opening lines of this predominantly first-hand account by two members of the
American intelligence services of events in Bucharest from the coup of 23 August
1944 to the departure of King Michael from Romania on 3 January 1948, tend to
detract from the authors' pretensions to sound historical judgement: 'The
conquest of Rumania was really accomplished by the American and Royal Air
Forces – not by the Red Army, as the Russians would like the world to believe'.
Nevertheless, the book is fascinating for it imparts detailed information about
many of the significant steps in the communist take-over of the government. The
authors' tendency to rely on rumour does not impair the overall accuracy of their
account.

175 **Romania's Ceauşescu.**
Donald Catchlove. Tunbridge Wells, England: Abacus Press,
1972. 120p.

A hagiography of the Romanian leader.

176 **Le traité de paix avec la Roumanie du 10 février 1947 (The peace
treaty with Romania of 10 February 1947.)**
Émile C. Ciurea. Paris: Éditions A. Pedone, 1954. 284p.

The most detailed account of the negotiations leading up to the conclusion of the
treaty between the Allies and Romania, and an assessment of its provisions and
their importance for the latter.

177 **Captive Rumania: a decade of Soviet rule.**
Edited by Alexandre Cretzianu. New York: Praeger, 1956. 424p.

A collective volume of articles on aspects of life in Romania under communist
rule. Written chiefly by émigrés, they emphasize the loss of personal and religious
freedom, and the subordination of the country's activities to Soviet dictates.

178 **A history of the people's democracies.**
François Fetjö, translated from the French by Daniel Weissbort.
Harmondsworth, England: Penguin Books, 1974. 565p.

A detailed study of the reaction against Soviet hegemony in Eastern Europe and
the emergence of liberalizing and nationalistic trends there following Stalin's
death. Developments in Romania are set alongside the major upheavals of the
Hungarian revolution in 1956 and the invasion of Czechoslovakia in 1968.

179 **The new Rumania: from people's democracy to socialist republic.**
Stephen Fischer-Galaţi. Cambridge, Massachusetts: MIT Press,
1967. 126p. bibliog. (Centre for International Studies,
Massachusetts Institute of Technology. Studies in International
Communism, no. 10).

A brief study of the imposition of communist rule in Romania and of the strategy of the party in the transformation of the country into a people's democracy and, later, into a socialist republic.

180 **Romania.**
Edited by Stephen Fischer-Galaţi. New York: Praeger, 1956. 339p. bibliog.

A survey of developments in Romania since 1945 that is particularly useful for the contributions on the economic situation between 1945-55. Other subjects covered in this collective work include political and cultural conditions in the country.

181 **Twentieth century Rumania.**
Stephen Fischer-Galaţi. New York: Columbia University Press, 1970. 248p. bibliog.

The author confines himself to political history and examines the present régime's claim to represent the aspirations of the Romanian people. The identifiction of Gheorghiu-Dej and Ceauşescu with nationalist sentiment is emphasized in this study.

182 **Rumania: Russia's dissident ally.**
David Floyd. London: Pall Mall Press, 1965. 144p.

Floyd charts Romania's transition under Gheorghe Gheorghiu-Dej from its position as one of the Soviet Union's model satellites in the 1950s to its more independent stance in the early 1960s which challenged the Soviet Union's supranational pretensions.

183 **La Roumanie dans l'engrenage** (Romania enmeshed.)
Nicolette Franck. Paris, Brussels: Elsevier Sequoia, 1977. 269p. bibliog.

A description of the transition of Romania from a monarchy to a people's republic between 1944 and 1947 as witnessed by the author, who is said to have enjoyed the confidence of King Michael and several key figures in the governments of the period while researching her book. The work is fascinating for the further light it sheds on the King's initiative in the coup of 23 August 1944 which is ignored in works published in Romania since 1948.

184 **Nicolae Ceauşescu and the Romanian road to socialism.**
Robert Govender. London: Unified Printers & Publishers, 1982. 190p.

A myopic view of contemporary Romania which performs a disservice to those who seek to appreciate the contribution of its present leader to its development.

185 **Communism in Rumania 1944-1962.**
Ghiţa Ionescu. London: Oxford University Press for the Royal Institute of International Affairs, 1964. 378p. bibliog.

Ionescu's penetrating study of the Romanian Communist Party since its foundation in 1921 and of its post-war rule is a study in both historiography and history. As the former it is an examination of the manner in which the Party, as its own historian, sees events and as the latter, a synopsis of political engineering, economic development and international relations in the post-war era.

186 A history of the Romanian Communist Party.
Robert R. King.   Stanford, California: Stanford University, Hoover Institution Press, 1980. 190p. bibliog.

As a former assistant director of research and senior analyst for Romania at Radio Free Europe the author has considerable experience of contemporary Romanian affairs which he demonstrates in this well-written study. Based on an extensive use of Romanian sources, he charts the political and organizational development of the Party from its accession to power in 1944 on the back of the Red Army to its increasing identification with Romanian nationalism during the late 1960s. The Party's exploration of the limits of Soviet indulgence, first under Gheorghiu-Dej, and later under Ceauşescu, enabled it to increase its popular support in Romania but, as King emphasizes, the failure to solve economic problems in the late 1970s and early 1980s severely tarnished the Party's image.

187 Romania.
Robert R. King. In: *Communism in Eastern Europe.* Edited by Teresa Rakowska-Harmstone, Andrew Gyorgy.   Bloomington, Indiana: Indiana University Press, 1979. 338p.

The contribution on Romania (p. 147-67) focuses on its geopolitical background, the distinctive characteristics of the population, the relevant features of the nation's historical development, sociological forces and Party political structures, and leads in to the imposition of communist rule after the war.

188 Communist power in Europe 1944-1949.
Edited by Martin McCauley.   London: Macmillan in association with the School of Slavonic and East European Studies, University of London, 1977. 242p.

The thirteen essays in this book attempt to explain why and show how all the countries east of the Elbe and in the Balkans had by 1948 been subjected to communist rule. Bela Vago's contribution on Romania shows how the communists' bid for power, after King Michael's coup d'état of 23 August 1944 against Marshal Antonescu, was based on accusations against the National Peasant Party and the National Liberal Party of anti-democratic and pro-Fascist tendencies and of sabotaging the implementation of the armistice agreement; the establishment of front organizations, the most significant of which was the Ploughmen's Front led by Petru Groza; and the splitting of the Social Democrats by discrediting their leader Titel Petrescu.

189 Rumania under the Soviet yoke.
Reuben H. Markham.   Boston, Massachusetts: Meador, 1949. 601p. bibliog.

A first-hand and, in places, virulently anti-communist account of the Soviet takeover in Romania by a former correspondent of the *Christian Science Monitor* that provides much incidental detail of Soviet actions in the country after August 1944.

190 Romania in the 1980s.
Edited by Daniel N. Nelson.   Boulder, Colorado: Westview Press, 1981. 313p.

A compilation volume of nine articles arranged under three headings entitled 'The setting of Romanian communism', 'Leaders and citizens in Romanian politics' and 'Foreign and economic policies'. Among the more original contributions are: M. E. Fischer's, 'Idol or leader? The origins and future of the Ceauşescu cult' (p. 117-41), W. Bacon's, 'Romanian military policy in the 1980s' (p. 202-18), R. Linden's, 'Romanian foreign policy in the 1980s' (p. 219-53) and M. R. Jackson's, 'Perspectives on Romania's economic development in the 1980s' (p. 254-305).

191 Nicolae Ceauşescu: the man, his ideas, and his socialist achievements.
Stan Newens.   London: Spokesman Books for the Bertrand Russell Peace Foundation, 1972. 235p.

An uncritical presentation of the Romanian leader's achievements on a national and international plane during the late 1960s that makes much use of extracts from his speeches.

192 Contemporary Romania.
Ion Raţiu.   Richmond, England: Foreign Affairs Publishing, 1975. 138p. bibliog.

A history of Romania since the advent to power of the communists that is particularly interesting for its appraisal of Gheorghiu-Dej. The author challenges the view that Gheorghiu-Dej was a nationalist communist and shows him as a dedicated Stalinist who exploited the natural response of a people who are deeply anti-Russian. Raţiu also paints a vivid picture of life in the 1970s under the present regime, highlighting the economic shortcomings.

193 Rumania: political problems of an agrarian state.
Henry L. Roberts.   New Haven, Connecticut: Yale University Press; London: Oxford University Press, 1951. Reprinted, Hamden, Connecticut: Archon Books, 1969. 414p. bibliog.

A most objective study of Romania between 1922 and 1945 that combines political analysis with economic survey. The author served with the American military mission to Romania in 1944-45 and his first-hand knowledge of the communist takeover, combined with a use of primary sources, provides illuminating detail of this event.

194 **Roumania at the peace conference.**
Paris, 1946. 145p. maps.
A publication by prominent Romanian politicians in exile, led by Alexandre
Cretzianu, Grigore Gafencu and Viorel Tilea. Submitted to the Paris Peace
Conference on 6 January 1946 it draws the attention of the Western Allies to the
fact that the Romanian people 'have learned to their cost, that good-will and loyal
fulfilment of their obligations alone cannot ensure to them either peace or
security, so long as ideas such as those proclaimed by the Atlantic Charter do not
find prompt and complete realization'. The authors clarify the point of view of the
Romanian democratic parties concerning the various problems awaiting their
solution in the Peace Treaty.

195 **Russia's Danubian empire.**
Gordon Shepherd. London: Heinemann, 1954. 262p.
In attempting to do justice to events inside the USSR's satellite states between
1945 and 1952 Shepherd examines the significance of the Kremlin's struggle with
the peasants and industrial workers of these countries, charts the spiritual contest
between Christianity and Communism, and discusses the impact of these events
on the quality of life of the sixty million people involved. Romania is well covered
in this comparative interpretation which contains insights that have retained their
value.

196 **Communist régimes in Eastern Europe.**
Richard F. Staar. Stanford, California: Hoover Institution Press,
1982. 4th ed. 375p. bibliog.
The chapter on Romania 'gives a brief sketch of post-1945 history and describes
current developments in industry, agriculture, foreign trade, defence, religion and
the handling of ethnic problems. The book includes numerous tables and charts
portraying trends in politics, economics and other important features of national
life combined with information drawn from extensive use of primary sources'.

197 **Treaties of peace with Italy, Roumania, Bulgaria, Hungary and
Finland. (Texts for signature in Paris on 10 February 1947).**
London: HM Stationery Office, 1947. 147p. (Cmd. 7022.
Miscellaneous no. 1 (1947)).
The text of the treaty with Romania is on p. 79-98.

198 **Trial of the former National Peasant Party leaders: Maniu,
Mihalache, Penescu, Grigore Niculescu-Buzeşti and others; after the
shorthand notes.**
Bucharest Military Tribunal. Bucharest: Dacia traiană, 1947.
228p.
On 30 October 1947 Iuliu Maniu and Ion Mihalache, the President and Vice-
President respectively of the National Peasant Party, were brought to trial with
seventeen other persons on charges of plotting against the security of the state,
armed insurrection and treason. The plot, according to the prosecution, was the
work of three interconnected groups, the first being the leaders of the NPP who

were charged with conspiring with two intelligence officers attached to the American mission to Romania, Major Tom Hall and Lt. William Hamilton, to organize an armed insurrection. The second group consisted of a resistance organization abroad, made up of leading political figures such as Alexandru Cretzianu, Grigore Gafencu, Grigore Niculescu-Buzeşti and Constantin Vişoianu, all of whom had managed to leave Romania. The third group was that of the 'treacherous Foreign Office', represented in the trial by career diplomats such as Victor Rădulescu-Pogoneanu and Vasile Serdici, who were accused of maintaining links with the resistance group abroad and with the American and British missions in Romania. All nineteen persons were found guilty, Maniu and Mihalache being sentenced to life imprisonment, Rădulescu-Pogoneanu to twenty-five years and Serdici to ten years, and the others to terms ranging from two to fifteen years. Maniu died in Sighet prison, purportedly on 3 February 1953, Mihalache and Rădulescu-Pogoneanu in Rîmnicu-Sărat jail, the former on 5 March 1963.

199 **Trial of the group of spies and traitors in the service of espionage of Tito's fascist clique.**
Bucharest: Military Tribunal, 1950. 64p.

The leadership of the Romanian Workers' Party was one of the most virulent in the anti-Tito campaign of 1949 and 1950. Romania sheltered anti-Tito refugees, beamed anti-Tito broadcasts to Yugoslavia, and Gheorghiu-Dej was the rapporteur of the first Cominform denunciation of Tito. This trial was organized in the spirit of the campaign.

200 **No fruit more bitter.**
Lawrence Wilkinson. London: Cape, 1958. 252p.

An account of an attack on the Romanian legation in Berne in 1957 by émigré anti-communists.

201 **The Balkans in our time.**
Robert Lee Wolff. Cambridge, Massachusetts: Harvard University Press, 1974. 647p. maps. bibliog.

Romania is one of four countries (the others are Albania, Bulgaria and Yugoslavia) that form the subject of this book. The emphasis is upon the twentieth century history of these countries. The first seven chapters cover the period before the Second World War, the eighth chapter deals with the war itself, and the remaining seven chapters consider the process by which all four countries were brought under communist rule.

Biographies and memoirs

202 **Des geôles d'Anna Pauker aux prisons de Tito** (From the jails of
Ana Pauker to the prisons of Tito.)
Nicolas Baciu.   Paris: Le Livre Contemporain, 1951. 298p.

'Out of the frying-pan into the fire' would be a suitable sub-title for this
description of the author's escape from Romania to Yugoslavia by swimming the
Danube. After being imprisoned in the Văcăreşti jail in Bucharest for being a
member of the 'bourgeois' bar, the author decided to flee Romania, only to be
incarcerated by the Yugoslav authorities on suspicion of being an anti-Tito spy.
His experiences in a succession of prisons in Kladova, Ruzika, Pantchevo,
Kovatchica, Zdrenjanin and Zagreb, and his eventual escape on foot across the
frontier into Austria are graphically described.

203 **Religion and politics: bishop Valerian Trifa and his times.**
Gerald J. Bobango.   Boulder, Colorado: East European
Monographs. Distributed by Columbia University Press, 1981.
294p. (East European Monographs, no. 92)

Valerian Trifa of the Romanian Orthodox Episcopate of America surrendered his
certificate of naturalization in 1980 to the courts in the United States following
charges against him that he was a 'Romanian Nazi' and a 'war criminal'.
Bobango's book examines these charges in a dispassionate manner. Trifa left the
USA on 13 August 1984.

204 **A Roumanian diary.**
Hans Carossa, translated from the German by Agnes Neill
Scott.   London: Martin Secker, 1929. 252p.

A sensitive, moving diary of a German officer's experience of the First World
War on the Eastern Front in Romania in an excellent translation.

205 **The lost footsteps.**
Silviu Crăciunaş, translated from the Romanian by Mabel Nandriş.
London: Collins & Harvill Press; New York: Farrar, Straus &
Cudahy, 1961. 318p.

A thrilling account of the author's clandestine flight from Romania in 1949 and his
subsequent illegal visits to the country. The author was persuaded by the
Romanian National Committee in Paris to return to the country in order to assist
in the smuggling out of opponents of the régime. He was eventually caught,
tortured, and imprisoned for four years before escaping once again to the West in
1957.

206 **King Carol, Hitler and Lupescu.**
A. L. Easterman.   London: Gollancz, 1942. 272p.

King Carol II (1893-1953) reigned in Romania between 1930 and 1940. His
colourful love-life permeates most of this book, written by the former foreign

editor of the *Daily Express*. In 1918 he became infatuated with Zizi Lambrino, a commoner, while the court was in Iaşi and, after smuggling her into Russia, married her in Odessa. When the couple returned to Romania Carol was ordered by his father King Ferdinand into confinement and the Supreme Court pronounced the marriage illegal and annulled it. During his confinement in Bistriţa Carol met Helena Tîmpeanu, wife of a cavalry officer whose regiment was garrisoned in the town, with whom he formed a close, and as it was to prove, permanent relationship. In March 1921, however, he married Princess Helen of Greece, and in October their son, Prince Michael, was born. Carol's link with Helena Tîmpeanu derived further strength from the incompatible temperaments of Carol and his royal wife. Their irreconcilability led to divorce in 1928. Helena Tîmpeanu's marriage was dissolved and she reverted to her maiden name of Lupescu. The notoreity of Carol's liaison with Madame Lupescu became one of the world press's best 'human interest stories', as is shown by the title of this book. Nevertheless, the presentation of Carol's attempts to steer Romania during the 1930s, including interviews with the King and leading political personalities, contains a great deal of interesting incidental material.

207 **Marie of Romania: the intimate life of a twentieth century Queen.**
Terence Elsberry. London: Cassell, 1973. 298p. bibliog.

Queen Marie Alexandra Victoria of Romania (1875-1938) was the eldest daughter of the Duke of Edinburgh, second son of Queen Victoria, and of the Grand Duchess Marie Alexandrovna, only daughter of Tsar Alexander II. In 1893 she married Ferdinand, Crown Prince of Romania, nephew of King Carol and son of Prince Leopold of Hohenzollern. She became a national symbol through her work amongst Romanian troops striken by cholera in 1913 during the invasion of Bulgaria, when she organized a hospital camp at Zimnicea. When King Carol died in October 1914 the Crown Prince and Princess became King and Queen of Romania. During the First World War she was again indefatigable in her care for the wounded, and when the court withdrew to Iaşi, she provided an example of optimism and energy to those who despaired at Romania's future. She was deeply upset by the failure of her elder son Carol's marriage to Princess Helen of Greece and, later, distressed by his continual maltreatment of her when he ascended the throne. Elsberry has based this biography on the reminiscences and papers of Queen Marie's youngest daughter, Ileana, and of George I. Duca, son of the former Prime Minister Ion Duca.

208 **There's a German just behind me.**
Clare Hollingworth. London: Right Book Club, 1943. 300p

An eyewitness account by a correspondent of the *Daily Express* of events in Southeastern Europe between 1940 and 1941 with particular emphasis on Romania and Greece. The author writes in her preface: 'The reader may wonder why Greece and Romania are treated at such length in comparison with Hungary and Bulgaria. The reason is that Romania for over a year provided one sensation after another, and Greece took the unusual line of fighting the Axis'.

209 **A Roumanian diary 1915, 1916, 1917.**
Lady Kennard. London: Heinemann, 1917. 191p.

A first-hand account of the author's impressions of Romania in the months prior to its entry into the war in 1916, supplemented by letters received from friends of the author who remained to work in Iaşi as Red Cross nurses. The latter provide a vivid picture of conditions in the Moldavian capital during the war.

210 Prisoner of red justice: an account of ten years' captivity in communist Roumania.
Leonard Kirschen. London: Arthur Barker, 1963. 224p.

This is an account of the prison experiences of the author who was an Associated Press correspondent in Bucharest after the Second World War. Arrested in April 1950 and tortured, he was tried nine months later and sentenced to twenty-five yeas imprisonment, of which he served ten, from 1950 to 1960.

211 Helen, Queen Mother of Rumania.
Arthur Gould Lee. London: Faber & Faber, 1956. 296p.

An authorized biography of Queen Helen (1896-1982), wife of King Carol II and mother of King Michael. Although divorced from Carol when he reigned, she was known as Queen Mother of Romania because of the support and counsel that she gave her son during his period of rule (1940-47). Her life was characterized by extremes of fortune. She was the eldest daughter of Constantine, Crown Prince and later King of the Hellenes. Her grandfather King George was assassinated in 1913 and, four years later, her father was forced by foreign intervention to renounce his throne and go into exile for three years. In 1921 she married Crown Prince Carol of Romania but the latter's association with Madame Lupescu led him to renounce his rights to the throne in 1925, to leave Romania and to cause great distress and humiliation to his wife. Helen was divorced from Carol in 1928 but remained at her son's side until 1930 when Carol returned to seize the throne and force her into exile. She went to Florence, seeing her son for a month each year until Carol's abdication in September 1940 when Michael summoned her to Bucharest. She performed untiring service for the war-wounded and sustained King Michael throughout the war and during his daring coup d'état of 23 August 1944. During the three difficult years that followed she demonstrated great resolution and discretion, offering advice to her son in the face of the threats of the Soviet and Romanian communists until Michael was forced to abdicate in December 1947. Her years of exile were spent near Florence.

212 The story of my life.
Marie, Queen of Roumania. London: Cassell, 1935. 3 vols.

In essence, this is the Queen's diary from her early childhood to the end of the First World War. Born at Eastwell Park, Kent on 29 October 1875, Marie was the eldest daughter of the Duke of Edinburgh, second son of Queen Victoria, and of the Grand Duchess, Marie Alexandrovna, only daughter of Tsar Alexander II. In 1893 she married Ferdinand, Crown Prince of Romania, nephew of King Carol and son of Prince Leopold of Hohenzollern. She was indefatigable in her care for the wounded during World War 1 and retained the affection and admiration of her subjects up to her death in July 1938.

213 **The wall between.**
Annie Samuelli. Washington, DC: Robert B. Luce, 1967. 227p.

A sensitive and moving account of the author's experiences of almost twelve years in prison in Romania. She and her sister were detained in 1949 in Bucharest by the communist authorities in a mass arrest of all Romanian nationals working for the US and British legations. After nine months of torture and interrogation, the sisters were sentenced to twenty and fifteen years penal servitude respectively. Released in 1961 upon payment of a ransom, they were exiled to the West.

214 **Athene Palace Bucharest: Hitler's new order comes to Rumania.**
R.G. Waldeck. London: Constable, 1943. 279p.

An American journalist's first-hand appreciation of the impact of the activities of the Iron Guard in Romania and of the German occupation under the Antonescu régime, seen from her base in the Athenée Palace Hotel in Bucharest. The cession of Bessarabia and Transylvania, the abdication of King Carol II, the accession of Ion Antonescu, and the significance of the arrival of German troops are discussed in this work.

215 **Death at my heels.**
David Walker. London: Chapman & Hall, 1942. 256p.

A vivid account of 'an ignominious personal retreat spread over a couple of years. It is not properly speaking a book: it is simply a reportage of what did happen in the countries concerned, without any conscious attempt to philosophize, moralize or prophesy'. The author, as correspondent for the *Daily Mirror*, describes his experiences in Romania, Bulgaria, Greece and Yugoslavia between 1939 and 1941. Political events in Romania take up one third of the book and are graphically presented.

51

Population

Demography and general studies

216 Romania's 1966 anti-abortion decree.
    B. Berelson. *Population Studies*, vol. 33, no. 2 (1979), p. 209-22.

In the mid-1960s the birthrate in Romania showed a marked decline which 'threatened the future of the nation' according to some party officials. In an attempt to halt this decrease two decrees were issued in October 1966 banning abortion and divorce. Although the result was a sudden increase in births, this was not maintained, and by 1981 the birth-rate had declined to virtually the 1966 level. This article examines the background to the abortion decree and comments on its effectiveness.

217 Romania's population. A demographic, economic and socio-political essay.
    Ion Blaga, translated into English by Doina Glăvan, Nora
    Scurtulescu.   Bucharest: Meridiane Publishing House, 1972. 156p.

The author highlights several features of demographic change in Romania during the post-war period. Details are given in tabulated form of the distribution of the population by sex and age, of the territorial distribution, of numbers employed in agriculture, industry and the service industries, of the social structure of the population, of the school population, and of the changes in the standard of living.

218 Romania.
    V. Cucu. In: *Essays on World urbanization*. Edited by R.
    Jones.   London: George Philip, 1975. p. 297-307.

A brief paper outlining the growth of towns in the 1960s and early 1970s which resulted from industrialization.

219 **Demografie historique de la Roumanie, 1972-1978: bibliografie analytique** (Romanian historical demography: analytical bibliography.)
Louis Roman. *Revue Roumaine d'Histoire*, vol. 19, no. 1 (1980), p. 85-127.

An invaluable international bibliography of publications on Romanian demography incorporating both books and periodical articles. It is divided into the following sections: working materials (bibliographies, dictionaries, encyclopaedias); sources; studies; and book and article reviews.

220 **The changing demographic structure of the population of Transylvania.**
G. D. Satmarescu. *East European Quarterly*, vol. 8, no. 4 (Jan. 1975), p. 425-49.

A critical analysis of the demographic statistics for Transylvania published since the Second World War. The author argues that the Hungarian population was closer to 2 millions in 1966 than to the 1.6 millions listed in the census for that year. The Saxon and Swabian population fell considerably after the war through emigration, as have the numbers of Jews. The conclusions of the author are that Transylvania is as distinct demographically from Moldavia and Wallachia as it is in geography, history, culture and economy, and that the population density and rates of increase are lower.

221 **The de-legalization of abortion in Romania.**
M. Teitelbaum. *Family Planning*, vol. 23 (1974), p. 38-41.

A brief presentation of the anti-abortion decree of October 1966 and its effects.

222 **Romania's population and demographic trends.**
Vladimir Trebici, translated from the Romanian by Caterina Augusta Grundbock. Bucharest: Meridiane Publishing House, 1976. 139p. bibliog.

A detailed presentation of demographic trends in Romania with copious tables. The study examines: population density; population distribution by age and sex; the structure of the population by marital status; its distribution by educational status; the incidence of general and infant mortality; marriage and its influence on fertility; population reproductivity and Romania's 'population policy'.

223 **Restricting legal abortion: some maternal and child health effects in Romania.**
N. Wright. *American Journal of Obstetrics and Gynecology*, vol. 121, no. 2 (1975), p. 246-56.

Making abortion illegal in 1966 and imposing stiff penalties on those who broke the law had only a temporary effect on the birthrate and on the numbers of abortions performed. By 1975 the birthrate was falling towards the 1966 level and was almost equalled by the incidence of illegal abortion. The dangers for mothers and children inherent in illicit abortion in Romania are presented in this article.

53

Nationalities and Minorities

Policy towards minorities

224 **Rumania's violations of Helsinki final act provisions protecting the rights of national, religious and linguistic minorities.**
Committee for Human Rights in Rumania. New York: American Transylvanian Federation, 1980. 105p. bibliog.

A series of papers on alleged Romanian violations against the human rights of the Hungarian minority, prepared for the Conference on Security and Cooperation in Europe held at Madrid in 1980-81.

225 **Nation and nationality in Romania.**
Mary Ellen Fischer. In: *Nationalism in the USSR and Eastern Europe in the era of Brezhnev and Kosygin*. Edited by George W. Simmonds. Detroit, Michigan: University of Detroit Press, 1977. p. 504-21.

'A survey of the nationality policies of the Romanian Communist Party to 1975 which provides comparative data on the socioeconomic characteristics of the various national minority groups. The intensive industrialization effort after 1958 produces a number of trends "inducing" but not "forcing" assimilation of the small groups: upward mobility through technical education in Romanian, for example, or internal migration to better jobs in the less developed but predominantly Romanian areas of the country. The author concludes that, despite the use of Romanian nationalism by Ceauşescu to mobilize majority support for régime policies, as of 1975 official party policies were not being directed against the minority nationalities any more than against other citizens of Romania'.

226 **The politics of national inequality in Romania.**
Mary Ellen Fischer. In: *Communism and the policies of inequality*.
Lexington, Massachusetts: Lexington Books, 1983. p. 189-220.
'An attempt to place nationality relations in contemporary Romania into the
context of comparative theories of political inequality. The ethnic complexity is
becoming simplified as the smaller ethnic groups emigrate (the Germans and
Jews) or come to identify themselves officially in census interviews as Romanians.
However, the largest nationality, the Hungarians, seems to be more unified and
actively hostile than before 1975. There is a striking contrast between the
Hungarians and the other minorities in their attitudes toward the Romanian
polity, and here the concept of inequality is crucial: the Hungarians perceive the
rhetoric of equality to be persecution. Ceauşescu's strategies of political control,
particularly the use of nationalism, have been rewarded by the quiescence of the
Romanian population but have intensified the fears of the Hungarian minority.
The author concludes that tension between Romanians and Hungarians will
probably increase over the next decade as the Romanians emphasize "equal"
treatment and the Hungarians demand "special" treatment'.

227 **Ethnic minorities in Romania under socialism.**
Trond Gilberg. *East European Quarterly*, vol. 7, no. 4 (winter
1973), p. 435-64.
An evaluation of the socioeconomic change inherent in Romania's rapid
industrialization during the 1960s and its effect upon the Hungarians, Germans,
Jews and Gypsies. The author concludes that generally speaking this process did
not result in the cultural assimilation of minorities into the predominant
Romanian culture. 'The Hungarians and Germans have remained true to their
ethnic heritage'. Only amongst Gypsies and Jews has there been more outward
assimilation.

228 **Minorities under communism: nationalities as a source of tension
among Balkan communist states.**
Robert R. King. Cambridge, Massachusetts: Harvard University
Press, 1973. 326p. maps. bibliog.
An excellent analysis of the tensions arising from the conflict between nationalism
and communism in Central and Eastern Europe and from the treatment of
national minorities in neighbouring communist states. Romania is covered on p.
146-69 while the historical debate over Bessarabia is aired on p. 220-41.

229 **Eagles in cobwebs: nationalism and communism in the Balkans.**
Paul Lendvai. London: MacDonald; Garden City, New York:
Anchor Books, 1970. 396p. bibliog.
A subjective yet thought-provoking study of attempts to reconcile nationalism and
communism in Albania, Bulgaria, Romania and Yugoslavia.

230 **Handbuch der europäischen Volksgruppen** (Handbook of
European nationalities.)
Edited by M. Straka. Vienna: Braumüller, 1970. 658p.

One of the most complete surveys of the nationalities of Romania in a Western
European language. This study of minority nationalities throughout Europe
contains separate chapters on the Hungarians and Germans in Romania and,
conversely, the Romanians in Hungary and Yugoslavia. An excellent reference
work with statistical data and a bibliography.

Hungarians

231 **National minorities in Romania: change in Transylvania.**
Elemér Illyés. Boulder, Colorado. Distributed by Columbia
University Press, New York, 1982. 355p. bibliog. (East European
Monographs, no. 112).

This work is devoted to the cultural policies affecting both Hungarians and Saxons
in Transylvania with the emphasis on the situation of the Hungarians. It is
impressive for its detailed and dispassionate presentation which covers territorial
and population changes in Transylvania since 1918, the situation of the national
minorities between 1918 and 1956, Romanian policy towards the minorities since
1956, the provision of educational facilities since the last war, the churches of the
national minorities, and publishing in Hungarian and German. The selective
bibliography is particularly valuable.

232 **The Hungarian nationality in Romania.**
The Institute of Political Science and of Studying the National
Question. Bucharest: Meridiane Publishing House, 1976. 53p.

A presentation of Romanian data concerning the participation of the Hungarian
minority in the political, economic and social life of Romania, religious worship
and the use of the Hungarian language in education, the mass media and in
cultural institutions.

233 **At the Danube: Gyula Illyés and Zsigmond Pál Pach versus Mihnea
Gheorghiu.**
New Hungarian Quarterly, (winter 1978), p. 120-28.

A summary in English of the articles that appeared in *Magyar Nemzet* (Christmas
1977 and New Year 1978), *Luceafărul* (16 May 1978) and *Élet és Irodalom* (8 July
1978) on the treatment of the Hungarian minority in Transylvania.

234 **The Hungarians of Rumania.**
George Schöpflin. London: Minority Rights Group, 1978. 20p.
(MRG report, no. 37).

A laudable attempt to present a picture of Hungarian and Romanian views on the
role of Transylvania in Hungarian and Romanian history and to offer an appraisal

of the position of the Hungarians there from an assessment of the polemical and partial publications that have appeared in recent years.

235 **Kinship terms and address in a Hungarian-speaking peasant community in Rumania.**
Lajos Vincze. *Ethnology*, vol. 17, part 1 (Jan. 1978), p. 101-17.
The author examines the kinship terms of the Erdögyarak and concludes that they attest to a system of hierarchical division in this particular peasant community.

Hungarians in Rumania and Transylvania: a bibliographical list of publications in Hungarian and west European languages. *See* item no. 787.

Germans

236 **The German nationality in Romania.**
Monica Barcan, Adalbert Millitz, translated from the Romanian by Anda Teodorescu-Bantaş. Bucharest: Meridiane Publishing House, 1978. 120p. bibliog.
The German population in Romania, according to the 1977 Romanian census, numbered 358,732 people. Of these some 170,000 were Saxons living in Transylvania and 138,000 Swabians from the Banat. The remaining 50,000 Germans are comprised mainly of the Styrians (Steirer) around Reşiţa (c. 16,000), the Germans of Timişoara who are of Austrian origin, the Swabians of Satu Mare (3,500), the Zipser of Vişeul de Sus in northern Maramureş (3,500), the Germans of Bukovina (Buchenländer) (2,200) and those in Bucharest (5,000). This booklet gives a brief history of their settlement, details of cultural history, education and mass media in German and of the Evangelical Church of the Augsburg Confession and of the Roman Catholic Church to which most Germans belong.

237 **Marriage traditions and customs among Transylvanian Saxons.**
Frederick H. Barth. *East European Quarterly*, vol. 12, no. 1 (spring 1978), p. 93-110.
A fascinating account of the wedding traditions amongst Saxons that have persisted to this day by a native of Transylvania. The article describes: courting and wedding traditions, engagement procedures in the author's native village of Seiden (Jidvei) and in the village of Schonau (Sona), and traditions of the wedding feast.

238 **Documents on the expulsion of the Germans from Eastern Central-Europe.**

Bonn, GFR: Federal Ministry for Expellees, Refugees and War Victims. 1955-61. 4 vols.

This is an abridged English translation of *Dokumentation der Vertreibung der Deutschen aus Ost-Mitteleuropa* published by the same ministry. Volume 3 outlines the fate of ethnic Germans in Romania during the immediate post-war years and their living conditions in the Romanian People's Republic. There is an annex of laws and decrees affecting the German population as well as a corpus of documents relating to the transfer of the Germans from Bessarabia, Bukovina and the Dobrogea in 1940 and to the deportation of Germans for compulsory labour to the Soviet Union in January 1945.

239 **The Germans of Rumania.**

Georges Castellan. *Journal of Contemporary History*, vol. 6, no. 1 (1971), p. 52-75.

A presentation of the history of the Germans of Transylvania (the Saxons), of the Banat and Satu Mare (the Swabians), and of Bukovina, Bessarabia and the Dobrogea from the first settlements in the 12th century to the present. The emphasis is upon the 20th century for which the author gives one of the few accounts in English of the fate of the Germans in Romania.

240 **German minorities and the Third Reich.**

Anthony Komjathy, Rebecca Stockwell. New York, London: Holmes & Meier Publishers, 1980. 221p.

Chapter 5 of this study on the ethnic Germans of East Central Europe between the World Wars deals with the Saxons and Swabians of Romania. In detail and scope this presentation in English is invaluable. The political organization of the Saxons, the split in 1935 between the 'moderates' under Fritz Fabritius and the Nazi sympathizers under Alfred Bonfert, the creation in November 1940 of a 'German Ethnic Group' in Romania under Volksgruppenführer Andreas Schmidt, is particularly well chronicled.

241 **Die siebenbürger Sachsen in Vergangheit und Gegenwart** (The Transylvanian Saxons, past and present.)

Friedrich Teutsch. Hermannstadt (Sibiu), Romania: W. Krafft, 1924. 2nd ed. 367p. bibliog.

Still unsurpassed in most respects as the most authoritative history of the Transylvanian Saxons.

242 **The Transylvanian Saxons. Historical highlights.**

Ernst Wagner, Edward R. Schneider, Max Gross, Martin Intscher. Cleveland, Ohio: Alliance of Transylvanian Saxons, 1982. 144p. map.

Three papers on 'The Saxons in Transylvania', 'The Saxons in America' and 'The Saxons in Canada' constitute this valuable little volume. The cornerstone is Ernst

Wagner's contribution on the Transylvanian Saxons (p. 7-94) which provides an excellent historical survey of the Saxon presence in Transylvania from the 12th century until the present.

Siebenbürgische Zeitung (Transylvanian Daily.)
See item no. 709.

Other minorities

243   **Cartea neagră: suferinţele evreilor din România, 1940-1944** (The black book: the sufferings of the Jews in Romania, 1940-1944.)
M. Carp.   Bucharest: Socec, 1945-1948. 3 vols. illus.
The most comprehensive account of the fate of Romanian Jewry during the Second World War. Includes eye-witness accounts of the uprising among members of the Iron Guard in Bucharest between the 21st and the 23rd of January 1941 when several hundred Jews were murdered.

244   **A bibliography of sources concerning the Czechs and Slovaks in Romania.**
Zdenek Salzmann.   *East European Quarterly*, vol. 13, no. 4 (winter 1979), p. 465-88.
An alphabetical but not thematic list of some 175 items on the sparsely scattered communities of Czechs and Slovaks in Romania. The published and manuscript sources mentioned here, including works from the 19th century, cover aspects of the history, demography, education, language, literature and economic activity of these communities, with emphasis on the Czech-speaking villages of the southern Romanian Banat.

245   **Les minorités bulgares en Roumanie. Conditions d'une entente bulgaro-roumaine. (The Bulgarian minorities in Romania. Conditions for a Bulgarian-Romanian entente.)**
Malomir Zaharieff.   Paris: Domat-Montchrestien, 1940. 99p.
Superficial details of the Bulgarian minority in the Dobrogea. This booklet was published to coincide with the negotiations, forced upon Romania by Hitler, with the Bulgarians which led to the cession of the southern Dobrogea and a transfer of population in September 1940.

Romanians in Bessarabia

246 **Bessarabia and beyond.**
Henry Baerlein. London: Methuen, 1935. 278p.

A colourful, entertaining account of travel in Bessarabia, the region between the Prut and the Dniester, in the early 1930s. Many of the accompanying photographs, however, are not from Bessarabia but from other Romanian provinces.

247 **National movements. National history, ancient and modern, as presented in the Moldavian Soviet Encyclopaedia.**
Michael Bruchis. *Crossroads. An International Socio-Political Journal*, vol. 10 (spring 1983), p. 165-95.

The Moldavian Soviet Socialist Republic was created in August 1940 from Bessarabia, northern Bukovina and north-western Dorohoi county which were ceded by Romania under duress to the USSR. Only the central counties of Bessarabia were incorporated by Moscow in the Moldavian SSR along with part of the Autonomous Moldavian SSR which had been formed on the left bank of the Dniester in 1924. The remaining greater part of the Autonomous Moldavian SSR was absorbed into the Ukrainian SSR in 1940. This dismemberment of Bessarabia and the liquidation of the Autonomous Republic conflicted with Soviet propaganda during the period 1924-1940 which advocated the union of Bessarabia with the Autonomous Republic. The problem that this posed for Soviet historians of the Republic and Moscow's post-war policy of discouraging the association of Moldavians with their mother Romanian history and culture are both thoroughly analysed in this article. *Crossroads* is published by the Israel Research Institute of Contemporary Society, POB 687, Jerusalem.

248 **One step back, two steps forward: on the language policy of the Communist Party of the Soviet Union in the national republics.**
Michael Bruchis. Boulder, Colorado: East European Monographs. Distributed by Columbia University Press, 1982. 371p. (East European Monographs, no. 109).

A unique account of language policy in the Moldavian SSR. The use since 1944 of the Cyrillic alphabet in Soviet Moldavia, and the avoidance in the written language of words of Romanian origin, is a major aspect of the drive to give the Moldavians and their language an identity distinct from their fellow Romanians. The changes of nuance in this policy are ably chronicled and examined by the author.

249 **Bessarabia: Russia and Roumania on the Black Sea.**
Charles Upson Clark. New York: Dodd, Mead & Co., 1927. 333p. bibliog.

The author's complaint that 'nowhere could I find any comprehensive and reasonably impartial discussion of Bessarabia' led him to pay two extended visits to the province and consult Romanian and Russian sources for information. The result is this judicious study which provides a history of the province, an examination of the impact of the revolution of 1917, and descriptions of the creation of the Bessarabian republic, of the ensuing period of anarchy, of Christian Rakovsky's Romanian career and Bessarabia's incorporation into Romania. The definition of the boundaries of the Autonomous Moldavian Soviet Socialist Republic, created in 1924, completes this still valuable work.

250 **Romania and the Moldavian SSR.**
Dennis Deletant.   *Soviet Analyst*, vol. 12, no. 1 (Jan. 12, 1983), p. 6-8.

The author's visit to the Moldavian SSR in 1982 provides the basis for a number of observations on the position of the Moldavians in the republic and on the status of their language, Romanian. The article is supplemented by a digest of the turbulent history of this land which is reflected in the partly synonymous names of Moldavia, Bessarabia and the Moldavian SSR.

251 **Bessarabia and Bukovina: the Soviet-Romanian territorial dispute.**
Nicholas Dima.   Boulder, Colorado: East European Monographs, 1982. 173p. bibliog. (East European Monographs, no. 108).

This study, while faithfully chronicling the propaganda conflict between the Soviet Union and Romania over Bessarabia and Bukovina, is far more valuable for its analysis of socioeconomic development in the Moldavian SSR which it amply illustrates with tabular details.

252 **Moldavians or Romanians?**
Nicholas Dima. In: *The Soviet West: Interplay between nationality and social organization.* Edited by Ralph S. Clem.   New York: Praeger, 1975. p. 31-45.

This article presents a resumé of the history of Moldavia, of Soviet policy towards the Moldavians, of the linguistic features of Moldavian which are almost identical with Romanian, and of the character of Moldavian literature since 1924.

253 **Facts and comments concerning Bessarabia, 1812-1940.**
Compiled by a group of Romanian press correspondents.
London: Allen & Unwin, 1941. 63p. bibliog.

A booklet designed to inform the British public of the Romanian character of Bessarabia and Northern Bukovina, both of which were occupied by the Soviet Union on 3 July 1940 on the basis of a secret protocol to the German-Soviet non-aggression pact of August 1939. Preceded by a chronology of the main events that shaped the history of the province, the booklet contains summaries and extracts reprinted from articles, studies and research on the subject, as well as part of the memorandum submitted to the Peace Conference in 1919 by the official delegation of representatives of the province.

254 **Moldavia and the Moldavians.**
Stephen Fischer-Galaţi. In: *Handbook of major Soviet nationalities*. Edited by Zev Katz. New York: Free Press, 1975. p. 415-33.

This contribution provides general information on the economy, history, demography and cultural activity of the Moldavians in the Moldavian SSR. Contains statistical information in tabular form on education in the Moldavian (that is, Romanian) language.

255 **The Moldavian Soviet Republic in Soviet domestic and foreign policy.**
Stephen Fischer-Galaţi. In: *The influence of East Europe and the Soviet West on the USSR*. Edited by Roman Szporluk. New York: Praeger, 1975. p. 229-50.

This article outlines the history of Bessarabia down to its incorporation into a Moldavian Republic in 1940 and 1944, Soviet rule in this republic after 1944, and its place in Soviet-Romanian relations since the war.

256 **Bessarabia: the thorny 'non-existent' problem.**
Jack Gold. *East European Quarterly*, vol. 13, no. 1 (spring 1979), p. 47-74.

A review article of a history of Bessarabia by a Soviet scholar, A. M. Lazarev, the publication of which reopened old Romanian wounds. The polemical character of this Soviet work affords the reviewer the opportunity to examine the history of Bessarabia and to reassert the Romanian case in the covert yet festering territorial dispute with the USSR over this province which today is largely constituted in the Moldavian SSR.

257 **The Russian annexation of Bessarabia, 1774-1828: a study of imperial expansion.**
George F. Jewsbury. Boulder, Colorado: East European Quarterly, 1976. 199p. bibliog. (East European Monographs, no. 15).

The title of this monograph is misleading since Bessarabia was not annexed by Russia until 1812. In November 1806 the Russian army crossed the Dniester and within two months occupied Iaşi and Bucharest. The action was met by a declaration of war from the Porte and the state of hostilities was ended by the Treaty of Bucharest of 1812. The Russians withdrew from Wallachia and Moldavia but assumed sovereignty in the area between the Prut and the Dniester which was renamed Bessarabia. Jewsbury's book examines the Russians' attempts to set up a local administration there. A period of limited autonomy ended in 1828 when by a new statute Bessarabia was absorbed politically into the Russian Empire, the local boyars losing a considerable part of their powers of self-government.

258 **Russian colonialism and Bessarabia: a confronttion of cultures.**
Ladis K. D. Kristof. *Nationalities Paper*, vol. 2, no. 2 (autumn 1974), p. 1-20.

259 **The tragic plight of a border area: Bassarabia and Bucovina.**
Edited by Maria Manoliu-Manea. Los Angeles, California: American Romanian Academy of Arts and Sciences, 1983. 280p. bibliog. (American Romanian Academy of Arts vol. 3).

A mosaic of contributions which advocate Romanian rights to Bessarabia and Bukovina. The first part of the volume presents historical, economic and political aspects of Bessarabia (of the twelve papers only two deal directly with Bukovina) in such papers as 'The principle of self-determination as applied to Bassarabia' by Ion Stere, 'Bassarabia and the policy of Russia at the mouths of the Danube (1812-1980)' by Ion Vardala, 'The Russian ultimatum of 1940' by Mircea Ionniţiu, and 'The Romanian communists on Bassarabia' by Ion Manea Manoliu. Part two covers the language and cultural heritage of the Romanian population in the two provinces. The work is supplemented by an extensive bibliography on Bessarabia and Bukovina.

260 **Bessarabia and Bucovina: the Trojan horse of Russian colonial expansion to the Mediterranean.**
Grigore Nandriş. London: Editura societăţii pentru cultură, 1968. 126p. 5 maps.

A collection of impassioned speeches and articles by a native of Bukovina relating to the history of Bessarabia and Bukovina. Contains a great deal of interesting data about the populations of both provinces but little original historical material.

261 **Die rumänische Nationalbewegung in der Bukowina und der Dako-Romanismus.** (The Romanian national movement in Bukovina and the Daco-Roman idea.)
Erich Prokopowitsch. Graz, Cologne, GFR: Böhlau, 1965. 192p. bibliog. (Studien zur Geschichte der österreichisch-ungarischen Monarchie. Bd. 3.)

A well-researched and documented study of the emergence of a national consciousness in Bukovina from the end of the 18th century to the First World War, with particular emphasis on the Daco-Romanian idea which envisaged the union of all Romanians in a Greater Romania.

Romanians abroad

262 **A magyarországi nemzetiségek néprajza.** (The ethnography of the
Hungarian nationalities.)
I. Balassa. Budapest: Hungarian Ethnographic Society, 1975. 4
vols. bibliog.

A detailed study of the popular customs of the national minorities in Hungary.
Volume 4, written in Romanian and entitled *Din tradiţiile populare ale românilor
din Ungaria* (The popular traditions of the Romanians in Hungary), is the
standard work on this subject.

263 **The Union and League of Romanian Societies: an 'assimilating
force' reviewed.**
Gerald J. Bobango. *East European Quarterly*, vol. 12, no. 1
(spring 1978), p. 85-92.

A review of the role played by the Union and League of Romanian Societies in
helping Romanians to assimilate to American life. The nucleus of the union was
formed in 1906 but it has never attracted more than fifteen per cent of the total
number of American Romanians to its membership. Thus in 1976 no more than
5000 of the 175,000 Americans of Romanian origin belonged to the affiliated
groups of the union that could still be identified as ethnically based.

264 **Some aspects of Romanian as spoken in the United States.**
Charles M. Carlton. *Yearbook of Romanian Studies*, no. 5 (Dec.
1980), p. 3-8.

The author concludes from his brief survey of reports on the character of
Romanian spoken in the United States that 'the American Romanian language,
while perhaps not exceedingly vital today, can hardly be said to be moribund.
From the evidence (not only the increase in periodicals, but also in the numbers
of Americans studying Romanian), it would seem to be undergoing a renaissance.
As to its exact description, however, as well as its social status, the real labor
remains to be done'.

Macedo-Romanians

265 **The Vlachs of Macedonia: some British perspectives.**
Richard Clogg. In: *Anglo-Romanian relations after 1821. Anuarul
Institutului de istorie şi arheologie 'A. D. Xenopol'.* Iaşi,
Romania: Editura Academiei Republicii Socialiste România, 1983.
p. 17-26.

A review article of mainly British accounts of the Vlachs of Macedonia in the half
century preceding the First World War. Clogg concludes: 'The Vlachs of
Macedonia were, as a result of the efforts of such writers as Eliot, Brailsford,

Wace and Thompson, no longer a completely unknown quantity. They could not now simply be dismissed, as Gibbon had done over a century earlier, as "vagrant Wallachians" '.

266 **What is an ethnic group? Ecology and class structure in northern Greece.**
Muriel D. Schein. *Ethnology: an International Journal of Cultural and Social Anthropology*, vol. 14, no. 1 (Jan. 1975), p. 83-97.
An analysis of the ethnicity of two groups of nomadic shepherds in Greece, the Macedo-Romanians or Vlachs, who speak a language closely related to Romanian, and the Sarakatsanoi who speak Greek.

267 **Les pasteurs de Pinde septentrional** (The shepherds of the northern Pindus.)
M. Sivignon. *Revue de Géographie de Lyon*, vol. 43, no. 1 (1968), p. 5-43.
A more recent account of life in those villages of northern Pindus inhabited by Macedo-Romanians (Vlachs) that were described by Wace and Thompson a half-century earlier

268 **The nomads of the Balkans: an account of life and customs among the Vlachs of northern Pindus.**
A. J. B. Wace, M. S. Thompson. London: Methuen, 1914. Reprinted 1972. 332p.
The Romance-speaking populations of the Balkans may be divided into four groups which are separated from each other by Slavonic and Greek-speaking peoples: the Romanians or Daco-Romanians inhabiting the Socialist Republic of Romania, Soviet Moldavia (Moldavian SSR), parts of Yugoslavia and Hungary; the Macedo-Romanians (Vlachs, Aromanians) living in communities in northern Greece, Albania and Yugoslavia; the Megleno-Romanians, now largely absorbed; and the Istro-Romanians, also virtually assimilated, who lived in a small number of villages in the peninsula of Istria on the Adriatic. This invaluable description of the life of the nomadic Macedo-Romanian or Vlach communities of northern Pindus on the eve of the First World War, provides a unique record in English of their customs, folklore and language which have now partially disappeared.

269 **Die Aromunen: etnographisch-philologisch-historische Untersuchungen über das Volk der sogenannten Makedo-Romanen oder Zinzaren** (The Aromanians: ethnographical, philological and historical studies on the so-called Macedo-Romanian or Zinzar people.)
Gustav L. Weigand. Leipzig, GDR: J. A. Barth, 1894-95. 2 vols.
In spite of their age these two volumes are a rich source of information on the cultural heritage of the Romance-speaking pastoral people living in a number of communities in Epirus and western Macedonia. These people are known to the Greeks as Vlachs, and to others as Macedo-Romanians or Aromanians because of the features their language shares with Romanian.

Religion

270 **Discretion and valour. Religious conditions in Russia and Eastern Europe.**
Trevor Beeson. London: Collins, Fount Paperbacks, 1982. rev. ed. 416p. bibliog.

This informative survey of the religious cults in Eastern Europe is based on material gathered by representatives of the British Council of Churches. Chapter 12 (p. 350-79) presents a well-balanced account of the situation of the various cults in post-war Romania, although sometimes the author does not distinguish clearly between the fate of the Roman Catholic and Uniate hierarchy. The unique status of the Orthodox Church in Romania is boldly underlined.

271 **The Rumanian church.**
Marcu Beza. London: Society for the Promotion of Christian Knowledge, 1943. 64p.

A brief outline of the history of the Orthodox Church in Romania that highlights the Byzantine heritage and the role of the Orthodox Church in preserving a cultural identity amongst the Romanians. More recent research has rendered part of Beza's Romanian church chronology inaccurate.

272 **Biserica ortodoxă română. The Romanian Orthodox Church.**
Bucharest: The Institute of the Bible and Orthodox mission, 1967. 255p.

A collection of largely black and white photographs depicting Romanian orthodox churches and monasteries. The subject matter of the photographs is arranged hierarchically: the Romanian patriarchate and the metropolitanates of Ungrovlahia, Moldavia and Suceava, Transylvania, Oltenia, and the Banat.

273 **Religious persecutions in captive Romania.**
Raoul Bossy. *Journal of Central European Affairs*, vol. 15, no. 2
(July 1955), p. 161-81.

A well-documented analysis of the persecution to which religious denominations
were subjected in the period 1948 to 1952 in the Romanian People's Republic and
of the methods used to enforce their subjection. The fate of the Orthodox,
Uniate, Roman Catholic, Armenian, Jewish and Moslem denominations is
covered.

274 **Eastern Churches Review.**
London: Oxford University Press, 1966-. bi-annual.

Occasionally contains articles on developments within the Romanian Orthodox
Church and on its contribution to Orthodox theology.

275 **The Uniate Church: catalyst of Rumanian national consciousness.**
Radu R. Florescu. *Slavonic and East European Review*, vol. 45,
no. 105 (July 1967), p. 324-43.

Historians in the Romanian People's Republic have disregarded the significance
of the Romanian Uniate Church (created in 1700) in fostering a national
awareness amongst the Romanians. It was this fact which prompted this
reappraisal by Florescu.

276 **Ten years ago: the story of the persecution of the Catholic Church
of Byzantine Rite in Romania.**
P. Gherman. Youngstown, Ohio: Gaspan Printing Company,
1958. 43p.

A shortened version of the author's passionate and highly subjective account of
church-state relations in the period 1945 to 1950 entitled *L'ame roumaine
écartelée; faits et documents* (Paris: Éditions du Cèdre, 1955. 258p. illus. maps).
The author, as a priest of the Uniate church (the Catholic Church of the
Byzantine Rite), concentrates on its disestablishment through a forced reunifica-
tion with the Romanian Orthodox Church in 1948.

277 **The Romanian Orthodox Church and the state.**
Keith Hitchins. In: *Religion and atheism in the USSR and Eastern
Europe*. Edited by Bohdan R. Bociurkiw, John W. Strong, assisted
by Jean K. Laux. Toronto: University of Toronto Press; London:
Macmillan, 1975. p. 314-27.

The relationship between the Orthodox Church and the State changed profoundly
when the Romanian Communist Party came to power. The Church was made
subservient to the State and the Party preached that religion was 'obsolete', being
a product of the class system. Nevertheless, harmony between the Orthodox
Church and the Party has been achieved, largely as a result of the leadership
given by Patriarch Justinian and of the historical role of the Orthodox Church as
the repository of a national consciousness. Thus the Romanian Orthodox Church
benefits from far greater tolerance from the Party than any other Orthodox

Religion

Church in the socialist bloc. As Hitchins concludes, 'this relative prosperity has largely been at the pleasure of the state' and that, as never before in its history, the Church is part of the State and is deeply dependent for its continued existence upon changes in the State's domestic priorities and the vicissitudes of its international relations.

278 **Handbuch der Ostkirchenkunde** (A handbook of the Eastern Churches.)
   Edited by Endre von Ivanka, Julius Tyciak, Paul Wiertz.
   Düsseldorf, GFR: Patmos Verlag, 1971. 839p. bibliog.

A compendium of information about the history, organization and discipline of the Orthodox Churches of the East, including that in Romania.

279 **Orthodox monasticism in Romania today.**
   Sister Eileen Mary. *Religion in Communist Lands*, vol. 8, no. 1 (spring 1980), p. 22-27.

A rare appreciation by a Western visitor of the significance of monastic life for the past and present of the Romanian people. 'Christians and non-Christians alike must realize the value of these centres of ancestral faith as a potent force in uniting and strengthening a people who throughout their history have had their identity threatened by one set of invaders or another'.

280 **Istoria bisericii ortodoxe române** (The history of the Romanian Orthodox Church.)
   Mircea Păcurariu. Sibiu, Romania; Bucharest: Editura Institutului Biblic şi de Misiune al Bisericii Ortodoxe Române, 1972-81. 3 vols. illus. maps. bibliog.

An easily digestible history of the Orthodox Church in Romania from its establishment there in the 14th century to the present day. For the period since the last war it presents the official view of church-state relations.

281 **Perspective** (Perspectives.)
   Munich: 1978-. quarterly.

This bulletin from the Romanian Uniate mission in West Germany contains bilingual articles in Romanian and German on aspects of Romanian Uniate Church history and on the activities of the church in Europe.

282 **Kirche unter Hammer und Sichel: die Kirchen Verfolgung in Rumänien, 1945-51.** (Church under hammer and sickle: the persecution of the churches in Romania, 1945-51.)
   Nicolae Pop. Berlin: Morus Verlag, 1953. 146p.

An account of the measures taken by the communist régime to ensure the subservience of the church in Romania. Particular attention is paid to the disestablishment of the Uniate Church in 1948.

283 **Orthodoxie heute in Rumänien und Jugoslawien** (Orthodoxy today in Romania and Yugoslavia.)
Flaviu Popan, Čedomir Drašković. Vienna: Herder, 1966. 190p.

Part of this work is a description of the organization of the Romanian Orthodox Church and its relations with the communist state.

284 **Ecumenism in Eastern Europe: Romanian style.**
Earl A. Pope. *East European Quarterly*, vol. 13, no. 2 (summer 1979), p. 185-212.

This article highlights the ecumenical activity of the Romanian Orthodox Church from the early 1920s down to the present and conveys something of the vigour of Romanian Orthodoxy and its willingness to enter into dialogue with the Western churches.

285 **Stolen church: martyrdom in communist Romania.**
Father Alexander Raţiu, Father William Virtue. Huntington, Indiana: Our Sunday Visitor, 1979. 192p.

A book based on the experiences of Raţiu, a Romanian Uniate priest imprisoned for his faith by the communist authorities in 1948 and released during the general amnesty of 1964. It is also a useful source of information on the fate of other Catholic prelates in Romania.

286 **Die Geschichte des Gottesdienstes der Siebenbürger Sachsen** (The history of the divine worship of the Transylvanian Saxons.)
Erich Roth. Göttingen, GFR: Vandenhoeck und Ruprecht, 1954. 281p. bibliog.

A scholarly account of the religious life of the Transylvanian Saxons and of the foundation of the Lutheran Church, the first bishop of which was elected in 1553 in Hermannstadt (Sibiu). In 1572 the Lutheran synod of the Saxons accepted the Augsburg Confession.

287 **Die Reformation in Siebenbürgen. Ihr Verhältnis zu Wittenberg und der Schweitz** (The Reformation in Transylvania. Its relationship to Wittenberg and Switzerland.)
Erich Roth. Cologne, GFR; Graz, Austria: Böhlau Verlag, 1962-64. 2 vols. bibliog.

The fundamental study of the influence of Luther amongst the Transylvanian Saxons and of the proselytizing activity of his disciple from Kronstadt (Braşov) Johannes Honterus (1498-1549). The Reformation of Kronstadt was achieved on the basis of Honterus's *Reformation booklet* which had been published in 1542/43. In 1550 the University of the Saxon Nation decided to introduce the Lutheran doctrine in Saxon settlements throughout Transylvania.

Religion

288 **Bible work in Eastern Europe since 1945 (Part 2).**
Walter Sawatsky. *Religion in Communist Lands*, vol. 3, no. 6
(Nov.-Dec. 1975), p. 4-14.

A review of the printing and distribution of the Bible in several communist
countries in Eastern Europe, including Romania.

289 **The evangelical wing of the Orthodox Church in Romania.**
Alan Scarfe. *Religion in Communist Lands*, vol. 3, no. 6 (Nov.-
Dec. 1975), p. 15-19.

Describes two evangelical movements within the Romanian Orthodox Church
that emerged around the priests Tudor Popescu of Bucharest in the late 1920s and
Josef Trifa of Sibiu a decade later.

290 **Patriarch Justinian of Romania: his early social thought.**
Alan Scarfe. *Religion in Communist Lands*, vol. 5, no. 3 (autumn
1977), p. 164-69.

Patriarch Justinian of the Romanian Orthodox Church died on 26 March 1977.
He left behind a church of 10,000 parishes with a trained priesthood to fill them
all, two theological institutes with 1,400 students, and a renewed monastic life.
His ministry was based on beliefs expressed in his *Apostolat social*, a collection of
his orations, writings and sermons from the period of his Patriarchate. The early
volumes from this series are examined by the author for evidence from the late
1940s of Justinian's social thought by which he sought to define the role of the
Church in the world at large.

291 **Romanian Baptists and the state.**
Alan Scarfe. *Religion in Communist Lands*, vol. 4, no. 2
(summer 1976), p. 14-20.

A valuable summary of the Baptist movement's history in Romania and the
problems that it faces from the State. These derive partly from the fact that over
recent years the Romanian Baptist Church has grown considerably and that it
cannot be identified historically with the Romanian nation, having been
introduced by German and Hungarian missionaries in the mid-19th century.

292 **Solia** (The Mission.)
Cleveland, Ohio. 1936-. monthly.

Published by the Romanian Orthodox episcopate in America, this Romanian
language journal presents information about the activities of the episcopate.

293 **Eastern politics of the Vatican 1917-1979.**
H. Stehle, translated by Sandra Smith. Athens, Ohio: Ohio
University Press, 1981. 466p.

Chapter eight of this study briefly covers the fate of the Uniate bishops in
Romania following the liquidation of their church in 1948.

294 **The Rumanian Orthodox Church and the West.**
Eric D. Tappe. In: *Studies in Church History, vol. 13: The Orthodox Churches and the West*. Edited by D. Baker. Oxford, England: Blackwell, 1976. p. 277-91.

A summary of the history of the Orthodox church in Transylvania, Wallachia and Moldavia from its earliest times down to the present, and a description of its contacts with Western churches throughout its history. The author draws on his considerable research into the activity of the British and Foreign Bible Society in Wallachia and Moldavia during the 19th century.

295 **Unirea** (The Union.)
East Chicago, Indiana: Association of Romanian Catholics of America Inc. 1949-. monthly.

News and information in English and Romanian for Catholics in the USA. Particularly useful for its coverage of developments in the Roman Catholic Church in Romania. Its members number some 1,300,000 of whom about 875,000 are Hungarian and 230,000 German, principally Swabians of the Banat. The church has two bishoprics, in Alba Iulia and Iaşi, and 660 parishes with 875 priests, 668 of whom receive a state stipend. The appointment of bishops requires the approval of the Romanian department of cults.

296 **The Orthodox Church.**
Timothy Ware. Harmondsworth, England: Penguin Books, 1963. 352p. bibliog.

A well-written introduction to the history and theology of the Orthodox Church by an English convert to the faith.

297 **In God's underground.**
Richard Wurmbrand, edited by Charles Foley. London: Hodder & Stoughton, 1969. 253p.

A powerful testimony to the triumph of faith and human dignity over the harrowing brutality of the prison under the communist régime in post-war Romania. The author, a Lutheran pastor, spent fourteen years in jail for his beliefs before being released under the general amnesty of 1964.

298 **The pastor's wife.**
Sabina Wurmbrand, edited by Charles Foley. London: Hodder & Stoughton, 1969. 218p.

An account by the wife of Richard Wurmbrand of her own imprisonment in Romania between 1950 and 1953 and the conditions in the several prisons and labour camps, including the Black Sea canal, through which she passed.

Society and Social Change

Anthropology

299 **National styles in the development and profession of anthropology: the case of Romania.**
G. James Patterson. *East European Quarterly*, vol. 14, no. 2 (summer 1980), p. 207-17.

A discussion of the nature of anthropological studies in Romania. The author argues that 'Romanian anthropology is descriptive and emphasizes data collection more than it stresses the development of theory; the training of anthropologists stresses traditional methodological approaches. With the focus on national needs there is continued study of peasants in rural areas as well as some development of applied anthropology to look at adjustment of rural migrants to urban areas'.

300 **Cultural anthropology in Romania.**
Paul Henri Stahl. *East European Quarterly*, vol. 4, no. 3 (Sept. 1970), p. 319-27.

A definition of the principal branches of cultural anthropology in which research is being conducted in Romania and an outline of that research. The branches are: ethnography and ethnology; folklore; rustic art; sociology; anthropology (both physical and social); and human geography.

301 **Some special aspects of Rumanian ethnology: phases of development and the contemporary scene.**
Romulus Vulcănescu, Paul Simionescu. *Rumanian Studies*, vol. 2 (1971-1972), p. 195-215.

A summary presentation of contemporary studies in Romanian ethnology that includes some discussion of theoretical and methodological views.

Sociology

302 **Sociological thought in Romania.**
Miron Constantinescu, Ovidiu Bădina, Ernö Gall, translated from the Romanian by Silviu Brucan. Bucharest: Meridiane Publishing House, 1974. 200p.

A historical survey of what the authors term 'sociological thinking' in Romania. The most interesting part is the interpretation given to the ideology of the pre-Marxist socialist movement in Romania (1875-1884), to Constantin Dobrogeanu-Gherea's application of a Marxist sociological model, and to the works of Ştefan Zeletin and Constantin Stere. Sections on the 'monograph school' of Bucharest and on sociological thought in contemporary Romania are also included.

303 **A concise history of Romanian sociology.**
Ştefan Costea, Ion Ungureanu. Bucharest: editura ştiinţifică şi enciclopedică, 1981. 78p. bibliog.

An outline of sociological thought in Romania from the middle of the last century to the present. Post-war sociological investigation in Romania constitutes an interesting section in this survey. A table of content analysis of sociological themes is provided and comparison made with J. Viet's *Thesaurus*. The organization of sociological research is discussed and a summary made of the results achieved by investigations carried out between 1965 and 1978.

Social change and conditions

304 **Industrialization and migration of the Transylvanian peasantry at the end of the 19th and the beginning of the 20th century.**
Ion Aluas. *East European Quarterly*, vol. 3, no. 4 (Jan. 1970), p. 499-508.

An examination of the social and professional migration of the rural population to industrialized centres in Transylvania before the First World War, and of its effects upon the structure of society.

305 **The transformation of the peasantry's consciousness and the economic relations in the countryside.**
M. Cernea. *Romanian Journal of Sociology*, vol. 1 (1962), p. 205-21.

A discussion of the problems encountered in forming a 'socialist consciousness' amongst the peasantry. One conclusion that may be drawn from the article is that the free consent of the peasant is essential if the cooperativization of agriculture is to be effective.

306 **Social change in communist Romania.**
Daniel Chirot. *Social Forces*, vol. 57, no. 1 (1978), p. 457-99.
A social anthropologist's analysis of the influence of post-war Romania's economic policies on labour mobility and urban development.

307 **Urban growth processes in Romania.**
Miron Constantinescu, Henri H. Stahl, Ion Drăgan. Bucharest: Meridiane Publishing House, 1974. 292p.
A collection of papers by a number of scholars, including some not mentioned on the title page, that are centred on the themes of the town and its problems, and on urbanized zones. The towns of Piteşti and Slatina provide the models for some of the research presented here.

308 **Rural community studies in Europe. Trends, selected and annotated bibliographies, analyses. Volume 1. Rural community studies in Rumania.**
Edited by J. L. Durand-Drouhin, L. M. Szwengrub, I. Mihăilescu. Oxford, England: Pergamon Press, 1981. 254p.
The principal author of the three sections of this volume is Mihail Cernea. Part 1 covers 'Trends and methodological development in village monographs', part 2 an 'Annotated bibliography of village studies', and part 3 'Selected analytical summaries'. Part 1 presents stages in the history of monographic research, namely: socioeconomic monographs of administrative rural zones; monographs of village communities; systematic sociology and monographic research; typological diversification of rural community research; and rural community research in the period of the cooperative farm.

309 **Social change in Romania, 1860-1940.**
Edited by Kenneth Jowitt. Berkeley, California: Institute of International Studies, University of California, 1978. 207p.
A collection of articles based on papers delivered at a conference on social change in Romania that analyse aspects of the relationship between economic growth and political independence. There are contributions by K. Jowitt, Daniel Chirot, John Michael Montias, Andrew C. Janos and Philippe C. Schmitter. Keith Hitchins's essay on the significance of the journal *Gîndirea*, and Virgil Nemoianu's study of the aesthetic doctrine of Eugen Lovinescu, complete this stimulating volume.

310 **Influences of the process of industrialization on social mobility.**
C. Murgescu. *Romanian Journal of Sociology*, vol. 4-5 (1966), p. 181-93.
This is an illustration with statistics of changes in the social composition of Romania during the post-war period.

311 **The planners and the peasant: an anthropological study of urban development in Romania.**
Steven Sampson. Esbjerg, Denmark: University Centre of South Jutland. Institute of East-West Studies, 1982. 96p. bibliog. (Monographs in East-West Studies, no. 4).

A valuable anthropological study of the movement from the village to the town in the wake of Romania's industrialization over the last twenty years. It provides a perceptive examination of the implications for the social cohesion of the peasant community when it is fragmented as a result of this migration, and of the changing nature of the town which has been developed to cater for the newcomer.

312 **Traditional Romanian village communities.**
Henri H. Stahl, translated by Daniel Chirot, Holley Coulter Chirot. Cambridge, England: Cambridge University Press; Paris: Editions de la Maison des Sciences de l'Homme, 1980. 227p.

'A study of the evolution of Romanian peasant society from the 13th century to the present, focusing particularly on the village communities of Wallachia and Moldavia'. By comparing communal villages, firstly with villages whose population was subjected to serfdom and, secondly, with those which were free but had private property, the author gives a fresh interpretation of Romanian agrarian history.

313 **Internal colonialism in Austria-Hungary.**
Katherine Verdery. *Ethnic and Racial Studies*, vol. 2 (1979), p. 378-99.

In this article the model of 'internal colonialism' is used to discuss Transylvania's position in the late Habsburg Empire. It is argued that 'internal colonies' are importantly different in different parts of a structured world-system; that the complexity of ethnic relations in the 'semi-peripheral' Habsburg Empire makes the model very difficult to apply meaningfully to that case; and that the model itself fails to account for *why* an ethnic phrasing rather than some other should become the dominant-idiom for social relations.

314 **Transylvanian villagers: three centuries of political, economic and ethnic change.**
Katherine Verdery. Berkeley, Los Angeles; London: University of California Press, 1983. 431p. bibliog.

'An investigation of the changing political economy within which a specific community of villagers underwent the shift from feudalism to socialism. It focuses particularly upon the meaning of ethnic and nationalist identifications, seen in the context of state centralization and relative economic backwardness. The study is both localized, treating a single community in which ethnographic and historical research was carried out, and macrosocial, using secondary sources and theoretical works to discuss wider processes in the eastern part of the Habsburg Empire from 1700 on. This larger social frame determined the character of ethnic meanings and national consciousness for villagers, yet specific features of their local social environment contributed to the form of this consciousness as well'.

75

Customs

315 **Paganism in Roumanian folklore.**
Marcu Beza. New York: Dutton; London: Dent, 1928. 162p.
bibliog.

A collection of papers based on public lectures delivered by the Romanian consul to London on remnants of pagan rites in Romania. The work includes the following contributions: 'Christmas and the New Year', 'The Paparude and Kalojan', 'The Hobby-horse dance' and 'St John's eve'.

316 **Zamolxis: the vanishing god.**
Mircea Eliade, translated by Willard R. Trask. Chicago: University of Chicago Press, 1972. 260p.

Essays on the religions and folklore of Dacia and Eastern Europe. Among the themes are: 'The Dacians and Wolves'; 'Zamolxis'; 'The Devil and God'; 'Prince Dragoş and the Ritual Hunt'; 'Master Manole and the Monastery of Argeş'; 'The Cult of the Mandragora in Romania'; and 'The Clairvoyant Lamb'.

Social Services, Health and Welfare

317 **A systematic approach to the ageing process of living beings.**
A. Aslan, C. Bălăceanu, V. Jucovschi, C. Angel. In: *Modern trends in cybernetics and systems.* Berlin: Springer Verlag, 1977. p. 909-17.

One of many contributions co-authored by Ana Aslan, the patentor of *Gerovital*, (a preparation claiming to give renewed vigour to older people) to the investigation of the ageing process in humans.

318 **Istoria medicinii româneşti** (The history of Romanian medicine.)
Edited by I. V. Bologa, M. Milcu, B. Duţescu, Gh. Brătescu.
Bucharest: Editura medicală, 1972. 566p.

A collective work presenting the development of the medical sciences in Romania, with particular stress on post-war innovations,

319 **Balneary and climatic treatment in Romania.**
Carpaţi-Bucharest National Tourist Office. Bucharest: Publiturism, 1975. 48p.

Shortly after their conquest of Dacia the Romans developed the sulphurous thermal springs at Băile Herculane which they dedicated to Hercules, calling them *aquae Herculi sacrae*. The *thermae Herculi* (baths of Hercules) and their waters have retained their curative properties and during recent years this, and new spas and resorts have been opened. This excellent guide gives details of such centres and of the therapeutic mud treatments available at resorts on the Black Sea.

320 **Public health in Romania.**
T. Ilea, D. Enachescu. Bucharest: Meridiane Publishing House, 1969. 74p.

A survey of the facilities for health care available at the end of the 1960s in the Socialist Republic.

321 **Index bibliographic al lucrărilor ştiinţifice medicale şi farmaceutice, 1970-1977. Bibliographical index of Romanian medical and pharmaceutic scientific papers, 1970-1977.**
Ministerul Sănătăţii. Bucharest: Editura medicală, 1979. 1,219p.

An almost exhaustive Romanian and English bilingual list of 19,446 books and papers by Romanian doctors, surgeons and veterinarians published in Romania and abroad between 1970 and 1977. Supplemented by an alphabetical index of authors.

322 **Health care in the Soviet Union and Eastern Europe.**
Michael Kaser. Boulder, Colorado: Westview Press, 1976. 278p. bibliog.

Chapter 8 is devoted to Romania (p. 235-60). Separate sections deal with: 'Legislation and Policy'; 'Demographic patterns'; 'Health conditions'; 'Health service administration'; 'Health care facilities and finance of care'.

323 **On the organization of social welfare units in rural areas.**
I. I. Matei. *Romanian Journal of Sociology*, vol. 4-5 (1966), p. 259-67.

A description of the principles governing the establishment of medical and welfare centres in rural areas. The steps taken by the authorities to determine the needs of village communities for social services are adumbrated here.

324 **Child care in Romania: a comparative analysis.**
William Moskoff. *East European Quarterly*, vol. 15, no. 3 (autumn 1981), p. 391-97.

The large percentage of women in the Romanian labour force (seventy per cent of all Romanian women were in employment in 1975) means that the state has to make adequate provision for the care of the children of working mothers. This article summarizes that provision with the help of tabulated statistics.

325 **Psychiatry in Romania.**
V. Predescu, D. Christodorescu. In: *International encyclopaedia of neurology, psychology and psychoanalysis*, vol. 2. New York: Aesculapius, 1977. p. 1259.

An outline of the practice of psychiatry in Romania that, inevitably, leaves much ground uncovered.

326 **A concise history of psychology in Romania.**
Alexandru Roşca, Constantin Voicu.   Bucharest: Editura ştiinţifică şi enciclopedică, 1982. 51p.

Principally a bibliographical essay on works by Romanian specialists in psychology from the middle of the last century to the present.

327 **The sanitary organization for the protection of mother and child in the Socialist Republic of Romania.**
Virginia Russ.   Bucharest: The Ministry of Health, 1971. 12p.

Outlines the facilities available for child health care in Romania in the early 1970s.

Politics, Government, Constitution and the Law

Constitution and Parliament

328 **Buletinul oficial al Republicii Socialiste România.** (The official bulletin of the Socialist Republic of Romania.)
Bucharest: Consiliul de Stat, Serviciul Buletinului oficial şi al publicaţiilor legislative, 1949-. Irregular.

Published in four parts: laws, decrees of the Council of Ministers and of the president; proceedings of the Grand National Assembly; official communiqués; and prices fixed by the Ministry of domestic trade.

329 **Socialist democracy: principles and political action in Romania.**
Ioan Ceterchi, translated from the Romanian by Dan Hurmuzescu.
Bucharest: Meridiane Publishing House, 1975. 99p

The official interpretation of socialist democracy and the constitutional channels through which it is implemented in Romania.

330 **The state system of the Socialist Republic of Romania.**
Ioan Ceterchi.   Bucharest: Meridiane Publishing House, 1967. 130p.

A description of Romania's bureaucratic structure.

331 **Constitution of the Socialist Republic of Romania.**
Bucharest: Meridiane Publishing House, 1975. 32p.

An English translation of the Romanian constitution with amendments to 21 March 1975.

332 **Constituţia Republicii Socialiste România** (The Constitution of the
Socialist Republic of Romania.)
Bucharest: Consiliul de Stat, Sectorul Buletinului oficial şi al
publicaţiilor legislative, 1980. 31p.

The constitution of Romania incorporating amendments to 19 December 1979.
The first communist constitution was passed by the Grand National Assembly in
April 1948. It was superceded by a second in September 1952. The present
constitution was passed in July 1965 when Romania was styled a 'socialist
republic'.

333 **The Grand National Assembly of the Socialist Republic of Romania:
a brief outline.**
Bucharest, 1974. 104p.

The Grand National Assembly (Marea Adunare Naţională) was established by
the constitution of 1948 and until 1972 was elected every four years (since then
every five years to coincide with party congresses). Since 1975 more than one
candidate has been allowed to stand in each constituency but all candidates must
represent the Front of Socialist Democracy and Unity. The assembly meets briefly
in two sessions each year and frequently amends the constitution. The prime
minister is elected by the assembly which also appoints standing commissions to
act in an advisory capacity to the government.

334 **Rumania.**
Traian Ionaşco. In: *International encyclopaedia of comparative
law*. Tübingen, GFR; The Hague, Paris: International
Association of Legal Science, 1974. Vol. 1, p. 25-38.

A concise presentation of the constitutional and legal system of Romania divided
into the following sections: 'Constitutional system'; 'Sources of law and historical
development'; 'Civil law, family law and cooperative law'; 'Commercial law';
'Planning and management of the national economy'; 'Principles of judicial
procedure'; and 'Private international law and the law of international procedure'.

335 **The Romanian socialist constitution of 1965.**
Traian Ionaşcu. *Review of Contemporary Law*, vol. 13, no. 1
(1966), p. 85-101.

The author's abstract speaks for itself: 'The constitution of 21 August 1965 reflects
the advanced stage of the development of our society, presents the picture of an
advanced socialist society whose tasks are now being completed with a view to
gradually going forward to the construction of communism'.

Political system and political trends

336 **The political system of the Socialist Republic of Romania.**
Edited by Ioan Ceterchi, Ovidiu Trăsnea, Constantin Vlad.
Bucharest: Editura ştiinţifică şi enciclopedică, 1979. 280p.

A collection of thirteen articles including 'The class structure of socialist Romania', 'The exercise of state power and workers' self-management', 'Democracy and lawfulness. Human rights in socialism', 'Political values and moral values in socialism' and 'The evolution of the political factor in the process of advancing towards communism'.

337 **Romania: problems of independence and development.**
Robert L. Farlow. In: *East Central Europe: yesterday, today, tomorrow.* Edited by Milorad M. Drachkovitch. Stanford, California: Hoover Institution Press, 1982, p. 327-48.

The view of contemporary Romania as a country of paradox is highlighted by this incisive and stimulating paper which identifies the principal political trends in Romania today. These are the personality cult of Ceauşescu and his wife, nationalism, and sporadic workers' protests. Whether the emergence of domestic discontent with the failure to solve the serious internal economic problems will obstruct Ceauşescu's independent foreign policy is the central question that the author poses for the 1980s.

338 **Nicolae Ceauşescu and the Romanian political leadership: nationalization and personalization of power.**
Mary Ellen Fischer. Saratoga Springs, New York: Skidmore College, 1983. 56p. (The Edwin M. Mosely Faculty Research Lecture 1982).

An excellent detailed study that reviews the political techniques used by Ceauşescu in consolidating his power over the RCP. 'A brief survey of his origins and early career is followed by a detailed discussion of the 1965-1969 period when he used policy compromise and ambiguity, personnel manipulation, promises of constitutionality and legality, participatory reforms, and a populist style reminiscent of Khrushchev to establish his personal control. Ceauşescu's anti-Soviet policies gained him a measure of popular support in Romania by the late 1960s, but his popularity waned as his economic priorities favoured industrial growth instead of higher living standards. His techniques of rule came to include the personality cult, tight control of personnel and policies, and skillful use of coercion. Since 1979 Romania has faced a severe economic crisis, and the author evaluates the possibilities for political change including élite opposition or mass revolt. She concludes that Ceauşescu's political skills will probably enable him to maintain the existing stalemate for some time to come'.

339 **Nicolae Ceauşescu: his political life and style.**
Mary Ellen Fischer. *Balkanistica*, vol. 5 (1979), p. 84-99.

'A brief summary of the information available on Ceauşescu's early life. Much is

from "approved" biographies and the descriptions are as valuable for their
revelations about the myths created in Romania regarding Ceauşescu as for the
actual information provided'.

340 **Participatory reforms and political developments in Romania.**
Mary Ellen Fischer. In: *Political development in Eastern Europe.*
Edited by Jan Triska, Paul Cocks.   New York: Praeger, 1977. p.
217-37.
'This study examines the 1975 elections to the Grand National Assembly and
places these first "multi-candidate" elections into the context of other participatory reforms introduced by Ceauşescu after 1965. The author sees these
reforms as part of a strategy to increase régime legitimacy, and neither the
strategy as a whole nor these reforms were very successful through 1975.
Participation remains formal and without influence on policy; this is clear in the
Assembly itself and in its electoral process'.

341 **Political leadership and personnel policy in Romania, 1965-1976.**
Mary Ellen Fischer. In: *World Communism at the crossroads.*
Edited by Steven Rosefielde.   Boston, Massachusetts: Martinus
Nijhoff, 1980. p. 210-33.
'The focus of this article is the RCP apparatus: the individuals surrounding
Gheorghiu-Dej and Ceauşescu in the top leadership group, and the regional party
secretaries who supported Ceauşescu during his consolidation of power'.

342 **The Romanian Communist Party and its central committee:**
patterns of growth and change.
Mary Ellen Fischer.   *Southeastern Europe*, vol. 6, part 1 (1979), p.
1-28.
'The author describes in detail the changes in size and socioeconomic
characteristics of the RCP and its central committee from the interwar period to
1978. The author finds that the size and composition of the RCP was affected by
conscious policy on the part of the leadership as well as by the perceptions of
citizens about the potential benefits of membership for themselves or for the
country. In contrast, changes in the CC are related to the needs of the individual
party leader, Gheorghiu-Dej or Ceauşescu. The author concludes that the party
has become an indigenous Romanian organization, reflective of the total
population, and thus has potential for widespread support. However, the internal
structure remains hierarchical, and the CC is a body of the political and economic
elite'.

343 **Myths in Romanian history.**
Stephen Fischer-Galaţi.   *East European Quarterly*, vol. 15, no. 3
(Sept. 1981), p. 327-34.
A brief survey of historical mythology, as practised in contemporary Romania, in
an attempt to establish legitimacy in two principal spheres: firstly, to justify
Romanian historical rights to the possession of Bessarabia and Transylvania;
secondly, to justify the policies of the present régime as a continuation of the
national and 'revolutionary' traditions of the Romanian people.

Politics, Government, Constitution and the Law. Political system and political trends

344 **Political leadership at the regional level in Romania: the case of the judeţ party, 1968-1973.**
Trond Gilberg. *East European Quarterly*, vol. 9, no. 1 (spring 1975), p. 97-119.

The Romanian term *judeţ* means 'region', 'county' and this analysis is based on an examination of the effects of the provincial reorganization that took place in Romania in 1968 when the previous regions were replaced by *judeţe*. This reorganization required the appointment of party personnel at both first and second secretary levels and provided Ceauşescu with an opportunity to strengthen his hold over the regional party structure. The author lists the new appointments, examines their significance, and concludes that most of them were party faithfuls and not 'skilled specialists'.

345 **Political innovation in Rumania.**
Kenneth Jowitt. *Survey*, vol. 20, no. 4 (autumn 1974), p. 132-51.

'The probability of a major crisis in Soviet-Romanian relations' was predicted by the author following political innovations in Romania in the early seventies. Yet the years 1972-74, with the fusion of party and state hierarchies, and the creation of the office of President of the Republic, will be remembered as the period of Ceauşescu's enhancement of his own power.

346 **Revolutionary breakthrough and national development. The case of Romania, 1944-1965.**
Kenneth Jowitt. Berkeley, California: University of California Press, 1971. 371p. bibliog.

The first study of contemporary Romania based on the techniques of political science. The author applies his own theory about the process of 'nation-building' to the experience of Romania between 1944 and 1965, and although the result has not found universal acceptance, it does offer a reconsideration of Romania's independent course.

347 **Reinterpretation of history as a method of furthering communism in Rumania: a study in comparative history.**
Michael J. Rura. Washington, DC: Georgetown University Press, 1961. 123p. bibliog.

A critique of the communist reinterpretation of Romania's past as reflected by the publications of Romanian historians between 1948 and 1954. Comparisons are made between pre-war histories and those of the Stalinist period.

348 **Rumanian nationalism.**
George Schöpflin. *Survey*, vol. 20, no. 2-3 (spring-summer 1974), p. 77-104.

An astute analysis of the manifestation of Romanian nationalism in foreign and economic relations, in language, and in historiography. The article demonstrates that official and popular conceptions of nationality coincide and, therefore, the Romanian Communist Party enjoys popular support in its defence of the national interest against what are construed as external threats to the country's integrity.

349 **The men of the archangel revisited: anti-semitic formations among
communist Romania's intellectuals.**
Michael Shafir. *Studies in Comparative Communism*, vol. 16, no.
3 (autumn 1983), p. 223-43.
A unique analysis of the apparent revival of anti-semitism in intellectual circles in
Romania. The analysis employs the 'interest group' approach and compares
developments in Romania with those in the Soviet Union.

350 **Political culture, intellectual dissent and intellectual consent.**
Michael Shafir. *Orbis*, vol. 27 (summer 1983), p. 393-420.
A fascinating and perceptive analysis of Romanian political culture and
intellectual sub-culture, focusing on issues such as submissiveness to the régime.
The approach is mainly comparative.

351 **The socialist republic of Romania.**
Michael Shafir. In: *Marxist governments: a world survey, vol. 3.*
Edited by B. Szajkowski. London: Macmillan, 1981. p. 589-693.
A general review of Romanian politics and social developments under the
communist régime.

352 **Ideology and political community in Eastern Europe: the case of
Romania.**
Ilie J. Smultea. *East European Quarterly*, vol. 5, no. 4 (Jan.
1972), p. 505-36.
A synopsis of Romania's internal and external policies since the Second World
War that is used to demonstrate the country's unique position in the Eastern bloc.

Law and the legal system

353 **Digest of the general laws of Romania.**
Legislative Council of the Socialist Republic of Romania.
Bucharest: Editura ştiinţifică şi enciclopedică, 1980. 256p.
This volume incorporates changes made during 1978 and 1979 to legislation
relating in particular to economic and financial procedures in Romania. It
presents the articles which amended: the law on the planned economic and social
development of Romania; the law on economic contracts; the law on health; the
customs code of the republic; the law on education; and the law on dealing with
proposals, complaints and petitions from the populace.

Politics, Government, Constitution and the Law. Law and the
legal system

354 **A concise history of Romanian law.**
Compiled by P. Gogeanu, L. P. Marcu. Bucharest: Scientific and
Encyclopaedic Publishing house, 1981. 84p. bibliog.

The most informative part of this misleadingly entitled survey is the bibliography
which does relate to the legal system in Romania. The chapter on 'Contemporary
law in socialist Romania' describes aspects of constitutional, civil and criminal
law.

355 **The obligation to conclude economic contracts.**
Traian Ionaşcu, Eugène A. Barasch. *Review of Contemporary
Law*, vol. 12, no. 1 (1965), p. 51-66.

Explains the necessity and importance of contracts concluded between socialist
organizations for delivery of goods, execution of work and provision of services in
fulfilment of the five-year plan then current.

356 **The Romanian procuratura.**
H. B. Jacobini. *East European Quarterly*, vol. 14, no. 4 (winter
1980), p. 439-59.

A clear and concise evaluation of the functions of the *procuratura* in Romania.
An analogous role is played in Britain and the USA by the Attorney General and
the State's attorney respectively. This article examines the role of the *procuratura*
in criminal proceedings, the supervision of the application of court decisions, and
the action taken by the procuracy regarding complaints against state officials.

357 **Roumanie.**
In: *La vie juridique des peuples*, tome 4. Edited by Henri Lévy-
Ullmann, Boris Mirkine-Guetzévitch. Paris: Librairie Delagrave,
1933. 452p.

A collection of articles surveying public and private law in Romania in the inter-
war period.

358 **Legislation on oil exploration and exploitation.**
I. Rucareanu. *Review of Comparative Law*, vol. 8, no. 1 (June
1961).

A survey of legislation relating to oil exploration and exploitation in Romania
from 1923 to 1960.

359 **Legal sources and bibliography of Romania.**
Virgiliu Stoicoiu. New York: Praeger, 1964. 237p.

An invaluable catalogue of selected publications chiefly in Romanian on the
corpus of laws enacted in the Romanian principalities from the 17th century to
1918, and in Greater Romania from 1918 to 1963. Section 9 presents a list of the
principal laws, decrees and resolutions in force in the People's Republic of
Romania from 1st January 1963. Some items in English, French, German, Italian
and Russian are also included.

360 **The penal code of the Romanian Socialist Republic.**
Translated and with an introduction by S. M. Vrabiescu Kleckner.
South Hackensack, New Jersey: Fred B. Rothman; London: Sweet
& Maxwell, 1976. 143p. (The American Series of Foreign Penal
Codes, no. 20).

A translation of the Romanian penal code with a summary of its distinctive
features.

Human rights

361 **Amnesty International briefing: Romania.**
London: Amnesty International, 1980. 19p.

A reference paper summarizing information on the official penalization of
Romanian citizens who attempt to exercise internationally recognized human
rights in a non-violent manner in the Socialist Republic of Romania. Among
details provided are those concerning: the confinement of prisoners of conscience
in psychiatric institutions; the number of prisoners; the location of prisons; prison
conditions; and action taken by Amnesty International.

362 **The Kremlin's dilemma: the struggle for human rights in Eastern
Europe.**
Tufton Beamish, Guy Hadley. London: Collins & Harvill Press,
1979. 285p.

An analysis of the nature and source of demands in six countries of Eastern
Europe for the implementation of the Final Act of the Helsinki Conference on
Security and Cooperation in Europe. Chapter five chronicles the emergence of a
human rights movement in Romania in the mid-1970s, one of the principal
architects of which was Paul Goma.

363 **Romanian dissent: its ideas.**
Vlad Georgescu. In: *Dissent in Eastern Europe*. Edited by Jane
Leftwich Curry. New York: Praeger, 1983. p. 182-94.

The author, director of the Romanian services of Radio Free Europe, has
personal experience of the treatment accorded to those citizens of the Socialist
Republic of Romania who attempt to act positively to achieve greater civil,
political and human rights in the country. Most Romanian dissidents consider
their country's independent policies to be more harmful than helpful since
Romania's élite is using its autonomy to implement a strict Stalinist system at
home. The cult of the personality has led to a strengthening of the police state,
and the internal chaos produced by short-sighted economic measures has
produced a moral perversion of the population. 'One of the main effects of both
the cult of the personality and this negative independence has been the rise of a
new official nationalism. None of the dissidents, however, accept the régime's
obsession with the past or its hollow appeal to what it terms "national values", an

appeal that makes Romanian communism look very similar to the interwar Romanian fascist movement'.

364 **Who is Paul Goma?**
Michael Shafir. *Index on Censorship*, vol. 7, no. 1 (1978), p. 29-39.

Written shortly after the arrest of dissident writer Paul Goma in Romania, this article traces Goma's literary and political development and the roots of his conflict with the authorities.

Defence forces

365 **The armed forces of the Socialist Republic of Romania.**
Constantin Antip, Gheorghe Bejancu. Bucharest: Military Publishing House, 1966. 78p.

The title of this booklet is misleading since it offers an appreciation of the role of the Romanian army in the defeat of the Germans following the overthrow of Marshal Antonescu on 23 August 1944.

366 **Pages from the history of the Romanian army.**
The Centre for Military History and Theory Studies and Research. Translated by Carol Kormos, Georgeta Bolomey, Florin Ionescu. Bucharest: Editura Academiei R. S. România and Editura militară a Ministerului Apărării Naţionale, 1975. 244p.

The work of a collective containing nineteen articles on such themes as the army of the Romanian principalities from the 14th to the 16th century (N. Stoicescu), the contribution of Stephen the Great to Romanian military tactics (I. Cupşa), the battle of Călugăreni in 1595 (M. Neagoe), the Romanian army in the First World War (V. Mâciu), and the army of the Socialist Republic of Romania (I. Coman).

367 **National defence: the Romanian view.**
Edited by Iulian Cernat, Emanoil Stanislav, translated by Carol Kormos, Georgeta Bolomey, Florin Ionescu. Bucharest: Military Publishing House, 1976. 267p.

A collection of twelve articles to which sixteen officers of the Romanian armed forces have contributed outlining the structure of Romania's national defence system, the conduct of such a defence, the anticipated features of a conflict with an aggressor, and the role of a resistance movement. As a member of the Warsaw Pact, it is noteworthy that no mention is made of the part that Romania's consignatories might play in her defence.

Foreign Relations

368 **Les relations entre Israel et la Roumanie de la guerre des six jours à la guerre de Kippour, 1969-1973.** (Relations between Israel and Romania from the Six-Day War to the Kippur War, 1969-1973.) Joseph Alpern. *Politique étrangère*, no. 6 (1973), p. 725-52.

A rare and valuable presentation of Romania's relations, unique for an East European socialist country, with Israel.

369 **The political and military limits of autonomy.** Aurel Braun. New York: Praeger, 1978. 201p. bibliog.

A detailed analysis of Romanian foreign policy under Ceauşescu. Romanian deviations from Soviet foreign policy lines are placed against the background of Soviet policy towards Eastern Europe and an attempt is made to define the political and military limits of Romania's autonomy in foreign policy.

370 **Romania and the United Nations.** Traian Chebeleu. Bucharest: Editura ştiinţifică şi enciclopedică, 1978. 125p. bibliog.

An examination of Romania's participation in the work of the United Nations and of its specialized agencies. This work underlines the importance attached by Romania to these institutions.

371 **Socialist Romania in international relations.** Nicolae Ecobescu, Sergiu Celac, translated from the Romanian by Sergiu Celac. Bucharest: Meridiane Publishing House, 1975. 132p.

An official presentation of the tenets of Romania's foreign policy, which examines the development of bilateral relations with all states, Romanian activity in international organizations, and Romania's contribution to European security.

372 **Romania and the policy of partial alignment.**
R. L. Farlow. In: *The foreign policies of Eastern Europe*. Edited
by James A. Kuhlmann. Leiden, Netherlands: A. W. Sijthoff,
1978. p. 191-207.

A survey of Romanian foreign policy during the 1960s and 1970s. In the course of
the construction of an independent foreign policy, 'Romania had performed the
paradoxical feat of remaining within the constellation of party-state institutions
and commitments, which constitutes the Soviet-East European alignment system
or bloc, while at the same time engaging in numerous policies directly opposed by
the other members of the bloc, particularly by the leading member, the Soviet
Union'.

373 **Foreign policy.**
Stephen Fischer-Galaţi. In: *Südosteuropa-Handbuch. Band II.
Rumänien.* (Handbook of Southeastern Europe, vol. 2. Romania.)
Edited by K.-D. Grothusen. Göttingen, GFR: Vandenhoeck und
Ruprecht, 1977. p. 198-231.

A·summary of the tenets applied by Ceauşescu to Romania's foreign policy with
regard to relations with the USSR, China and the West during the late 1960s and
1970s.

374 **Rumania: background to autonomy.**
Graeme J. Gill. *Survey*, vol. 21, no. 3 (summer 1975), p. 94-113.

An analysis of the conditions which made independent Romanian initiatives in
economic and foreign policy possible during the mid-1960s and early 1970s.

375 **Detente and disarmament: the Romanian view.**
Robert Govender. London: Unified Printers & Publishers, 1982.
190p.

A presentation of President Nicolae Ceauşescu's statements on detente and
disarmament between 1975 and 1981. An annex of documents includes details of
Romania's initiatives at the Belgrade meeting of the Conference on Security and
Cooperation in Europe (1977-78), and the text of a speech by Ceauşescu in
December 1981 to mark the fifth anniversary of the signing of the all-European
Conference Final Act.

376 **The break-up of the Soviet empire in Eastern Europe.**
Ghita Ionescu. Harmondsworth, England: Penguin Books, 1965.
168p. bibliog.

An examination of Eastern Europe's erosion of their domination at the hands of
the USSR, with an account of Romania's assertion of national independence and
her challenge to Comecon in the early 1960s.

377 **The reluctant ally: a study of communist neocolonialism.**
Ghita Ionescu. London: Ampersand Books, Allen & Unwin,
1965. 133p.

A brief study of the course of Soviet-Romanian relations during and after the
crisis in Comecon between 1962 and 1963, and a description of the subsequent
change of emphasis in Romanian diplomacy.

378 **R and D in Bucharest.**
Lloyd Jordan. *Survey*, no. 76 (summer 1970), p. 122-36.

A summary of Romania's efforts to expand her scientific and technical relations
with the West during the late 1960s and their political significance.

379 **Rumanian foreign policy.**
Robert R. King. *Survey*, vol. 20, no. 2-3 (spring-summer 1974),
p. 105-20.

The external considerations which permitted and encouraged the Romanian
leadership to develop its autonomy in the early 1960s changed during the decade
and forced the country to seek new ways of maintaining its position. This article
provides a penetrating account of the efforts which were made to achieve that
goal.

380 **Socialism, nationalism and underdevelopment: research on**
Romanian foreign policy making.
Jeanne Kirk Laux. In: *Foreign policy making in communist*
countries. Edited by Hannes Adomeit, Robert Boardman.
Farnborough, England: Saxon House, 1979. p. 49-78.

This paper provides answers to the following four questions: Why did Romania
embark upon an independent foreign policy?; Why did Romania's development
priorities differ from those of other small socialist partners?; Why did the
Romanian political élite choose to pursue a divergent strategy rather than defer to
its allies' preferences?; and Why should a narrow confrontation over industrialization have been extrapolated into a general foreign policy orientation?

381 **Romanian foreign policy in the 1980s: domestic-foreign policy**
linkages.
Ronald H. Linden. In: *Foreign and domestic policy in Eastern*
Europe in the 1980s. Edited By Michael J. Sodaro, Sharon L.
Wolchik. London, New York: Macmillan, 1983. p. 47-80.

The author of this paper describes it as 'an effort to explore the range of domestic
and international factors which have stimulated and allowed Romanian foreign
policy to take the unique course that it has'. This policy has served to reduce
Romania's dependence on the USSR and Comecon by enabling her to obtain
technology and raw materials from elsewhere, and to secure for Ceauşescu the
status of national leader through his identification with the policy and his constant
promotion of it in the international arena.

382 **The uses of Beijingpolitik: China in Romanian foreign policy since 1953.**
Mark Hunter Madson. *East European Quarterly*, vol. 16, no. 3 (autumn 1982), p. 277-309.

An overview of Romanian foreign policy since the early fifties, in which the author concentrates on 'the process through which leaderships in Bucharest and Beijing have maneuvered to construct and delimit, justify and express, a stable formal relationship which effectively serves the compatible formal and informal goals of the two régimes'.

383 **Romanian diplomacy. A historical survey.**
Mircea Malița. Bucharest: Meridiane Publishing House, 1970. 224p. bibliog.

Written by Romania's senior ambassador (Malița has held the post of ambassador to the USA), this survey traces the history of Romanian diplomatic activity abroad through its emissaries from the 16th century until the institutionalization of diplomatic representation in the form of representatives and ministers in the 19th and 20th centuries.

384 **European security. A Romanian point of view.**
Romulus Neagoe, translated from the Romanian by Anda Teodorescu-Bantaş. Bucharest: Meridiane Publishing House, 1977. 152p.

A presentation and explanation of President Ceauşescu's views on the means of reducing tension in Europe and of ensuring peace. The principal features of the Romanian proposals, as put forward at the Conference on Security and Cooperation in Europe which opened at Helsinki in 1972, are reproduced here. They advocate the peaceful settlement of disputes, refrain from the use and threat of force, respect for national independence, non-intervention in the internal affairs of a country, and military disengagements and disarmament in Europe.

385 **Romania's special diplomatic position: a case study of China's role.**
David W. Paul. *East European Quarterly*, vol. 7, no. 3 (autumn 1973), p. 311-29.

The author sees China's support of Romania's foreign policy during the late 1960s and early 1970s as a crucial element in the Soviet Union's tolerance of its maverick neighbour.

386 **For a better and juster world: a collection of treaties and solemn joint declarations concluded by socialist Romania with other states.**
Edited by E. Popa with an introductory study by G. Macovescu. Bucharest: Meridiane Publishing House, 1975. 159p.

Romania's vigorous and independent foreign policy is reflected in this collection. The second twenty-year treaty with the USSR, signed in July 1970, may also be found in R. A. Remington's *The Warsaw Pact*, Cambridge, Massachusetts, MIT Press, 1971, p. 242-45.

387 **Rumanian foreign policy after 1945.**
Gabriel Ronay. In: *The Soviet Union and Eastern Europe: a handbook*. Edited by George Schöpflin. London: Blond, 1970. p. 269-75.

A brief but perceptive assessment of Romanian foreign policy with special emphasis on the period since 1965.

388 **Romanian policy in the Middle East.**
Michael Shafir. Jerusalem: Hebrew University of Jerusalem, Soviet and East European Research Centre, 1974. 53p. (Research paper, no. 7).

An analysis of Romanian policies in the Middle East, focusing upon political and economic interests pursued by Bucharest in this region.

389 **The foreign policy of Romania in the sixties.**
Horia Socianu. In: *The foreign policies of Eastern Europe*. Edited by James A. Kuhlmann. Leiden, Netherlands: A. W. Sijthoff, 1978. p. 167-89.

A study of Romanian foreign policy in the 1960s which seeks to answer two questions: Why did Gheorghiu-Dej and Ceauşescu initiate and expand foreign policy consonant with Romania's national interest but opposed to Soviet interests? and why did Soviet leaders tolerate the Romanian insubordination? The author concludes that 'even though reluctantly, the Romanian deviation has been incorporated in the eastern bloc in an attempt to keep under control the impact of a disrupting force'.

390 **The limits of national independence in the Soviet bloc: Rumania's foreign policy reconsidered.**
Vladimir Socor. *Orbis. A journal of world affairs*, vol. 20, no. 3 (autumn 1976), p. 701-32.

In a critical re-examination of Romania's foreign policy since the early 1960s, the author suggests an alternative interpretation of the evidence adduced to support the view that this policy is independent of the Soviet Union. The conclusion reached is that 'Rumania's semblance of independence in foreign policy, and Soviet permisiveness towards it, have probably been the result of an enlightened comprehension by each side of the advantage to be drawn from such a course. This, and the minimal risks involved, have led to the emergence of Communist Rumania in her "independent" posture. To expect that an East European Communist régime would, or could, under the international conditions prevailing in the 1960s and 1970s, embark upon a genuine policy of emancipation and independence running counter to Moscow's interests would be as unrealistic as to expect that Moscow would tolerate the challenge'.

Economy, Finance and Banking

General

391 Romania's development over 1971-1975.
Bucharest: Chamber of Commerce of the Socialist Republic of
Romania, 1973. 95p

A digest of statistics which show the expansion of the Romanian economy during
the late sixties and the projected targets for the period 1971-75.

392 The national income in the Socialist Republic of Romania.
Bucharest: Editura Academiei R. S. România, 1975. 252p.

A detailed presentation, using official statistics, of the growth in national income
during the late sixties and early seventies.

393 Structural patterns of the Romanian economy.
Emilian Dobrescu, Ion Blaga, translated from the Romanian by
Elena Hârşan.   Bucharest: Meridiane Publishing House, 1973.
204p. bibliog.

A descriptive work that presents the general trends in Romania's economic
development since 1948, the development and organization of industry and
agriculture, the influence of structural modifications in the areas of industry and
transport on the national economy, the territorial distribution of productive
forces, the modifications in the structure of the labour force, and the social
consequences of economic development during the period mentioned.

394 **Modernization in Romania since World War II.**
Trond Gilberg. New York, London: Praeger, 1975. 261p. bibliog.
(Praeger Special Studies in International Economies and
Development.)

The author provides an impressive array of data on economic indicators, societal
changes, and party membership in his analysis of modernization and development
(i.e. socioeconomic changes) in Romania. The author suggests that these
socioeconomic changes have produced political change in Romania although the
evidence can lend equal support to the conclusion that the reverse is true. The
contradictions in the relationship between these two types of change are
highlighted by this work.

395 **Regional development strategy in Southeast Europe: a comparative
analysis of Albania, Bulgaria, Romania and Yugoslavia.**
G. W. Hoffman. New York: Praeger, 1972. 322p. bibliog.

Although the emphasis of the work is on Yugoslavia, this comparative study
contains significant details on the planning and execution of regional development
policies in Romania.

396 **New economic systems of Eastern Europe.**
Edited by Hans Hermann Höhmann, Michael Kaser, Karl C.
Thalheim. London: Hurst, 1975. 585p.

This collective work contains studies of reforms in each of the nine socialist
economies of Eastern Europe. It also comprises comparative analyses of
planning, finance, foreign trade, legislation, and of the regulation of agriculture.
The chapter on Romania (p. 171-98), written by Michael Kaser, deals with a
number of aspects of the economic reforms including the reorganization of central
authorities, investment planning, wage and profit reform, and the private sector.

397 **Industrialization, trade and mobilization in Romania's drive for
economic independence.**
Marvin R. Jackson. In: *East European economies Post-Helsinki. A
compendium of papers presented to the Joint Economic Committee,
95th Congress, 1st session.* Washington, DC: Government
Printing Office, 1977. p. 886-940.

Although Romania is an oil producing country, it is a net importer of oil. It must
also import iron ore, metallurgical coke, asbestos, cellulose, copper, nickel and
titanium. Jackson's paper presents a comprehensive analysis of Romania's
progress in industrialization and towards economic independence.

398 **Perspectives on Romania's economic development in the 1980s.**
Marvin R. Jackson. In: *Romania in the 1980s.* Edited by Daniel N.
Nelson. Boulder, Colorado: Westview Press, 1981. 313p.

A judicious inquiry into the prospects for Romania's economy in the 1980s which
proceeds from an elucidation of a confusing statistical record of the Romanian

95

economy. It goes on to evaluate official Romanian projections of economic development from 1980 to 1990.

399 Romania's economy at the end of the 1970s: turning the corner on intensive development.

Marvin R. Jackson. In: *Joint Economic Committee, US Congress, East European Assessment. Part 1 – Country Studies, 1980.* Washington, DC: Government Printing Office, 1981. p. 231-98, 571-618.

A detailed analysis of the performance of the Romanian economy during the 1970s and an assessment of prospects for the following decade.

400 Comecon: integration problems of the planned economies.

Michael Kaser. London, New York: Oxford University Press, 1965. 215p.

Romania's opposition to economic integration within Comecon is highlighted in this study of the organization. The author examines Comecon's trade problems, the difficulty of applying Soviet-type central planning to the economies of the member states, and the achievements in mutual technical assistance.

401 National independence and reciprocal advantages: the political economy of Romanian-South relations.

Colin W. Lawson. *Soviet Studies*, vol. 35, no. 3 (July 1983), p. 362-75.

Romania, unlike any other East European Socialist state, is a member of the South's UNCTAD negotiating body, the Group of 77. By her own definition 'a socialist developing country', Romania has adopted the group's resolutions and has sought to benefit from West-South concessions, and to diversify her trade. 'This paper provides a description, an explanation, and an evaluation of Romanian policies towards the South. It will suggest that these policies can be explained largely by the Romanian desire to benefit from West-South concessions, and to diversify trade'.

402 Economic development in communist Rumania.

John Michael Montias. Cambridge, Massachusetts: MIT Press, 1967. 327p. bibliog.

An objective evaluation of Romanian economic development from the inception of communist rule to the mid-1960s with emphasis on the expansion of Romanian industry and the doubling of industrial output between 1953 and 1963. The effects of collectivization on Romanian agriculture are also surveyed.

403 The East European economies in the 1970s.

Edited by Alec Nove, Hans Hermann Hohmann, George Seidenstecher. London: Butterworth, 1982. 353p.

A survey of the development of economic policy in Eastern Europe in the 1970s that also traces the process of differentiation of aims, institutions and instruments of economic policy among individual countries. The themes of the section on Romania (p. 253-79), written by Michael Kaser and Iancu Spigler, are: 'Publications on the Romanian system'; 'The period between reforms (1972-1978)'; and 'The new economic mechanism and its implementation 1978-1980'.

404 **Selected trade and economic data of the centrally planned economies.**
Washington, DC: Bureau of East West trade, US Department of Commerce. 1970-. annual.

Charts, tables and graphs of economic data on fifteen industrialized non-socialist and eight socialist countries including Romania.

405 **Romanian economic relations with the EEC.**
Alan H. Smith. *Jahrbuch der Wirtschaft Osteuropas/Yearbook of East European Economics*, vol. 8 (1977), p. 323-61.

The summary of this lucid article reads: 'In 1967 Romania embarked on a policy of acquiring Western technology by importing substantial volumes of machinery from the West and encouraging cooperation ventures with Western firms. In 1971 foreign equity (49:51) participation on Romanian territory was permitted. Her major suppliers have been based in the EEC, but Romania has experienced difficulties in marketing her predominantly agricultural exports to those countries'. Until her debt crisis of 1981 Romania enjoyed more extensive commercial relations with the West than any of her CMEA partners, with the exception of Hungary.

406 **Economic reform in Rumanian industry.**
Iancu Spigler. Oxford, England; New York: Oxford University Press, 1973. 176p. bibliog. (Institute of Soviet and East European Studies, University of Glasgow, Economic Reforms in East European Industry Series).

This work complements and expands Montias' earlier work on the economy by analysing developments that have taken place since the mid-1960s. It presents detailed information on Romanian macro-, micro-, and branch-planning, outlines industrial management, discusses the criteria for investment allocation, and surveys budgetary procedures and banking.

407 **Romania: the industrialization of an agrarian economy under socialist planning.**
Andreas C. Tsantis, Roy Pepper. Washington, DC: The World Bank, 1979. 707p. bibliog.

The most comprehensive study in English of the Romanian economy. Presented in a historical framework this book 'describes the growth and changes within the economy over the past three decades, looks at the major sectors, and shows the present level of the economy – all of which provides the basis for an assessment of what will happen to Romania during the current five-year plan and in the following decade. In addition, the book contains a comprehensive data base of the economy and describes the planning and management systems'. This work

97

also covers foreign trade, human resources, the construction industry, housing, tourism, transport and energy. Separate appendices describe local government and financing, national accounting, planning, investment, the social welfare system, and overall development prospects. This assessment of the Romanian economy was made before Romania's large external debt began to impose burdens on the economy, burdens that have made it more difficult to maintain the high growth rates of the past and that led in 1982 to rationing of bread, milk, cooking-oil, flour, sugar and petrol in many areas of the country.

Historical

408 The Danubian basin and the German economic sphere.
Antonin Basch. New York: Columbia University Press, 1943; London: Kegan Paul, Trubner, 1944. 272p. bibliog.

A study of the German trade drive in Southeastern Europe, including Romania, that is set within an analysis of the economic and political situation in the area in the 1930s. Special emphasis is placed on the effects of the world economic crisis upon this part of Europe.

409 Enciclopedia României (The encyclopedia of Romania.) Volume 4.
Bucharest: Imprimeria naţională, 1943. 1081p. illus. maps.

An invaluable reference source for the pre-war Romanian economy with descriptions, sector by sector, of manufacturing output and rare estimates of income.

410 Balkan economic history, 1550-1950.
John R. Lampe, Marvin R. Jackson. Bloomington, Indiana: Indiana University Press, 1982. 728p. bibliog.

A pioneering study of remarkable range and depth that fills a significant lacuna in scholarship of Southeast Europe. The authors have assembled an impressive amount of data from primary and secondary sources, many of which are in the languages of the Balkans, and have written a book that is not only unique in any language, but also intelligible to those who are not economists. The historical survey, supported by some 130 statistical tables, emphasizes the factors of modernization in the area and finds parallels in economic development there, despite the present differences between Greece's private market economy, Yugoslavia's planned market economy, and the centrally planned economies of Romania, Bulgaria and Albania.

411 **Rumania: agricultural production, output, expenses, gross and net product and productivity, 1938, 1948, 1950-71.**
Gregor Lazarchik, George Pall.   New York: Riverside Research Institute, 1973. 55p.

One of a series of occasional papers on national income in Eastern Europe with tabular information on the areas and production for the years mentioned in the title.

412 **Le III Reich et le petrole roumain, 1938-1940.** (The Third Reich and Romanian oil, 1938-1940.)
Philippe Marguerat.   Leiden, Netherlands: A. W. Sijthoff, 1977. 231p. bibliog.

This work goes beyond the confines of its title and offers an analysis of German economic policy towards Romania during the period mentioned. Based on German, British, French and American primary sources, it describes the struggle between Germany on the one hand, and Britain and France on the other, for control of Romania's raw materials, the most important of which was oil, and provides an authoritative interpretation of German actions in Romania between 1938 and 1940.

413 **Oil and the Romanian state.**
Maurice Pearton.   London: Oxford University Press, 1971. 361p. bibliog.

The most comprehensive and detailed study of the Romanian oil industry, from its birth in the final decade of the last century to its nationalization under the communist government in 1948. Drawing on a wide range of sources, including unpublished material, the author displays an authoritative knowledge of the subject, combining erudition as an economic historian with first hand experience of the oil industry.

414 **The agrarian economy of the Danubian countries, 1933-1945.**
S. D. Zagoroff, J. Vegh, A. D. Bilimovich.   Stanford, California: Standard University Press, 1955. 478p. bibliog. maps.

This is an invaluable account of the agricultural development in Southeast Europe in the inter-war period. It also includes data on agriculture and food in Hungary, Romania, Yugoslavia and Bulgaria during the Second World War. The section on Romania during the latter period (p. 231-88) covers the agricultural exploitation of occupied territories, the nutritional habits of the population, food rationing, the control of food prices, and details of the food industry.

Finance and banking

415 **Studii, probleme, comentarii bancare.** (Banking studies, problems and commentaries.)
Banca naţională a Republicii Socialiste România. Bucharest: Editura Academiei Republicii Socialiste România, 1972. 246p.

A work that describes the role and services of the National Bank of the Socialist Republic of Romania. The bank acts as a centre for credit, cash and payment operations. All state enterprises and institutions are obliged to deposit their reserves with it, and to effect their financial dealings through it. The book contains a three-page English summary of its contents.

416 **Romania: temporary difficulties.**
The Banker, vol. 131, no. 668 (Oct. 1981), p. 93.

In September 1981 a spokesman for the Romanian finance ministry announced that his country had run into 'temporary payments difficulties', that it wished to extend its short-term debt, but that this did not amount to a request for rescheduling. This brief article examines the background to this request.

417 **Sistemul bănesc al leului şi precursorii lui.** (The monetary system of the leu and its precursors.)
Costin C. Kiriţescu. Bucharest: Editura Academiei Republicii Socialiste România, 1964-71. 3 vols.

This is both a history of the coinage and paper money in the Romanian lands as well as a history of banking in Romania. Volume one charts the circulation of currencies, from that of Philip II's silver tetradrachmas in the Greek colonies of Histria, Callatis and Tomis at the end of the 4th century BC, down to the adoption of gold monometallism at the close of the last century. Volume two looks at the system based on the unit of the leu between 1900 and 1944, while volume three discusses, from a doctrinaire standpoint, the need for, and effects of, the nationalization of the National Bank in December 1946, the monetary reform of 15 August 1947, and a further reform of 26 January 1952 designed to stem the rise in prices of agricultural produce which had increased threefold since 1947. These price rises resulted from the disruption in agricultural production caused by the introduction of collectivization. The volume closes with a ten-page English summary of the work.

418 **Banking business in socialist economy with special regard to East-West trade.**
Ivan Meznerics. Leiden, Netherlands: A. W. Sijthoff, 1968. 383p.

This enlarged English version of the author's original work in Hungarian provides an excellent exposé of the legal regulations governing the banking system in the socialist countries of Eastern Europe, including Romania. Part two includes sections on the types of credit used in the financing of foreign trade, and on the purchase and sale of foreign exchange and on foreign currency operations.

Trade and Industry

Foreign trade

419 **Economic and commercial guide to Romania.**
Bucharest: Publicom Foreign Trade Publicity Agency, 1982. 272p.

An invaluable guide to the Romanian agencies that effect economic cooperation with foreign countries. Details are given of collaboration with socialist and capitalist countries, of manufacturing co-operation ventures, of joint companies, of technology transfer, and of addresses of Romanian economic and trade agencies. This handbook is complemented by sections on the banking and customs systems in Romania.

420 **Doing business with Romania. Opportunities for U.S. businessmen.**
Chamber of Commerce and Industry of the Socialist Republic of
Romania.   Bucharest: Publicom Foreign Trade Publicity Agency,
1977. 132p.

A handbook of information for companies engaged in or considering business with Romania. Information is given about Romanian-American agreements concerning businessmen, general marketing procedures, opening an office in Romania, registering patents, and Romanian foreign trade laws.

421 **Trade contacts in Eastern Europe.**
Compiled by the London Chamber of Commerce.   London:
Publishing and Distributing Co., 1977. 112p.

A directory of practical information for Western companies that wish to enter the East European market, including Romania.

422 **Directory of Soviet and East European companies in the West.**
Edited by Bruce Morgan. Ottawa: Carleton University, 1979.
235p.

A guide to East European companies with offices in the West. It lists Romanian commercial, banking, shipping, airline and tourist representatives.

423 **Romania's foreign trade: an overview.**
John Michael Montias. In: *East European Economies Post-Helsinki. A compendium of papers presented to the Joint Economic Committee, 95th Congress, 1st session.* Washington: Government Printing Office, 1977. p. 865-85.

A detailed analysis of the selective economic cooperation with both socialist and capitalist economies that Romania embarked upon after the disastrous floods of 1969.

424 **Romanian Foreign Trade.**
Bucharest: Publicom Foreign Trade Publicity Agency. 1950-.
quarterly.

An illustrated magazine in English that concentrates on foreign trade aspects of the Romanian economy with sections on fairs and exhibitions, and on Romania's international commercial links.

Industry

425 **The mining industry of Romania.**
Bujor Almăşan. Bucharest: Meridiane Publishing House, 1968.
71p.

This guide to the mines of Romania contains a brief history from Roman times to the present, information on the technology used at present, and details of miners' training. The following substances are mined in Romania: coal, lignite, bauxite, iron ore, kaolin, talc, barite, feldspar, dolomite, industrial sands, gold and silver ores, lead, zinc and copper ores, and rock salt.

426 **Twenty years of progress in socialist Romania's chemical industry.**
Mihail Florescu, translated from the Romanian by Anca Boicu, Călin Sergiu Stoicescu. Bucharest: Meridiane Publishing House, 1973. 281p.

A detailed presentation of the impressive development of the chemical industry between 1952 and 1972. Information is given about production costs, investments, the development of the inorganic chemical sector, the fertilizer, pesticide and biostimulator branches, the petrochemical industry, the plastic and synthetic resin industry, the chemical fibre and yarn industry, and the rubber, varnish, paint, dye, pigment and medical drug industries. The prospects outlined in the final chapter were, with hindsight, over optimistic.

427 **The evidence of industrial growth in Southeastern Europe before the Second World War.**
Marvin R. Jackson, John R. Lampe. *East European Quarterly*, vol. 16, no. 4 (Jan. 1983), p. 385-415.

Industrial growth in Romania between 1900 and 1930 is examined and illustrated with four tables of statistics.

428 **Soviet undertakings and Soviet mixed companies.**
Nicolas Spulber. *Journal of Central European Affairs*, vol. 14, no. 2 (July 1954), p. 154-73.

Once the Soviet Union abandoned its policy of removing 'war booty' from Eastern Europe, it had to decide what institutions should be purely Soviet in Eastern Europe, which assets should be used as the Soviet contribution towards the formation of joint companies, and which plants, machinery, ships and rolling stock should be sold back to the respective countries. This article describes how these options were exercised in Hungary, Romania and Bulgaria.

429 **The nationalization of Rumanian industry.**
P. B. Steanu. *Journal of Central European Affairs*, vol. 11, no. 1 (Jan.-April 1951), p. 47-56.

An account of how the act of 11 June 1948, which nationalized industrial, banking, insurance, mining and transport enterprises, was put into effect. Examples are also given of the attacks on private ownership which began in 1945.

430 **The industrial development of Romania from the unification of the principalities to the Second World War.**
David Turnock. In: *An historical geography of the Balkans*. Edited by Francis W. Carter. London, New York: Academic Press, 1977. p. 319-78.

A contribution that will be of interest to the geographer, economist and historian alike. The author surveys the development of large-scale industry to 1944 and then makes a special case-study of metallurgy and engineering in Romania from Dacian times until the Second World War.

Transport and
Communications

General

431 **The urban evolution of Timişoara in the last century with special emphasis on urban transport.**
A. Caranfil. *Revue Roumaine de Géographie, série géographie*, vol. 16, no. 1 (1972), p. 119-24.
An outline of urban transport development in this western Transylvanian town (Hungarian Temesvár) in the late 19th century.

432 **The steam locomotives of Eastern Europe.**
A. E. Durrant. Newton Abbot, England: David & Charles, 1972. rev. ed. 160p.
The reliance on steam traction by Romanian railways has diminished considerably since the last war and therefore their presentation (p. 41-49) in this finely illustrated volume is valuable for students of the country and steam buffs alike. A brief history of the railway network in the area which constitutes present-day Romania is followed by a catalogue of passenger and freight engines in service from the turn of the century until the mid-1960s.

433 **Romanian aeronautical constructions, 1905-1974.**
Ion Gudju, Gheorghe Iacobescu, Ovidiu Ionescu, translated from the Romanian by Carol Kormos. Bucharest: Military Publishing House, 1974. rev. ed. 388p.
A splendid testimony to the internationally renowned Romanian aircraft industry. This illustrated catalogue of Romanian aeroplanes, seaplanes, helicopters and gliders constructed since 1906 describes 148 aircraft with the aid of photographs and drawings. It is prefaced by an introduction on the evolution of Romanian aeronautical constructions in which the contributions made by Traian Vuia, who

made his first flight in his own plane on 18 March 1906, Henri Coandă and Aurel
Vlaicu to powered flight are naturally highlighted.

434 **Report on Danube navigation.**
Walker D. Hines, with the aid of Major Brehon Somervell.
Lausanne, Switzerland: League of Nations, 1925. 187p. map.

Although dated, this is an invaluable source of information on the nature of the
Danube traffic and on its role in the economy of its riverain states, including
Romania.

435 **British railway builders along the lower Danube, 1856-1869.**
J. Jensen, Gerhard Rosegger. *Slavonic and East European
Review*, vol. 46, no. 106 (1968), p. 105-28.

This article describes the activities and achievements of British railway engineers
in the Dobrogea during the period mentioned. Particular attention is paid to the
railway projects Cernavoda-Constanţa, Ruse-Varna, and Bucharest-Giurgiu with
which the engineer-entrepreneurs J. Trevor Barkley and his three brothers,
George, Henry and Robert, were associated.

436 **Aperçus sur l'organisation postale en Roumanie.** (Aspects of the
organization of the postal services in Romania.)
Virgil Şchiopârlan. Bucharest: Poşta Română, 1979. 2nd. ed.
240p.

An account in parallel French and Romanian texts of the organization of
Romanian postal services, of the method of distribution of letters and parcels, of
the problems posed by the introduction of mechanization and of planning
considerations. Several of the chapters in this work were previously published by
the author in the journal *Union Postale* (Berne, Switzerland) between 1974 and
1978.

437 **Bulgarian and Romanian tramways today. Part 2: Arad, Brăila and
Bucureşti.**
M. R. Taplin. *Modern Tramway*, no. 7 (July 1975), p. 233-42.

This historical presentation of the tramway system in the three towns mentioned
is accompanied by photographs of the trams in operation and diagrams of the
tramway network.

438 **Bulgarian and Romanian tramways today. Part 3: Galaţi, Iaşi,
Oradea, Sibiu and Timişoara.**
M. R. Taplin. *Modern Tramway*, no. 8 (Aug. 1975), p. 271-81.

The tramway systems in the five towns are described with the aid of diagrammatic
maps. Their history and the changes made to routes and rolling-stock are noted in
detail and illustrated by photographs.

Postage stamps

439 **Romanian philatelic studies.**
Romanian Philatelic Club.   Jamaica Estates, New York. 1977-. 3
issues annually.

A specialist bulletin devoted both to recent issues and to the history of the
postage stamp in the Romanian lands which, surprisingly, has a venerable
tradition there.

Agriculture and Forestry

Agriculture

440 The cooperativization of agriculture and the economic consciousness of the peasant.

M. Cernea. *Romanian Journal of Sociology*, vol. 2-3 (1964), p. 139-66.

An analysis of the rural revolution caused by the collectivization of agriculture in post-war Romania. Two farm budgets for individual farmers and two for farmers in a collective are used as illustration.

441 Lands alive.

René Dumont. London: Merlin Press, 1965. 247p.

A collection of essays on the problems of agricultural efficiency in a range of countries extending from South America to Asia. Romania is the subject of chapter 14 entitled 'Persisting Stalinism in 1956 Rumania' (p. 194-211) which includes a description of a collective farm in Transylvania and a breakdown of the taxes levied on a private farm in Wallachia.

442 Short introduction to the principal structural problems of agriculture in Romania.

M. Gormsen. Bucharest: Cartea Românească, 1945. 77p.

An interesting pre-collectivization report by a Danish specialist on Romania's agricultural difficulties.

443   **The wines of Central and Southeastern Europe.**
      R. E. H. Gunyon.   London: Duckworth, 1971. 132p.

Little has been published in English on the wines of Romania which deserve much wider international recognition. Unfortunately, exports are confined to the produce of the more prolific vineyards and several of the best varieties are unknown outside Romania. This sketch does a great deal to advance their cause with the author's conviction that 'the best of these wines will come to be accepted again as part of the fine ancient tradition of European wine-making'. The study records the place and grape-names for each of the countries covered, and the grape varieties common and peculiar to the various countries. Romania is covered in chapter nine with information about the vineyards of Tîrnave, Odobeşti, Cotnari, Dealul Mare, Murfatlar and others.

444   **Romania's experience and the problem of increasing agricultural output during the revolutionary transformation of agrarian relations.**
      C. Murgescu.   *Romanian Journal of Sociology*, vol. 2-3 (1966), p. 81-107.

After presenting an incomplete survey of collectivization in Romania (1949-1962), the author attempts to refute the claim that collectivization produces an initial drop in gross agricultural production.

445   **Regional fluctuations in Rumanian agriculture: a case study of grain production, 1956-1966.**
      C. Thomas.   *Balkan Studies*, vol. 15 (1974), p. 80-98.

Analysis of Romania's grain production is a significant barometer of the country's post-war development since grains are preponderant in Romania's agricultural performance. The author shows that the shortcomings in grain production over this period can be attributed to lack of investment in less productive regions and deficiencies in the internal transport system.

Forestry

446   **Forestry in Romania.**
      Filip Tomulescu.   Bucharest: Ministry of Agriculture, Food Industry, Silviculture and Waters. Department of Silviculture, 1971. 99p maps.

Forestry represents an important branch of Romania's economy. This work contains chapters on forest resources in Romania, natural vegetation zones, protection and development of the forest, forest restoration and maintenance, torrent control and degraded land amelioration.

Employment, Labour and Trade Unions

447 Labour code of the socialist republic of Romania.
Bucharest, 1973. 62p. (Supplement to *Trade Unions of Romania*, no. 1 (1973))
The text of the labour code observed by Romania's 'trade unions'.

448 Trade Unions of Romania.
Bucharest: Central Council of Trade Unions of the Socialist Republic of Romania, 1961-. quarterly.
Accounts in English of the activities of the 'trade unions', of working conditions, and of general economic developments in Romania. The trade unions are the mouthpiece of the state and consequently do not defend their members' interests.

Statistics

449 **Anuarul statistic al Republicii Socialiste România.** (Statistical
annual for the socialist republic of Romania).
Bucharest: Direcţia Centrală de Statistică, 1957-. annual.

The basic source of statistical data on Romania with chapters on population, the
labour force, industry, agriculture, investment, transport and telecommunica-
tions, internal and foreign trade, the budget, education, culture, the health
service, and comparative tables of international statistics.

450 **Romania: facts and figures.**
Bucharest: Editura ştiinţifică şi enciclopedică, 1964-. annual.

A brief but useful compendium of statistics on the population, economy,
transport, trade, education, sport and tourism in Romania. Between 1964 and
1978 it was published by Meridiane Publishing House.

Education

General

451 Education in the Rumanian people's republic.
Randolph L. Braham.   Washington, DC: US Government
Printing Office, 1963. 229p.

A detailed presentation of the educational system in post-war Romania that also
includes information on the pre-war structure. It highlights the steps taken to
wipe out illiteracy under communist rule and the progress that was achieved.
Contains an interesting list of textbooks used in primary and secondary education
during the 1950s.

452 A concise history of education in Romania.
Emilian Dimitriu, Octavian Ionescu, Iulian Nica, Ion Orghidan.
Bucharest: Editura ştiinţifică şi enciclopedică, 1981. 64p. bibliog.

A well-documented introduction to the history of education amongst the
Romanians, from the foundation of monastery schools in the 15th century in
Moldavia to the new education law of 1977. While the organization and extension
of educational provision from 1800 to the Second World War is outlined in some
twenty pages, more than half the book is devoted to the development of
primary and secondary education since 1948. The bibliographical notes are a
useful indication of the major works on the subject published by Romanian
scholars.

453 Society, schools and progress in Eastern Europe.
Nigel Grant.   London, New York: Pergamon Press, 1969. 363p.

Although modifications have been made to the educational system in Romania
since the publication of this book, the excellent outline presented here (p. 282-99)
holds good. The tabulated presentation of the eight-year basic school curriculum

and of the middle general school curriculum are the clearest of their kind in English-language works on the subject. Post-1980 reforms mean that kindergartens are no longer free and that vocational apprentice schools for industry and agriculture have replaced many middle schools of general education.

454 **Glimpses of education in Poland and Romania.**
G. E. Mitchell. *American Education*, vol. 13, no. 3 (April 1977), p. 16-24.
A report on a visit to kindergartens and secondary schools in Romania and Poland.

455 **Romania's younger generation.**
Vasile Nicolcioiu, Dan Mihai Bîrliba, Fred Mahler, Mihail Stoica, translated into English by Doina Motaş, Ştefanica Rotaru.
Bucharest: Meridiane Publishing House, 1974. rev. ed. 91p.
A compendium, with many photographs, of facts and figures showing the contribution made by Romania's youth to political and cultural life in the Socialist Republic. Information is given about education, youth movements, and their rôle in society.

456 **Principles and practices in Romanian education.**
Peter C. M. Raggat. *Compare. Journal of the Comparative Education Society in Europe, British Section*, vol. 4, no. 1 (Jan. 1974), p. 14-23.
A description of the structure of education in Romania which covers pre-school and secondary education.

457 **A concise history of pedagogy in Romania.**
Ion Gh. Stanciu. Bucharest: Editura ştiinţifică şi enciclopedică, 1982. 64p. bibliog.
A survey of the development of educational theory and practice in Romania from the late 18th century to the present.

458 **Contemporary educational policies in Transylvania.**
M. Szász. *East European Quarterly*, vol. 11, part 4 (1977), p. 493-501.
A brief analysis of educational policy in Transylvania and its disadvantages for the Hungarian minority.

459 **Les structures de l'apprentissage en Roumanie: unité et divsité.**
(The structure of learning in Romania: unity and diversity.)
George Văideanu. *International Review of Education*, vol. 28, no. 2 (1982), p. 209-22.
'This analysis concerns structures of learning at the pre-university level. Three categories of learning structure are examined: formal, non-formal and informal.

Other possibilities of grouping the structures are also indicated, including learning for society and for oneself'. The model for the author's analysis is the Romanian educational system.

460 **Romania pre-school.**
Brenda Walker. *Education*, vol. 163, no. 26 (29 June 1984), p. 534.

The author's three visits to Romania have enabled her to inspect primary and secondary schools, choreography and music schools, and a summer camp for pre-school children. This informative article is based on her experience there and fills an important lacuna in English-language reports on Romanian education.

Higher education

461 **The Al. I. Cuza University of Jassy, 1860-1960.**
Bucharest: Scientific Publishing House, 1960. 148p.

A commemorative volume celebrating the centenary of Romania's oldest university. It provides a pictorial record of the development of the university that is accompanied by a text replete with the socialist hyperbole of the 1950s.

462 **Bucharest University, 1864-1964.**
Edited by Alexandru Balaci, Ion Ionaşcu. Bucharest: Graphic Arts Printing Press, 1964. 84p.

A collection of brief studies marking the centenary of the foundation of the university. The emphasis is upon the period after 1948 when the educational system was completely reformed although there is an interesting contribution on the St Sava Academy, the first institution of higher education in Wallachia in which Romanian was used as the language of instruction.

463 **L'enseignement supérieur en Roumanie.**
Bucharest: CEPES, 1978. 108p. bibliog. (Études et documents edités par le centre européen pour l'enseignement supérieur UNESCO).

A presentation of the development of higher education in Romania since 1948, the year of the first reform of education in the socialist period. There are chapters on the organization of higher education, its content, the entrance qualifications required of students, the teaching staff, and the financing of higher education. A table of institutes of higher education with their specializations is annexed.

464 **The undergraduate programme for teaching future general practitioners in Romania.**
I. J. Farkas. *Medical Education*, vol. 11, no. 2 (March 1977), p. 125-28.

This survey article contains details of medical studies and practical medical education, practical work in the first, second and third years, externship and internship. Much of the information is based on practice at the Tîrgu Mureş Medical School in Transylvania.

465 **Higher education in Rumania.**
C. Ionescu-Bujor. Bucharest: Meridiane Publishing House, 1964. 55p.

A guide to the principles and organization of higher education in post-war Romania with a statistical illustration of achievements over the period 1944-1964.

Other (special) education

466 **Education in the languages of the coinhabiting nationalities in Romania.**
Marin Gaşpar, Gergely László, Nikolaus Kleininger, Murvai László, Sorin Teodorescu, translated by Veronica Focşeneanu. Bucharest: Editura didactică şi pedagogică, 1982. 213p.

The provision of teaching in Hungarian has been one of the yardsticks by which the Romanian authorities have been accused of cultural discrimination against the Hungarian minority in Transylvania. The sensitivity of the régime to such allegations is exemplified by a number of recent publications in Romania relating to the position of the minorities, of which this is one. Part one contains papers on the place and rôle of education in the languages of the coinhabiting nationalities within the system of education in Romania. Part two presents contributions by the teaching staff of these languages themselves, and Part three describes the main provisions of the Education Act of 1978 concerning education in these languages, and gives details of the curricula for schools offering such tuition.

467 **Some aspects of guidance and counselling in British and Romanian education.**
T. D. Vaughan. *Vocational Aspect of Education*, vol. 23, no. 55 (summer 1971), p. 57-64.

'The idea of guidance as a specialist sub-area in education, and the related concept of the specialist counsellor, appear superficially to be a similar phenomenon in Britain and Romania; but because of the wide differences in cultural tradition this may be misleading. The concepts involve others such as techniques and aims which cannot be studied in isolation from their cultural context'. This paper suggests, on the basis of a study of the development of guidance concepts in Britain, a typology broad enough to accommodate wide differences of theory and practice, but specific enough to allow some comparison of the concept in the two countries.

Science and Technology

468 **East European research index.**
Guernsey, Channel Islands: Hodgson, 1977. 697p.
A list of university and scientific personnel engaged in research in the fields of agriculture, engineering and medicine that includes Romanian specialists.

469 **Guide to world science.**
Series edited by R. J. Fifield.   Guernsey, Channel Islands: Hodgson, 1968-70. 20 vols.
Volume eleven, entitled *Communist Countries*, provides details of the activities of the Academy of Sciences, research centres and universities in the scientific field in Romania.

470 **Societies and associations in Romanian science.**
Bucharest: Association of Scientists in Romania, 1981. 103p.
A brief history of scientific societies in Romania from 1795 to the present. There is a useful section containing names, addresses, titles of publications and affiliations of numerous Romanian scientific associations.

471 **World guide to scientific associations.**
New York: Bowker; Munich: Verlag Dokumentation, 1974. 481p.
Bilingual English-German directory of scientific associations which includes a section on Romania.

472 **The world of learning, 1983-84.**
London: Europa Publications, 1983. 34th ed. 2 vols.
This is the standard reference work for information about academic institutions throughout the world. The material is arranged by country, Romania being well-

served with entries on the Academy, learned societies, research institutes, libraries and archives, museums, universities, and colleges.

Language

General

473 **The development of modern Rumanian: linguistic theory and practice in Muntenia 1821-1838.**
Elizabeth Close.   London: Oxford University Press, 1974. 316p. bibliog.

The only serious study in English that discusses the development of modern literary Romanian during the first half of the 19th century. This book offers a linguistic analysis of the work of Ioan Heliade Rădulescu (1802-72) and his associates that determined the direction that literary Romanian was to take.

474 **Rumanian.**
Dennis Deletant. In: *A guide to foreign language courses and dictionaries*. Edited by A. J. Walford, J. E. O. Screen.   London: Library Association, 1977. 3rd rev. enl. ed. p. 244-48.

A selection of published manuals, grammars and dictionaries available at the time of compilation. Brief descriptions and comments accompany the entries to provide a guide to suitability for teachers, students and librarians.

475 **The early history of the Rumanian language.**
André Du Nay.   Lake Bluff, Illinois: Jupiter Press, 1977. 275p. bibliog.

A long standing controversy in Romanian studies centres around the theory of continuity, that is, the argument that the Romanians are descended from Romanized Dacians from the Roman province of Dacia Traiana (roughly modern Transylvania and Oltenia) who remained in the province after its abandonment by the Romans c. 271 AD. One of the main arguments in favour of this theory is a linguistic one. This study, written under a pseudonym, provides a great deal of

118

linguistic evidence to refute the continuity theory and contends that the Romanized Dacians evacuated the province together with the Romans and moved south of the Danube. The author's theories, however, are far from flawless. The continuity debate has assumed an importance far beyond the realm of linguistics since it postulates the continuous occupation, since Roman times, of Transylvania by the Romanian people.

476 The Romance languages.
W. D. Elcock.   London: Faber & Faber, 1960. 573p. bibliog.

A comprehensive analysis of the historical development of the Romance languages. Romanian is well served in the chapter on the Latin foundation but the absence of written evidence of the language until 1521 has naturally led to emphasis in succeeding chapters on the other languages in the Romance family.

477 Introducing the Rumanian language.
Graham Mallinson.   Exeter, England: Language Centre, University of Exeter, 1980. 1 tape cassette and notes. (Exeter Tapes no. RM 816).

An introduction to the language for students of linguistics with particular reference to the development of its vocabulary and to its relationship with the other Romance languages. Side one covers the Romance and non-Romance character of the Romanian vocabulary, side two the phonological and morphological development of Romanian from Latin. The tape is accompanied by notes.

478 Outline history of the Romanian language.
Alexandru Niculescu.   Bucharest: Editura ştiinţifică şi enciclopedică, 1981. 187p. bibliog.

An excellent introduction to the history of Romanian that is refreshingly free of the dogmatism of similar works on the subject that have appeared in Romania. Balance is achieved in the presentation of the Latin heritage, Slavonic influence, and Turkish and Greek lexical features. The substratum is objectively examined and undue importance is not accorded to the so-called 'Dacian' element. The discussions of the 16th century texts, the structure of the language in the 17th and 18th centuries, the adoption of neologisms and late 19th century and 20th century developments are particularly useful for the student of Romanian.

479 The Romance languages: a linguistic introduction.
Rebecca Posner.   Garden City, New York: Anchor Books, Doubleday, 1966. 336p.

A comparative approach to the evolution of the five major Romance languages which is written in a conversational style that will not bemuse the non-specialist. Romanian is well represented and examples are provided.

Courses and grammars

480 Spoken Romanian.
F. B. Agard, M. Petrescu-Dimitriu.   Ithaca, New York: Spoken
Language Services, 1974. Textbook and 6 cassettes.

A sound, graduated course in thirty units, each consisting of taped dialogues
(which are transcribed in the textbook), vocabulary lists, grammar details, and
exercises. Very useful for those who wish to acquire a rapid conversance with
colloquial Romanian.

481 Modern Romanian.
James E. Augerot, Florin D. Popescu.   Seattle, Washington:
University of Washington Press, 1971. 329p.

An excellent graded manual of Romanian for English speakers, rich in exercises
and conversational drills, which is divided into two parts of sixteen lessons. It
contains an appendix on pronunciation and inflexion, and is supplemented by an
extensive Romanian-English vocabulary. More suitable for class use than self-
tuition.

482 Précis de grammaire roumaine (A summary of Romanian grammar.)
Ioan Baciu.   Lyon, France: Éditions l'Hermès, 1978. 111p.

A brief, reliable guide to the essential features of the Romanian grammatical
system.

483 Îmi place limba română (I like Romanian.)
Rodica C. Boțoman, Donald E. Corbin, E. Garrison Walters.
Columbus, Ohio: Slavica Publishers, 1981. 199p.

An extremely useful basic reader for elementary and intermediate students of
Romanian that is characterized by the practical nature of the texts and the
conversational style of its exercises.

484 A course in modern Rumanian.
Ana Cartianu, Leon Levițchi, Virgil Ştefănescu-Drăgănești.
Bucharest: Publishing House for Scientific Books, 1958. 359p.

A course of thirty-two graded lessons with reading passages, exercises and
grammar notes. The vocabulary does not indicate Romanian stress.

485 An advanced course in modern Rumanian.
Ana Cartianu, Leon Levițchi, Virgil Ştefănescu-Drăgănești.
Bucharest: Publishing House for Scientific Books, 1964. 2nd ed.
365p.

A reader and grammar for the more advanced student which is in two sections:
the first contains reading passages, vocabulary and exercises, and the second is
made up of copiously annotated extracts from works of Romanian literature. It is

120

notable for its excellent reading passages which richly illustrate the pitfalls of Romanian syntax.

486 **A course in contemporary Romanian.**
Boris Cazacu, Clara Georgeta Chiosa, Matilda Caragiu Marioţeanu, Valeria Guţu Romalo, Sorina Bercescu. Bucharest: Editura didactică şi pedagogică, 1980. 2nd rev. ed. 712p and 2 records.
An excellent graduated course for use primarily with a tutor. It contains thirty lessons with grammatical reference sections and indication of Romanian stress throughout. Each lesson consists of a reading passage (reproduced on the records), grammar notes, a vocabulary and exercises.

487 **Curs de limba română. A Romanian course for beginners.**
Oltea Delarăscruci, Ion Popescu. Bucharest: Editura didactică şi pedagogică, 1971. 2 vols and 4 records.
A graduated course with reading passages and exercises that is designed to give the student a grounding in elementary Romanian. The grammar reference sections are therefore brief and the range of vocabulary limited. It provides, nevertheless, a satisfactory introduction.

488 **Colloquial Romanian.**
Dennis Deletant. London: Routledge & Kegan Paul, 1983. 335p.
Designed primarily for those studying Romanian on their own, this is an introduction to the language in which stress has been placed on everyday situations and colloquial usage. The course contains twenty-five graded lessons, each including conversations and texts which use the grammatical points presented and discussed in the lesson, and the vocabulary given. Each lesson also includes a set of exercises and a key. The appendix has a verb table and an extensive Romanian-English vocabulary of words other than those used in the book.

489 **Gramatica limbii române** (The grammar of the Romanian language.)
Academia Republicii Socialiste România. Bucharest: Editura Academiei Republicii Socialiste România, 1972. 2nd ed. 2 vols. bibliog.
The standard reference grammar of Romanian that, surprisingly, does not give Romanian stress throughout. Vol. 1 covers morphology, vol. 2 syntax.

490 **La langue roumaine. Une presentation.** (The Romanian language. A presentation.)
Alf Lombard. Paris: Librairie C. Klincksieck, 1974. 396p.
This excellent guide to Romanian grammar, which includes stress, is, in many respects, more informative about popular usage than the Romanian Academy grammar. The material is admirably presented and simple to use for reference.

121

491 **English-Romanian conversation book.**
Mihai Miroiu. Bucharest: Editura Sport-Turism, 1982. 188p.
An excellent phrase-book that covers an extensive range of daily situations with a
high level of appropriate and uncontrived phrases accompanied by phonetic
notation.

492 **Ghid de conversaţie român-englez** (A Romanian-English
phrasebook.)
Mihai Miroiu. Bucharest: Editura Sport-Turism, 1982. 191p.
The companion volume to Mihai Miroiu's *English-Romanian conversation book*
(q.v.) that covers an extensive range of everyday situations.

493 **Romanian.**
Virgiliu Ştefănescu-Drăgăneşti, Martin Murrell. London: Hodder
& Stoughton; New York: David McKay, 1980. 5th impression.
428p.
One of the series of 'Teach yourself' language manuals, this volume offers an
admirable guide to pronunciation, provides many exercises for translation into
both Romanian and English with a key, and has an excellent general vocabulary.
It is vitiated only by the use of a grammatical terminology that the layman is
unlikely to understand.

494 **Romanian phrase book.**
Gabriela Vorvoreanu, Jillian Norman. Harmondsworth,
England: Penguin Books, 1973. 213p.
A practical phrase-book for the tourist that includes a substantial English-
Romanian vocabulary. The phrases, however, are not accompanied by phonetic
notation although the vocabulary section carries a guide to the pronunciation of
each Romanian entry.

Specialized works

495 **Romanian phonology: a generative phonological sketch of the core
vocabulary of standard Romanian.**
James E. Augerot. Bucharest: Editura Academiei Republicii
Socialiste România; Moscow, Idaho: Idaho Research Foundation
Inc., University of Idaho, 1974. 86p. bibliog.
A partial description of the phonological features of Romanian that is synchronic
rather than historical in approach.

496 **Les mots composés dans les langues romanes** (Compound words in the Romance languages.)
Anca Giurescu. The Hague: Mouton, 1975. 172p. bibliog. (Janua linguarum. Studia memoriae Nicolae van Wijk dedicata. Edenda curat C. H. van Schooneveld. Series practica 228).
A study of the formation of compound words in Romance with many Romanian examples.

497 **Bibliographie de phonologie romane** (Bibliography of Romance philology.)
Maria Grossman, Bruno Mazzoni. The Hague: Mouton, 1974. 115p. (Janua linguarum. Studia memoriae Nicolae van Wijk dedicata. Edenda curat C. H. van Schooneveld. Series practica 232).
Section 12 of this bibliography is devoted to studies on the phonology of Romanian and lists over 300 items that appeared between 1930 and 1970 in Romania and elsewhere.

498 **Essai sur la syntaxe des propositions subordonnées dans le roumain littéraire contemporain** (Essay on the syntax of subordinate clauses in contemporary literary Romanian.)
Alain Guillermou. Paris: Librairie Marcel Didier, 1962. 161p.
A detailed study of the formation of subordinate clauses in Romanian.

499 **The Rumanian verb system.**
A. Juilland, P. M. H. Edwards. The Hague: Mouton, 1971. 220p.
A structural approach to the classification of Romanian verbs according to their infinitives. The most detailed study of the Romanian verb is still Alf Lombard's *Le verbe roumain: étude morphologique* (The Romanian verb: a morphological study.) (q.v.)

500 **Transformational and structural morphology: about two rival approaches to the Rumanian verb system.**
A. Juilland. Saratoga, California: Anma Libri, 1978. 77p. bibliog. (Stanford French and Italian Studies no. 5)
Although curiously included in a series of studies on French and Italian, this paper discusses the problem of how to classify two small groups of Romanian verbs with infinitives in -ea and -e. Juilland defends the structural approach which he adopted as co-author of item no. 499 against the transformational alternative proposed by Merrit Ruhlen in an article in *Romance Philology*, vol. 28 (1974), p. 178-90.

123

Language. Specialized works

501 **Le verbe roumain: étude morphologique** (The Romanian verb: a morphological study.)
Alf Lombard. Lund, Sweden: C. W. K. Gleerup, 1954-55. 2 vols. bibliog.

An authoritative study of over 1,000 pages of the Romanian verb system. It is divided into two parts: the phonology of the verb, and its morphological classification. Complemented by an index of all the verbs discussed, including their variants.

502 **Les termes relatifs et les propositions relatives en roumain moderne** (Relative forms and relative clauses in modern Romanian.)
Elsa Nilsson. Lund, Sweden: C. W. K. Gleerup, 1969. 208p. bibliog. (Études romanes de Lund publiées par Alf Lombard XVII).

An analysis of the syntactical use of relative pronouns, adjectives and adverbs that is richly illustrated by examples and is easy to follow even by the non-specialist.

503 **L'influence du français sur le roumain** (The influence of French upon Romanian.)
Ana Goldiş Poalelungi. Paris: Société des belles lettres, 1973. 473p. bibliog. (Publications de l'université de Dijon XLIV).

France played a decisive part in the regeneration of the Romanians during the 19th century by providing the forms upon which much of Romanian cultural, social, and political life was moulded. While these aspects of French influence are well documented, the impact of French upon the Romanian language, which began to be felt at the beginning of the last century, had not received the attention that it deserved until the appearance of this solid study. This work chronicles French influence in the vocabulary (Part 1) and syntax (Part 2) of Romanian by examining journals and books from the period. In places, however, this influence is exaggerated, particularly in the section devoted to adjectival constructions.

504 **Les dérivés parasynthétiques dans les langues romanes: roumain, italien, français, espagnol** (Parasynthetic derivatives in the Romance languages: Romanian, Italian, French, Spanish.)
Sanda Reinheimer-Rîpeanu. The Hague: Mouton, 1974. 161p. bibliog. (Janua linguarum. Studia memoriae Nicolae van Wijk dedicata. Edenda curat C. H. Schooneveld. Series practica 229).

Parasynthetic derivation has been defined as 'the simultaneous enlistment of two affixes to a root, one a prefix, and one a suffix'. In this study the author broadens the definition to include verbs and adjectives derived by either a suffix or prefix, and illustrates her analysis with many examples from Romanian.

505   **Syntaxe roumaine** (Romanian syntax.)
Kristian Sandfeld, Hedvig Olsen.   Paris: Librairie E. Droz. (vol.
1). Copenhagen: Munksgaard. (vols 2, 3). 1936-62. 3 vols.
A fundamental study of Romanian syntax based on the literary language. Vol. 1
covers the use of nouns, pronouns, adjectives and verbs, vol. 2 that of
conjunctions and particles, and vol. 3 the structure of the sentence. The last two
volumes appeared after the death of the authors and were prepared for
publication by Holger Sten.

506   **The transformational syntax of Romanian.**
E. Vasiliu, S. Golopenţia-Eretescu.   Bucharest: Editura
Academiei Republicii Socialiste România; The Hague, Paris:
Mouton, 1972. 198p.
An analysis of the syntax of Romanian according to the principles of
transformational grammar and based on the authors' work with the same title
published in Romanian in 1969.

Dictionaries, monolingual

507   **Dicţionar enciclopedic illustrat 'Cartea românească'** (The 'Cartea
românească' illustrated encyclopedic dictionary.)
Ion-Aurel Candrea, Gheorghe Adamescu.   Bucharest: Cartea
românească, 1931. 1949p. illus. maps.
A one-volume encyclopaedic dictionary that, in several respects, remains
unsurpassed e.g. as a historical dictionary of the Romanian language. It lacks,
however, phonetic transcriptions of headwords.

508   **Dicţionar al limbii române contemporane** (A dictionary of the
contemporary Romanian language.)
Vasile Breban.   Bucharest: Editura ştiinţifică şi enciclopedică,
1980. 680p.
With approximately 20,000 headwords this dictionary can be used with profit by
most students and scholars of Romanian. Since it is not designed specifically for
use by foreign students, there are no phonetic transcriptions although stress is
given in entries.

509 **Dicţionarul explicativ al limbii române** (An explicatory dictionary of the Romanian language.)
Academia Republicii Socialiste România.   Bucharest: Editura Academiei Republicii Socialiste România, 1975. 1049p.

The most exhaustive one-volume monolingual dictionary of recent years. It incorporates many neologisms that have entered the language since the war and indicates stress but does not give phonetic transcriptions.

510 **Dicţionarul limbii române** (A dictionary of the Romanian language.)
Bucharest: Academia Română, 1906-44: 1965-.

The Romanian Academy published volumes 1 (A-B); 2 (C); 4 (F-I); and three fascicles of volume 5 (J-Loj) of this definitive dictionary of Romanian between 1906 and 1944. Publication was resumed in 1965 with vol. 6 (M) under the auspices of the Academia Republicii Populare Romîne (now Academia Republicii Socialiste România) and has reached vol. 11 part 1 (Ş) although vol. 10 (S) has still to appear. The stress of headwords and a guide to their pronunciation is provided.

511 **Dicţionarul limbii romîne literare contemporane** (A dictionary of the contemporary Romanian literary language.)
Academia Republicii Populare Romîne.   Bucharest: Editura Academiei Republicii Populare Romîne, 1955-57. 4 vols.

Although it is often claimed that this dictionary of literary Romanian is the standard reference work on the subject, it is far from exhaustive and has fewer entries than the item that follows.

512 **Dicţionarul limbii romîne moderne** (A dictionary of the modern Romanian language.)
Academia Republicii Populare Romîne.   Bucharest: Editura Academiei Republicii Populare Romîne, 1958. 961p. illus. maps.

An invaluable one-volume encyclopaedic dictionary compiled by a group of specialists under Dimitrie Macrea. It contains over 50,000 entries with stress indicated, 1000 more than the four-volume *Dicţionarul limbii romîne literare contemporane* (A dictionary of the contemporary Romanian language.) (q.v.) on which it is based. No phonetic transcription of entries is given. Sadly it has been out of print for several years.

513 **Mic dicţionar al limbii române** (Small dictionary of the Romanian language.)
Ana Canarache, Vasile Breban.   Bucharest: Editura ştiinţifică, 1974. 848p.

In spite of its modest title, this handy dictionary suits the needs of even advanced students of the language with over 30,000 entries. While indicating stress in headwords, it lacks phonetic transcriptions of them.

514 **Mic dicţionar enciclopedic** (Small encyclopaedic dictionary.)
Bucharest: Editura ştiinţifică şi enciclopedică, 1978. 2nd ed. rev.
1851p. illus. maps.

Modelled on the *Petit Larousse illustré*, this one-volume reference aid is divided
into two parts: part one is a dictionary of the contemporary Romanian language;
and part two is a biographical, geographical and historical dictionary. This second
edition contains an extra 151 pages in comparison with the first edition (1972).
However, in the new edition there are shorter entries on a number of leading
political figures in the Romanian Communist Party who are no longer alive.

Dictionaries, bilingual

515 **Dicţionar englez-român** (English-Romanian dictionary.)
Academia Republicii Socialiste România. Bucharest: Editura
Academiei Republicii Socialiste România, 1974. 825p.

Compiled under the direction of Leon Leviţchi, this admirable work is the most
comprehensive English-Romanian dictionary to appear in print. Intended for the
use of Romanian specialists, it lists about 120,000 words with their pronunciation
in both British and American varieties of English.

516 **Dicţionar de buzunar englez-romîn, romîn-englez** (English-
Romanian, Romanian-English pocket dictionary.)
Şerban Andronescu. Bucharest: Editura ştiinţifică, 1961. 2 vols.

While in print this dictionary was the most practical to use for the tourist and
casual traveller. Within the limits of its scope, it provides a wide range of
Romanian headwords but they lack phonetic transcription or indication of stress.

517 **Dicţionar de buzunar englez-român, român-englez** (English-
Romanian, Romanian-English pocket dictionary.)
Andrei Bantaş. Bucharest: Editura ştiinţifică, 1973. 2nd ed.
1131p.

Although described as a 'pocket' dictionary, the bulk of this single volume makes
it impractical for the tourist to carry around. Nevertheless, it provides an
adequate reference tool but, as it is aimed at the Romanian public, lacks a
phonetic transcription of Romanian headwords.

518 **Dicţionar englez-român, român-englez** (English-Romanian, Romanian-English dictionary.)
Andrei Bantaş. Bucharest: Editura ştiinţifică, 1968. 2nd ed. rev. and aug. 2 vols.

Each volume serves as a practical 'pocket' dictionary, containing some 16,000 headwords, but as it is designed for the use of Romanians the Romanian entries do not indicate stress nor do they have a phonetic transcription.

519 **Dicţionar frazeologic român-englez** (Romanian-English dictionary of phrases.)
Andrei Bantaş, Andreea Gheorghiţoiu, Leon Leviţchi.
Bucharest: Editura ştiinţifică şi enciclopedică, 1981. 2nd enlarged and rev. ed. 654p.

Over 25,000 Romanian expressions with English translations are listed in this dictionary. No distinction is made between outmoded and current expressions.

520 **Mic dicţionar englez-român, român-englez** (Small English-Romanian, Romanian-English dictionary.)
Andrei Bantaş. Bucharest: Editura ştiinţifică, 1971. 2 vols.

A miniature dictionary, each volume of which contains, nevertheless, over 15,000 entries. Very practical for the tourist and reliable for the vocabulary of colloquial Romanian. No phonetic transcriptions or indication of stress are given.

521 **Dicţionar englez-român** (English-Romanian dictionary.)
Leon Leviţchi, Andrei Bantaş. Bucharest: Editura ştiinţifică, 1971. 1068p.

An advanced learner's dictionary of English for the Romanian public, the companion of which is Leon Leviţchi's *Dicţionar român-englez* (Romanian-English dictionary.) (q.v.) Its rich variety of expressions and their Romanian equivalents makes it extremely useful to the student of Romanian.

522 **Dicţionar român-englez** (Romanian-English dictionary.)
Leon Leviţchi. Bucharest: Editura ştiinţifică, 1973. 3rd ed. revised by Leon Leviţchi, Andrei Bantaş. 1085p.

A dictionary of about 30,000 entries aimed at Romanian students of English to assist them in translating modern Romanian texts. Consequently, no phonetic transcriptions of Romanian headwords are provided, nor is stress indicated. It is, nevertheless, a useful source of Romanian expressions for students of Romanian.

523 **Dicţionar frazeologic englez-român** (English-Romanian dictionary of phrases).
Adrian Nicolescu, Liliana Pamfil Teodoreanu, Ioan Preda, Mircea Tatos. Bucharest: Editura ştiinţifică şi enciclopedică, 1982. 2nd. ed. rev. aug. 567p.

A comprehensive dictionary of English and American expressions, both antiquated and contemporary, with Romanian equivalents.

524 **Romanian-English, English-Romanian dictionary.**
Irina Panovf. Bucharest: Editura ştiinţifică şi enciclopedică, 1982. 828p.

A single-volume Romanian-English, English-Romanian dictionary that offers English-speaking users a guide to the pronunciation of the Romanian headwords. The stress of Romanian entries is given but not their phonetic notation (as in the case of the English-Romanian section). Contains over 30,000 entries.

525 **Romanian-English, English-Romanian dictionary.**
Irina Panovf. Bucharest: Editura ştiinţifică şi enciclopedică, 1983. 416p.

The most exhaustive bilingual dictionary of its kind for English speakers. 30,000 headwords are listed with the stress of Romanian entries marked. Grammatical tables illustrating the declension and conjugation of Romanian nouns and verbs make this an extremely practical aid to all students of the language.

526 **Rumanian-English and English-Rumanian dictionary.**
Marcel Schönkron. New York: Frederick Ungar, 1952. 501p.

This dictionary contains many anachronisms, with regard to both its vocabulary and its use of the now obsolete Romanian orthography of â for î. It is consequently of limited use to the student of the contemporary language.

Dictionaries, specialized

527 **Diccionario etimológico rumano** (An etymological dictionary of Romanian.)
Alejandro Cioranescu. La Laguna, Canary Islands: Biblioteca Filológica, Universidad de La Laguna, 1958-66. 918p.

This is the only completed etymological dictionary of Romanian although it is far from exhaustive. The 9,532 entries indicate stress and the annotations are in Spanish.

528 **Dicţionar de neologisme** (Dictionary of neologisms.)
Florin Marcu, Constant Maneca. Bucharest: Editura Academiei
Republicii Socialiste România, 1978. 3rd ed. 1,168p. bibliog.

A monolingual dictionary of recent borrowings by the Romanian language, the
vast majority of which are from French. Of great practical use as a reference tool
for colloquial vocabulary, it indicates stress but does not provide phonetic
transcriptions of headwords.

529 **Dicţionar onomastic romînesc** (Romanian onomastic dictionary.)
N. A. Constantinescu. Bucharest: Editura Academiei Republicii
Populare Romîne, 1963. 469p.

An excellent dictionary of names and proper nouns with copious annotations on
their etymologies and variant dialectal forms.

530 **Dicţionar poliglot. Construcţii, materiale de construcţii, şi
hidrotehnică** (Multilingual dictionary. Buildings, building
materials, and hydrotechnics.)
Bucharest: Editura tehnică, 1979. 828p. bibliog.

One of a series of specialized multilingual dictionaries with English headwords
and Romanian, German, French and Russian equivalents. Other dictionaries in
the series include Medicine and Mechanics.

531 **Dicţionar tehnic englez-român** (English-Romanian technical
dictionary.)
Bucharest: Editura tehnică, 1967. 1303p. bibliog.

An exhaustive dictionary of over 115,000 technical terms in current use in British
and American English with their Romanian equivalents.

532 **Dicţionarul dialectului aromân** (A dictionary of the Macedo-
Romanian dialect.)
Tache Papahagi. Bucharest: Editura Academiei Republicii
Socialiste România, 1974. 2nd. enlarged ed. 1,435p.

The standard dictionary of Macedo-Romanian spoken by the Vlachs living in the
Pindus mountains of northern Greece and Southeastern Albania. Stress is marked
in the headwords and there is a lucid and detailed introduction to the language (p.
5-97) in Romanian and French.

533 **Frequency dictionary of Rumanian words.**
A. Juilland, P. M. H. Edwards, I. Juilland. The Hague: Mouton,
1965. 513p.

A guide to the colloquial core vocabulary of Romanian. This volume is of great
practical benefit to the student and words are listed according to the frequency of
use and in an alphabetical index.

534 **Lexicon maritim englez-român** (An English-Romanian nautical lexicon.)

Gh. Bibicescu, A. Tudorică, Gh. Scurtu, M. Chiriță. Bucharest: Editura ştiinţifică, 1971. 852p.

The expansion of Romania's merchant navy and its increasing contact with the international maritime community explain the appearance of this admirable lexicon which defines over 8,000 English headwords in Romanian and also gives their equivalents in French, German, Spanish and Russian. A Romanian-English nautical dictionary with 3,500 headwords is annexed.

Literature

General

535 **A concise history of Romanian literature.**
     Ion Dodu Bălan. Bucharest: Editura ştiinţifică şi enciclopedică,
     1981. 119p.

A balanced introduction to the principal figures of Romanian literature and the anonymous masterpieces of Romanian oral literature. Arranged in the form of a biographical dictionary (chronologically not alphabetically), the entries on each writer often include a short passage in translation from his or her work. Most of the major talents of this century are included. Surprisingly, there is no bibliography.

536 **Rumanian travelogue.**
     François Bondy. *Survey*, no. 55 (April 1965), p. 21-37.

An appraisal of what the thaw in intellectual life in Romania in 1964 meant to the writers and artists living there.

537 **The new censorship model.**
     Anneli Ute Gabanyi. *Index on Censorship*, vol. 7, no. 6 (1978),
     p. 44-48.

In May 1977 Ceauşescu, in an address to the National Writers' Conference in Bucharest, referred to the intended withdrawal of the current censorship practices. The optimism that this announcement engendered proved to be misplaced for in June of the same year the Central Committee resolved that the main responsibility for control or censorship be borne by the author and full responsibility for published material be borne by the managements of newspapers, journals, and publishing houses. The implications of this new form of censorship, and of the new powers of control vested in the Council for Socialist Culture and Education in December 1977, are assessed by the author.

538 **The writer in Rumania.**
Anneli Ute Gabanyi. *Index on Censorship*, vol. 4, no. 3 (1975), p. 51-55.
In spring 1974 a new Press law was passed by the Grand National Assembly and a Central Committee resolution on 'Ways of improving the press and of economizing paper consumption' adopted. As a result the number of pages and copies of certain papers, and their frequency of publication, was reduced. The details of how these measures affected individual dailies and reviews are given, followed by a review of the cosmetic changes in the methods of censorship.

539 **Partei und literatur in Rumänien seit 1945** (Party and literature in Romania since 1945.)
Anneli Ute Gabanyi. Munich: R. Oldenbourg Verlag, 1975.
209p. (Untersuchungen zur Gegenwartskunde Südosteuropas.
Herausgegeben vom Südost-Institut München, no. 9).
A fascinating and unique analysis of the influence exerted by the Communist Party over the development of literature and literary criticism in Romania from the end of the war until the mid-1970s. A fundamental work for all students of post-war Romanian literature and politics.

540 **Literatur** (Literature.)
Anneli Ute Gabanyi. In: *Südosteuropa-Handbuch. Band II. Rumänien* (Handbook of Southeastern Europe, vol. 2. Romania.)
Edited by K-D. Grothusen. Göttingen, GFR: Vandenhoeck und Ruprecht, 1977. p. 527-56.
A splendid survey of the significant developments and the major talents in contemporary Romanian literature.

541 **The post-war literature of Rumania.**
D. Iliescu. In: *The Soviet Union and Eastern Europe: a handbook*.
Edited by George Schöpflin. London: Blond, 1970. 614p. bibliog.
P. 573-78 provide an informative guide to the major writers and trends in contemporary Romanian literature.

542 **Flights from reality: three Romanian women poets of the new generation.**
Michael H. Impey. *Books Abroad. An International Literary Quarterly*, vol. 50 (Jan. 1976), p. 16-35.
An illuminating presentation of the poetry of Ana Blandiana (1942-), Constanţa Buzea (1941-) and Gabriela Melinescu (1942-), characterized by the Romanian critic Ion Pop as among the poets of the post-war generation who, together with Nicolae Labiş (1935-56), injected a measure of candour and youthfulness into

Romanian poetry. All three women poets, as Impey points out, 'view their work as the expression of a particular age, a strange confluence of past, present and future'.

543 **Historical figures in the Romanian political novel.**
Michael H. Impey. *Southeastern Europe, L'Europe du sud-est*, vol. 7, part 1 (1980), p. 99-113.

A discussion of three novels: Marin Preda's *Delirul* (1975), Eugen Barbu's *Incognito* (1975), and Augustin Buzura's *Orgolii* (1977). The first two portray events and figures from the Second World War and the years immediaely preceeding it, and owed their success partly to the fact that they reintroduced the previously taboo figure of Marshal Antonescu. However, Barbu's character assassination of Antonescu contrasts with Preda's more sympathetic treatment of the private person who was motivated by a sense of patriotism. *Orgolii* may be called a historical novel in the sense that its protagonist, a professor of medicine, reflects the challenge to many professional figures in Romanian society during the advent to power of the communists, the Stalinist era and its aftermath. There is, however, a sympathetic portrayal of Iuliu Maniu, who was the leader of the National Peasant Party until its forced dissolution after the Second World War. As Impey argues, 'Buzura allows his protagonists greater psychological growth, while his interface technique provides for mutual relationships which are barely glimpsed even in Preda's novel'. *Orgolii*, which may be translated as 'forms of pride', interweaves the lives of a number of Transylvanians including Maniu and the professor of medicine, Ion Christian, who exemplified a sense of public duty and devotion to a belief. These qualities are defined by the author as pride and are offered as an example to his contemporaries.

544 **Yugoslav writers on Romania.**
Ante Kadic. *East European Quarterly*, vol. 9, no. 3 (autumn 1975), p. 331-44.

The brevity of this sketch suggests that Yugoslav writers have had very little to say about Romania and much of what they have said is a testimony to their own characters rather than to objective report. References to the country and its people have been culled from Ivan Gundulić (1589-1638), Dositej Obradović (1739-1811), Franjo Rački (1828-94), Miloš Crnjanski (1893-) and Prežihov Voranc (1893-1950).

545 **Literary Review, vol. 10, no. 4 (summer 1967).**
Teaneck, New Jersey: Farleigh Dickinson University. 133p.

A special issue devoted entirely to contemporary Romanian prose and verse with translations. Some thirty writers are represented, including Mihail Sadoveanu, Marin Preda, Tudor Arghezi, Marin Sorescu, Nichita Stănescu, Miron Radu Paraschivescu and Ion Alexandru.

546 **The new wave of Rumanian writers.**
Monica Lovinescu. *East Europe*, vol. 16, no. 12 (Dec. 1967), p. 9-15.

Three developments may be said to have characterized contemporary Romanian literature in the mid-1960s: the emergence of a group of young poets and novelists; the reappearance of a number of older writers whose talent was not allowed expression during the previous two decades; and the rehabilitation of several authors whose works were banned during the post-war era. This article describes the features of the younger generation's verse and the prose of such novelists as Marin Preda, Ştefan Bănulescu, Alexandru Ivasiuc and Dumitru Radu Popescu.

547 **Modern Roumanian literature.**
Basil Munteano, translated by Cargi Sprietsma. Bucharest: Editura Cuvântul, 1943. 322p.

Although written in a rhetorical style this work is still the only intelligible history of Romanian literature in English. Originally published as *Panorama de la littérature roumaine contemporaine* (Paris: Éditions du Sagittaire, 1938. 332p.), it opens its account in the middle of the 19th century and thus overlooks the emergence of a native literature in the late 1820s.

548 **Recent Romanian criticism: subjectivity as a social response.**
Virgil Nemoianu. *World Literature Today*, vol. 51 (1977), p. 560-63.

A profound analysis of two main lines of contemporary Romanian literary criticism which the author sees as finding expression in the works of Nicolae Manolescu and Ion Negoiţescu.

549 **The Romanian search for realism.**
Thomas Amherst Perry. *Yearbook of Romanian Studies*, no. 4 (1979), p. 29-39.

A discussion of the definition of realism in the Romanian context which leads the author to conclude: 'Most contemporary Romanian fiction, however, has remained within the mainstream of Realism. The demands for a literature of social significance and "historicity", the persistence of Social Realism as the official dogma of orthodox Marxism, the loyalty of neo-Hegelians to some form of Realism, as well as the past Romanian record of significant literary achievement in critical and psychological Realism – all anchor present day Romanian fiction in the homeland to the Realist mode'.

550 **The literary scene in Rumania**
Edgar Reichman. *Survey*, no. 55 (April 1965), p. 38-51.

A brief but judicious survey of the work of what the author considers to be the most representative writers in Romania of the early sixties – Tudor Arghezi, Mihail Sadoveanu, George Călinescu, Petru Dumitriu, Marin Preda, Eugen Barbu and Lucian Blaga.

135

Literature. General

551 Introduction to Rumanian literature.
Edited by Jacob Steinberg. New York: Twayne, 1966. 411p.

An anthology of 19th and 20th century Romanian prose in English translation that provides an introduction to the Romanian short story. Each translation is preceded by biographical notes about its author. Among the writers represented are Ion Creanga, Ion Luca Caragiale, Mihail Sadoveanu, Liviu Rebreanu, Camil Petrescu and Marin Preda.

552 Romanian essayists of today.
Translated by Anda Teodorescu, Andrei Bantaş. Bucharest: Univers Publishing House, 1979. 414p.

A collection of essays by a number of Romania's foremost literary critics on assorted themes of Romanian and foreign literature. Among the contributions on Romanian literature are E. Papu's, *The universal character of Eminescu's poetry*, N. Balotă's, *Lucian Blaga – an Orphic poet*, Ş, Cioculescu's, *Irony in Caragiale's work*, C. Ciopraga's, *Liviu Rebreanu or the assertion of the novel*, A. Martin's, *Nichita Stănescu or the state of poetry*, E. Simion's, *Marin Preda and the ways of realism*, I. Vlad's, *Contemporary Romanian fiction as history and aesthetic experience*, and S. Alexandrescu's, *The function of symbol with Tudor Arghezi*.

553 Communist literature in Romania.
Nicholas Timiras. *Journal of Central European Affairs*, vol. 14, no. 4 (Jan. 1955), p. 371-81.

An interesting survey of some Romanian literature of the early 1950s that has been largely forgotten or overlooked in recent appraisals of post-war writing in Romania.

554 Centres of literary activity in Moldavia, 1504-1552.
Emil Turdeanu. *Slavonic and East European Review*, vol. 34, no. 82 (Dec. 1955), p. 99-123.

This pioneering article recounts how the literary heritage of the reign of Stephen the Great (1457-1504) was developed under succeeding princes of Moldavia, and how the influence of the cultural centres of Neamţu, Putna and Suceava spread in the first half of the 16th century. Based on materials scattered throughout the Orthodox world, Turdeanu's impressive and unrivalled knowledge of his subject is conveyed lucidly and eloquently.

Oral tradition

555 **The artistic devices of Romanian folk poetry.**
Robert Austerlitz. In: *Romanian folk arts*. New York: Romanian Library, 1976. p. 70-76.

An analysis of two Romanian folk poems, one originating from the Second World War, the other first published in 1913. His study of the rhythm, rhyme and metre of the two poems leads the author to conclude: 'The building blocks of poetic language, words and grammatical constructions, are very much like the stuff of which designs (e.g. those on textiles) are made: both are deployed and recur symmetrically in space or time and both are governed by rules of repetition'.

556 **Another folk poem analysed.**
Robert Austerlitz. *Studii şi cercetări lingvistice*, vol. 31, no. 5 (1980), p. 505-09.

The importance of studying cohesion in folk poetry is stressed in this analysis of a short, nine-line Romanian folk poem. The formulaic synopsis of the poem reveals a high degree of cohesion in its metre, content and rhyme which, the author suggests, serves as a model for further popular creation and for the perpetuation of the genre.

557 **The maiden without hands.**
C. Bărbulescu. In: *Studies in East European folk narrative*. Edited by L. Dégh. Bloomington, Indiana: Folklore Institute, Indiana University, 1978. p. 321-65.

558 **Literary analysis of the Romanian folk ballad Mioriţa.**
Vasile C. Barsan. *Romanian Sources*, vol. 1, part 1 (Jan. 1975), p. 38-42.

The author of this article writes of this folk-ballad about a shepherd's fatalism in the face of death: 'the shepherd awaiting his death nobly reviews in his imagination all the magnificent aspects of reality in the midst of which he has lived. . . With great poetic skill the poet invokes stately mountains, the surrounding fir trees and sycamore maples, the birds singing rapturously and, above all, the conveying the great cosmic unity in the midst of which he lived and the contemplation of which charmed him'. An English translation of the ballad precedes the article.

559 **The legend of mesterul Manole – a literary study of sources and themes.**
Vasile C. Barsan. *Romanian Sources*, vol. 1, part 2 (July 1975), p. 33-38.

The belief that sacrifice of life will ensure the durability of a monument is reflected in the ballad of the masterbuilder Manole who entombs his wife while building the Argeş monastery. This article consists largely of a series of appreciations of both monastery and ballad made by a number of Romanian and foreign scholars.

560   **A storyteller from Hatzeg: imagination and reality in the life and magic tales of Sinziana Ilona.**
T. Brill, translated by A. Hershberger. In: *Studies in East European folk narrative*. Edited by L. Dégh. Bloomington, Indiana: Folklore Institute, Indiana University, 1978. p. 621-78.

561   **Die rumänische Volkskultur und ihre Mythologie** (Romanian popular culture and its mythology.)
Octavian Buhociu.   Wiesbaden, GFR: Otto Harrassowitz, 1974. 358p. bibliog. (Schriften zur geistesgeschichte des Östlichen Europa. Band 8).
One of the most comprehensive studies in a West European language of Romanian dirges, carols and folk legends. It is also distinguished by an extensive bibliography.

562   **Romanian folk tales.**
Translated from the Romanian by Ana Cartianu.   Bucharest: Minerva Publishing House, 1979. 335p.
A selection of seventeen folk tales preceded by a brief but perceptive introduction on their features by Vasile Nicolescu.

563   **Rumanian bird and beast stories.**
Moses Gaster.   London: Sidgwick & Jackson, 1915. 381p.
A fascinating collection in English translation of animal tales and incantations against animal illnesses that, in several cases, are peculiar to Romania. Their place in the study of folk literatures is analysed by the author in a lengthy introduction (p. 1-59).

564   **Le rite et le discours: introduction à la lecture de la versification populaire** (Ritual and discourse: an introduction to the 'lecture' of folk versification.)
Claude Karnoouh.   Ghent, Belgium: Communication and Cognition, 1983. 130p.
An interpretation of the matrimonial rites that survive in the north of Romania in the area of Maramureş which combines both description and analysis. The author's presentation of the precepts upon which his analysis is based provides the reader with an outstanding introduction to the techniques of a scientific, as opposed to Romantic, study of folklore, the bases of which were established by R. Jakobson and P. Bogatynev in 1929.

565 **Balade populare româneşti: Romanian popular ballads.**
Translated by Leon D. Leviţchi, Andrei Bantaş, Dan Duţescu,
Alfred Margul-Sperber, W. D. Snodgrass.   Bucharest: Minerva
Publishing House, 1980. 471p.

A Romanian-English bilingual anthology of Romanian folk-ballads. Some of
these probably date from the 16th century, since the incursions of the Tatars are
mentioned. The ballads are often grouped into the heroic, those devoted to
notorious outlaws, the 'fantastic', in which elements of the miraculous prevail,
and the pastoral and love types. The specific metre is trochaic, in contrast to the
English iambic, and deviations from the programmed syllabic line are more
frequent than in the English ballad. The refrain is less common in Romanian
ballads.

566 **Doine; or the national songs and legends of Roumania.**
E. C. Grenville Murray.   London: Smith, Elder & Co., 1854.
161p.

A collection of folk tales translated from Romanian and accompanied in the
postface by six 'national' airs of Romania arranged for the piano. The Romanian
noun 'doine' is normally used to describe Romanian folk poems reminiscent in
character to those of Ossian and its use by Murray is misleading.

567 **The Romanian folkloric vampire.**
Jan Louis Perkowski.   *East European Quarterly*, vol. 16, no. 3
(autumn 1982), p. 311-22.

An attempt to classify nineteen vampire texts that were collected from various
regions of Romania in the 1930s. The texts suggest precautions to be taken
against the creation of vampires and the remedies offered if these precautions
have not been heeded.

568 **Were-beings and *strigoi* legends in village life: Romanian folk
beliefs.**
Harry A. Senn.   *East European Quarterly*, vol. 14, no. 3 (autumn
1980), p. 303-14.

A brief examination of the role played by were-wolf, witch and vampire legends
in the folk belief of Romanians. The author concludes that these legends 'find
their place in a folk system that offers an explanation, a means of protection, a
method of protection for them that both relieves anxiety and maintains the
stability of the community'. In Romanian *strigoi viu* signifies a witch and *strigoi
mort* a vampire.

569 **Pacala and Tandala and other Romanian folktales.**
Compiled, translated and edited by Jean Ure.   London: Methuen,
1960. 194p. illus.

Thirty-five Romanian folk tales in an admirable English translation accompanied
by notes on the original Romanian story-tellers.

Anthologies

570 **46 Romanian poets in English.**
Translations, introductions and notes by Ştefan Avădanei, Don
Eulert. Iaşi, Romania: Junimea Publishing House, 1973. 362p.

A selection of principally Romanian verse of the 20th century, the major part of
which is devoted to poets of the post-war generation, such as Ştefan Augustin
Doinaş, Leonid Dimov, Nichita Stănescu, Marin Sorescu, Constanţa Buzea,
Mihai Ursachi, Ion Alexandru, Ana Blandiana and Adrian Păunescu. The
original introduction by Don Eulert highlights the position of the poet in
Romanian society.

571 **History and legend in Romanian short stories and tales.**
Translated by Ana Cartianu. Bucharest: Minerva Publishing
House, 1983. 298p.

A selection of short stories based on fact and legend in Romanian history. The
following tales are included: 'Prince Alexandru Lăpuşneanul' by Constantin
Negruzzi, 'Prince Mihnea the Wicked' by Alexandru Odobescu, 'Prince Cuza' by
Mihail Sadoveanu, 'Alcyon or the White Devil' by Vasile Voiculescu, 'Seven
Wooden Horns' by Dominic Stanca and 'Hunting Horn' by Alexandru Ivasiuc.

572 **Romanian fantastic tales.**
Translated from the Romanian by Ana Cartianu. Bucharest:
Minerva Publishing House, 1981. 341p.

Selections from the work of eleven Romanian authors from the 19th and 20th
centuries illustrating the fantastic element in Romanian prose. Among the writers
included are Mihai Eminescu, Ion Luca Caragiale, Vasile Voiculescu, Cezar
Petrescu and Mircea Eliade.

573 **Modern Romanian poetry: an anthology.**
Edited by Nicholas Catanoy. Oakville, Ottawa: Mosaic Press,
Valley Editions, 1977. 142p.

A collection of almost one hundred poems by more than fifty Romanian poets
sensitively translated into English by twenty-two Canadian writers. The editor
himself provided many of the translations from the Romanian from which English
versions were produced by Canadian translators. Biographical and bibliographical
notes on the Romanian poets, several of whom are living in exile, are provided.

574 **An anthology of contemporary Romanian poetry.**
Translated by Andrea Deletant, Brenda Walker. London;
Boston, Massachusetts: Forest Books, 1984. 128p.

This short anthology is nevertheless one of the most representative of its kind to
be published outside Romania. Containing selections from the work of Ioan
Alexandru, Ana Blandiana, Constanţa Buzea, Nina Cassian, Ştefan Augustin
Doinaş, Marin Sorescu, Nichita Stănescu and Ion Stoica, it illustrates the
remarkable breadth and vision of Romanian verse from the last two decades.

575 **100 de ani de poezie românească – 100 years of Romanian poetry.**
Translated by Ioana Deligiorgis. Iaşi, Romania: Junimea
Publishing House, 1982. 443p.

A bilingual compendium of verse covering poetry from the mid 19th century to
the present, in which the poets presented are arranged chronologically. Most of
the 131 poets are represented by one poem although Mihail Eminescu, Alexandru
Macedonski, George Bacovia, Tudor Arghezi, Ion Barbu and Lucian Blaga are
accorded three poems. There are no biographical notes.

576 **Romanian poems: an anthology of verse.**
Selected and translated by Dan Duţescu. Bucharest: Eminescu
Publishing House, 1982. 333p.

The most comprehensive anthology of contemporary Romanian verse in English
translation. Over one hundred poets are represented, in chronological order of
birth, in sensitive translations of their work by one of Romania's most
accomplished translators.

577 **Anthology of contemporary Romanian poetry.**
Edited, translated and with an introduction by Roy MacGregor-
Hastie. London: Peter Owen, 1969. 166p.

The first anthology of 20th century Romanian verse to be published in Britain
with a judicious selection from the work of several significant Romanian poets of
this century. The eccentric introduction mentions a Romanian 'library' at Hull in
the north of England but fails to point out that the largest library of Romanian
literature in the UK is housed in the School of Slavonic and East European
Studies of the University of London.

578 **Romanian short stories.**
Introduction by Olivia Manning. London: Oxford University
Press, 1971. 335p.

An anthology of eighteen short stories covering a century of Romanian writing
translated into English. No acknowledgement is given to the translators. Two
satirical sketches of urban society by I. L. Caragiale and stories of peasant life by
Mihail Sadoveanu and Ioan Slavici are included in this volume. The introduction
is brief but pithy and notes on the authors are provided in a postface.

579 **Cu bilet circular. With circular ticket.**
Anthology and foreword by Mircea Zaciu. Translated into English
by Fred Nădăban, John W. Rathbun. Bio-bibliographical notes by
Sever Trifu. Cluj-Napoca, Romania: Editura Dacia, 1983. 343p.

A bilingual anthology of Romanian short stories by eighteen authors spanning the
period from the last quarter of the 19th century to the present. The preface by
Zaciu is an essay on the short-story in Romanian which is dense in its coverage
and full of insights. The authors represented include Duiliu Zamfirescu, D. D.
Pătrăşcanu, Liviu Rebreanu, Tudor Arghezi, Ion Vinea, Urmuz, Pavel Dan,
Marin Preda and D. R. Popescu.

580 **Romanian songs and ballads.**

R. Stewart Patterson. London: John Long, 1917. 128p.

A compilation of Romanian folk ballads and cultivated verse brought together by the one-time chaplain to the British legation in Bucharest. This 'pot-pourri' in quaint English verse includes translations of Queen Elizabeth of Romania's (Carmen Sylva) laments.

581 **Romanian.**

Thomas Amherst Perry. In: *Contemporary East European poetry*. Ann Arbor, Michigan: Ardis, 1983. p. 293-341.

A brief introduction to contemporary Romanian verse followed by selections from the work of some of the major poets, translated by Perry himself and various other Romanian translators.

582 **Romania is a song: a sampler of verse in translation.**

Eli Popa. Cleveland, Ohio: America Publishing Co., 1966. 160p.

An anthology of Romanian verse with accompanying English translations that is unusual in that includes the work of a number of poets living abroad, such as Vasile Posteucă (b. 1912) and Nicolae Novac (b. 1919). The emphasis of the collection is upon poets of the 19th and early 20th century such as Eminescu, Coşbuc and Goga.

583 **Rumanian prose and verse.**

Eric D. Tappe. London: University of London, Athlone Press, 1956. 193p.

An anthology of Romanian literature in the original with English annotations. This is not a graded reader but a selection of extracts from the work of many of the most representative Romanian writers, arranged chronologically. Post-war literature is not represented. The introductory essay provides a valuable survey of Romanian literature for the non-specialist.

584 **Romanian poems: a bilingual anthology of Romanian poetry.**

Sever Trifu, Dumitru Ciocoi-Pop. Cluj, Romania: Dacia Publishing House, 1972. 311p.

Some twenty Romanian poets of the 19th and 20th century are represented in this bilingual anthology. The English versions are by Romanian and English translators and are preceded by brief biographical notes and a bibliography on each poet.

585 **15 young Romanian poets.**

An anthology of verse selected and translated by Liliana Ursu. Bucharest: Editura Eminescu, 1982. 109p.

The fifteen poets are Daniela Crăsnaru, Ioana Diaconescu, Mircea Dinescu, Dinu Flămînd, Ioana Ieronim, Carolina Ilica, Dumitru M. Ion, Ion Mircea, Lucia Negoiţă, Adrian Popescu, Mircea Florin Şandru, Grete Tartler, Doina Uricariu, Liliana Ursu and Dan Verona. Each is introduced by a brief description of the themes of his or her verse and is represented by a handful of poems in intelligible English translations.

Individual writers

586 **Vasile Alecsandri.**
Alexandre Cioranescu, translated by Maria Golescu, revised by Eric D. Tappe. New York: Twayne, 1973. 179p. bibliog. (Twayne's World Authors Series, no. 204).

An excellent appraisal of the life and work of one of the most outstanding Romanian literary figures of the 19th century. Alecsandri (1821-90), as bard of the union of Moldavia and Wallachia, as a collector of Romanian folklore, and as a founder of a national Romanian theatre, acquired the status of a Poet Laureate during his lifetime and became a father-figure of Romanian literature to succeeding generations.

587 **Vasile Alecsandri.**
G. C. Nicolescu. Bucharest: Meridiane Publishing House, 1967. 163p.

An unfortunately stilted English translation of an original Romanian monograph on Alecsandri that faithfully sets his achievements as poet, dramatist, prose-writer and politician in the context of his times.

588 **Selected poems of Tudor Arghezi.**
Translated by Michael Impey, Brian Swann. Princeton, New Jersey: Princeton University Press, 1976. 223p.

An admirable introduction to Arghezi's verse which appears in both the Romanian original and in sympathetic English translation. The preface by Michael Impey is a perceptive analysis of the threads of the poet's work which are: a search for the supreme being, an exploration of the creative act, and a return to man's origins, all of which constitute 'man's search for the self'. The cycles of poetry represented are *Cuvinte potrivite*, *Flori de mucegai*, *Versuri de seară* and *Una sută una poeme*.

589 **Tudor Arghezi: poet for contemporary man.**
George Ivaşcu. *Books Abroad: An International Literary Quarterly*, vol. 43, no. 1 (winter 1969), p. 32-36.

A brief but illuminating introduction to the nature of Arghezi's verse which is a painful self-examination, and a search for cognition, expressed in an oscillation between denial and belief in the existence of God – see the volume *Cuvinte potrivite* [Fitting words] (1927). All shreds of doubt are removed in his post-war volume *Cîntare omului* [Hymn to man] (1956) in which man is presented as cogniscent of his own self and thus able to fashion his own destiny.

590 **Tudor Arghezi.**
Dumitru Micu, translated from the Rumanian by H. A. Richard, Michael Impey. Bucharest: Meridiane Publishing House, 1965. 163p.

This is an uneven monograph, for the appraisal of the poet's post-war work is disproportionate to his achievement in *Cuvinte potrivite* (1927).

591 **Plumb: lead.**
George Bacovia, translated by Peter Jay. Bucharest: Minerva Publishing House, 1980. 233p.

George Vasiliu (1881-1957) took his pseudonym from his birthplace Bacău where the monotony of provincial urban life provided the setting for much of his poetry, including his first volume *Plumb* [Lead] (1916). Melancholy and pessimism are expressed in a repetitious use of stark colour words and phrases. The poet is haunted by damp, decay, rain, and snow. These are the elements that constitute Bacovia's universe, which is one of putrefaction and gloom. Dusk and night, autumn and winter, grey, black and violet characterize his neurosis of which his use of repetition is symptomatic. Grotesque faces and bodies, screaming and howling, add an expressionist note. Bacovia's use of a limited vocabulary gives it a symbolic rôle in his verse. Through the poet's exploration of the possibilities of association his poetry acquires an unexpected richness. Peter Jay's versions are an attempt to write 'English poems that are compatible with my intuition of the Bacovian style'. The attempt succeeds.

592 **Ion Barbu.**
Alexandre Cioranescu, edited and translated by Eric Tappe. New York: Twayne, 1981. 155p. bibliog. (Twayne's World Authors Series, no. 590).

A fascinating insight into one of the most enigmatic figures of Romanian literature. Ion Barbu (1895-1961) provides an unusual example of a person with two métiers, those of poet and mathematician. Barbu's preoccupation with the analogies between poetry and mathematics produced a verse characterized by mathematical metaphor which is perceptively analysed in this study.

593 **Doda.**
Marcu Beza, translated from the Roumanian by Lucy Byng. London: G. Bles, 1925. 155p.

The area of Macedonia settled by the Macedo-Romanians and the toen of Thessaloniki forms the background to this novel in which the eponymous heroine's aspirations for her children are sentimentally realized.

594 **Rays of memory.**
Marcu Beza, translated from the Roumanian by Lucy Byng. New York: E. P. Dutton; London: J. M. Dent & Sons, 1929. 144p.

A series of autobiographical sketches set largely in Greece and Turkey that exude the atmosphere and colouring of cities such as Thessaloniki and Istanbul in the 1920s.

595 **Poems of light: a Romanian-English bilingual edition.**
Lucian Blaga, English versions by Don Eulert, Ştefan Avădanei,
Mihail Bogdan. Bucharest: Minerva Publishing House, 1975.
349p.

Blaga (1895-1961) was a poet, dramatist, and philosopher who in 1937 was
appointed to the chair of the philosophy of culture at Cluj University. His poetry
is often expressed in symbols and myths. The theme of *Poemele luminii* [Poems of
light] (1919), is the mysterious character of light as a natural agent of the
universe. The poet's fascination with light is explored against a background of
myth. His use of metaphor reveals his association with the universe in visions of
space, and his identification with the mountains and the earth. The title of this
volume is misleading since many poems from Blaga's later cycles are included,
namely: *Paşii profetului* [The prophet's footsteps] (1921); *În marea trecere* [In the
great transition] (1924) which is translated here as 'In the great passage', *Lauda
somnului* [In praise of sleep] (1929); *La cumpăna apelor* [At the watershed]
(1933); *La curţile dorului* [In the courtyards of yearning] (1938); *Nebănuitele
trepte* [Unsuspected steps] (1943) and there are also some individual poems from
the post-war period which were not published in his life-time.

596 **Contributions à l'histoire de la versification roumaine: la prosodie
de Lucian Blaga.** (Contributions to the history of versification in
Romanian: Lucian Blaga's prosody.)
Ladislas Gáldi. Budapest: Akadémiai Kiadó, 1972. 205p.

A systematic analysis of the metre and rhyme of Blaga's verse which also
constitutes a major contribution to the study of the development of Romanian
poetry in this century. In this outstanding study the author highlights the
prosodical innovations made by Blaga (1895-1961).

597 **Poeme – poems.**
Ana Blandiana, translated into English by Dan Duţescu.
Bucharest: Eminescu Publishing House, 1982. 175p.

Ana Blandiana (1942-), in her first volume of poems *Persoana întîia plural* [First
person plural] (1964); practices an asceticism which brings her to a state of self-
knowledge and lucidity. A desire for purity is expressed in subsequent cycles
Călcîiul vulnerabil [The vulnerable heel] (1966); *A treia taină* [The third
sacrament] (1969); and *Octombrie, noiembrie, decembrie* [October, November,
December] (1972); where rain is its symbol. A withdrawal into the world of sleep
and dreams is symbolized in *Somnul din somn* [The sleep within sleep] (1977)
where once again purity is sought. This selection of Blandiana's verse is
distinguished by the sensitive translations offered by Dan Duţescu.

598 **Ion Luca Caragiale.**
Eric D. Tappe. New York: Twayne, 1974. 117p. bibliog.
(Twayne's World Authors Series, no. 276).

This monograph on Romania's most accomplished comic writer is illustrated by
Eric Tappe's excellent translations of extracts from his work which show how
Caragiale (1852-1912) excelled as a humorous playwright and short-story writer.

Literature. Individual writers

599 **The lost letter and other plays.**
Ion Luca Caragiale, translated by Frida Knight. London:
Lawrence & Wishart, 1956. 181p.

Competent translations of the farces *O scrisoare pierdută*, *D-ale carnavalului*, *O noapte furtunoasă* and *Conul Leonida faţă cu reacţiunea*. In places there are small omissions in the translations from the original Romanian.

600 **Sketches and stories.**
I. L. Caragiale, translated by Eric D. Tappe. Cluj-Napoca,
Romania: Dacia Publishing House, 1979. 285p.

The Romanian text of several of Caragiale's most accomplished short stories and tales, accompanied by faithful yet idiomatic English translations. Among the pieces included are 'Petiţiune' (An application), 'Bubico' (Bubico), 'La hanul lui Mînjoală' (Mînjoala's Inn) and 'Kir Ianulea' (Kir Ianulea). There is no table of contents.

601 **Poems.**
George Coşbuc, translated by Leon Leviţchi. Bucharest: Minerva
Publishing House, 1980. 329p.

Village life in his native Transylvania provides the inspiration for the verse of Coşbuc (1866-1918). Conceived as a folk epic, his poetry observes the daily life of the villagers as conditioned by the cycle of seasons. The unity of peasant and nature is evoked dramatically on a canvas of rural scenes, which are notable for their descriptive detail. The popular Romanian ballad is echoed in a number of his poems, especially those describing the ritual of peasant life. The idyllic character of Coşbuc's verse does not spring from a distorted picture of the village but rather from the poet's serene and genial view of life, one in which the harsher realities are attenuated.

602 **La vie et l'oeuvre de Ion Creanga (1837-1889).** (The life and work
of Ion Creanga, 1827-89.)
Jean Boutière. Paris: Librairie Universitaire J. Gamber, 1930.
254p.

This study of the life and work of Creangă, the Moldavian humourist, remains the only one of substance in a major European language. While the biographical chapters now need to be read with caution in view of more recent research into the author's life, the ensuing critical appraisal of his work remains unsurpassed in any language. The book is complemented by an invaluable glossary of 'Moldavianisms' used by Creangă which is based on an edition of his work by G-T. Kirileanu.

603 **Memories of my boyhood. Stories and tales.**
Ion Creangă, translated by Ana Cartianu, R. C. Johnston.
Bucharest: Minerva Publishing House, 1978. 352p.

The charm of *Amintiri din copilărie* (Memories of my childhood) lies in its picture of village life and traditional customs, and in Creangă's recording of Moldavian speech habits. This last feature is impossible to render in English in a universally acceptable manner and the translators have used archaisms and dialectal words. The result is largely successful.

604 Folk tales from Roumania.
Translated from the Roumanian of Ion Creangă by Mabel Nandriş.   London: Routledge & Kegan Paul, 1952. 170p. illus.

Fine translations of folk tales retold by the 19th century writer Ion Creangă, a master of the oral style. Creangă collected the themes of his stories from peasants in his native Moldavia and embellished them with unexpected allegories which have charmed children and adults alike.

605 Alibi and other poems.
Ştefan Aug. Doinaş, translated by Peter Jay, Virgil Nemoianu. London: Anvil Press Poetry in association with Rex Collings, 1975. 31p.

A selection of twenty poems from the verse of one of the outstanding contemporary Romanian poets that illustrates his various modes in their chronological development.

606 Family jewels.
Petru Dumitriu, translated by E. Hyams.   London: Collins, 1961. 437p.

A translation of the first volume of the author's three volume *Cronica de familie* (Family chronicle) which is set in the inter-war period and was published in 1956 in Bucharest before the author emigrated to the West.

607 The last romantic: Mihail Eminescu.
English versions and introduction by Roy MacGregor-Hastie. Iowa City: University of Iowa Press, 1972. 129p. bibliog.

A selection of the major poems of Romania's most celebrated poet, faithfully rendered into English.

608 Poems.
Mihai Eminescu. English version by Corneliu M. Popescu. Bucharest: Editura Eminescu, 1978. 215p.

These remarkable translations are a testimony to the precocity of this Romanian translator who died at the age of eighteen in the earthquake of 4 March 1977 in Bucharest. His rendering of the original rhyme in English and the restoration of the metre are generally extremely successful, and place these translations on a level with alternative versions.

609 **Poems.**

Mihai Eminescu, translated by Leon Leviţchi, Andrei Bantaş.
Bucharest: Minerva Publishing House, 1978. 509p.

A Romanian-English bilingual edition containing most of Eminescu's poems. The translators' insistence on rhyme in the English version has, in some cases, led to incongruities that distort the meaning of the original.

610 **La genèse intérieure des poésies d'Eminescu.** (The internal genesis of Eminescu's poems.)

Alain Guillermou. Paris: Librairie Marcel Didier, 1963. 470p.

A textual analysis of the development, through Eminescu's manuscript variants, of the versions of his poems published during his lifetime. While invaluable for the poet's sources of inspiration, the full texts of the poems analysed are not always reproduced.

611 **The twenty-fifth hour.**

C. Virgil Gheorghiu, translated from the Rumanian by Rita Eldon. London: Heinemann, 1950. 373p.

A critique of what the author calls 'modern technocracy' in Western civilization which regards man not as an individual but as an abstract conception. The author's indictment is largely based on his experiences and those of his wife at the hands of the Western Allies at the end of the Second World War. As refugees from Romania, they were interned by the Americans in West Germany as enemy aliens.

612 **Poezii – poems.**

Octavian Goga, translated by Leon Leviţchi. Bucharest: Minerva Publishing House, 1982. 283p.

A bilingual edition of the verse of Octavian Goga (1881-1938), a Transylvanian Romanian poet. His work is characterized by its protest against what he saw as the oppression of the Romanian peasant in Transylvania during his formative years, which is expressed in *Poezii* [Poems] (1906); and *Ne cheamă pămîntul* [The earth summons us] (1909). It is also a eulogy to the purity of village life which he contrasts with the corrupting influence of the town: *Din umbra zidurilor* [From the shadow of the walls] (1913); *Cîntece fără ţară* [Homeless songs] (1916). In Goga's own words 'I was born with my fists clenched tight, my soul set from the very beginning for protest, for revolt – the strongest feeling that has guided my life and from which I derived my literary formula'. After the First World War Goga's political ambitions brought him ministerial office and, in December 1937, the position of Prime Minister. His term of office, lasting three months, was notorious for its anti-semitic measures, a blight on his name which prevented publication of his verse in Romania after the war until the mid-1960s. The English versions of his poems presented here are sensitive to the original.

148

613 **The disguises of miracle: notes on Mircea Eliade's fiction.**
Matei Călinescu. *World Literature Today*, vol. 52 (1978), p. 558-
64.

These 'notes' on Eliade's fiction are rich in suggestion and constitute an
introduction to the writer's *oeuvre*. 'Not unpredictably, Eliade the writer is
confronted essentially by the same problems (sacred and profane qualities of time
and space, the "camouflage of myth" and the "unrecognizability of miracle" etc.)
that, from a different perspective and working with different materials, the
historian of religions has repeatedly encountered over the years. By saying this, I
in no way want to imply that Eliade the writer "treats" or "illustrates" motifs,
rituals and symbols, ideas and beliefs that Eliade the phenomenologist of religion
has previously studied in their historical and transhistorical connections. Actually
the opposite seems to be true in his case'. These observations of Călinescu form
the background to a presentation of Eliade's novels and novellas, culminating in
an analysis of *The Forbidden forest*, first published in a French translation of the
Romanian manuscript in 1955.

614 **The old man and the bureaucrats.**
Mircea Eliade, translated by Mary Park Stevenson. Notre Dame,
Indiana: University of Notre Dame Press, 1979. 128p.

A translation of *Pe strada Mântuleasa* (Mântuleasa Street), Eliade's accomplished
novella set in the Bucharest of the early 1950s. The theme of the novella is the
conflict between suspicion and trust, between fantasy and fact, between myth and
history. The central character is a retired school teacher who tells fabricated tales
about his former pupils. He attempts to contact a major in the security police
whose name reminds him of a former pupil, an attempt which eventually leads to
the teacher's arrest and interrogation. His reminiscences during the interrogation
arouse the suspicions of the security authorities about people working for the
security police itself and about high-ranking party officials, several of whom are
removed. The schoolmaster's tales are, in fact, inventions but, such is the degree
of suspicion amongst the police that they are interpreted as sources of important
information about various officials in the régime. The form of interpretation is
one of the themes of Eliade's writing and reminds us of his anthropological
studies on the interpretation of myths.

615 **The forbidden forest.**
Mircea Eliade, translated by Mac Linscott Ricketts, Mary Park
Stevenson. Notre Dame, Indiana: University of Notre Dame
Press, 1978. 596p.

First published in French in 1955 as *La forêt interdite*, Eliade's *Noaptea de
Sânziene* (The night of St. John the Baptist [24 June]) presents the hero Ştefan's
search to distinguish the sacred and the profane in everyday life in terms of
fundamental time as opposed to historical time. These concepts are expounded in
Eliade's philosophy of myth as expressed in *Le mythe de l'éternel retour* (Paris,
1949). Ştefan's quest takes place during the Second World War and its aftermath
in Romania. During this period his wife and son were killed in the bombing of
Bucharest by the Western Allies (1944), his close friend died under interrogation
by the communist authorities (1947), and he fled to the West. Ştefan seeks to
transcend this 'terror of history' in order to attain an historical paradise. The

narrative is punctuated in its logical sequence (in which events occur in chronological order and to which the characters respond predictably) by gaps filled with dreamlike images. The reader is left to ask himself whether Ştefan's dream is realized, for the last scene describes a car accident in which he and his love Ileana are killed. The accident occurs on the night of St. John the Baptist in 1948 in a French forest, twelve years, or one cosmic year, to the day, after the two first met in a forest outside Bucharest.

616 **Fantastic tales.**
Mircea Eliade, Mihai Niculescu, translated and edited by Eric D. Tappe. London: Dillon, 1969. 100p.

Three short stories in parallel Romanian-English texts intended for those with some knowledge of Romanian grammar. They are *Douăsprezece mii de capete de vită* and *Un om mare* by Mircea Eliade, and *Cizmarul din Hydra* by Mihai Niculescu. The tales are prefaced by brief biographical notes on both authors and postfaced with a page of annotations on the Romanian texts.

617 **Folklore motifs in Panait Istrati's fiction.**
Rodica C. Botoman. *Yearbook of Romanian Studies*, vol. 1 (1976), p. 6-12.

A glimpse of folklore motifs in the work of the Romanian-born francophone novelist Panait Istrati (1884-1935).

618 **The labyrinth.**
Francisc Păcurariu, translated from the Romanian by Eugenia Farca, Andrei Bantaş. Bucharest: Univers, 1977. 434p.

Păcurariu (1920-) has pursued a diplomatic career which has taken him to Argentina and Uruguay as minister, and Greece as Romanian ambassador (1968-73). His association with Latin America is reflected in several volumes of essays devoted to the literature of that area. His novel *Labirintul* (1974) is set in his native northern Transylvania during the last war. Through the diary of Sabin Popa, who returns to Cluj after the Vienna diktat, life in the Transylvanian capital under Hungarian rule is recounted. These years constitute the labyrinth from which Popa and his friends attempt to emerge. Stylistically, Păcurariu employs techniques characteristic of the modern novel – a collage of first and third person narratives, reminiscences, newspaper reports and flashbacks.

619 **A man amongst men.**
Camil Petrescu, translated from the Rumanian by Eugenia Farca. Verses translated by Dan Duţescu. Bucharest: Foreign Languages Publishing House, 1958. 2 vols.

Un om între oameni is a historical novel based on events leading up to the 1848 revolution in Wallachia and the part played in it by Nicolae Bălcescu (1819-52). Based on extensive research, this novel by Petrescu (1894-1957) is partly a historical document, and partly a work of the imagination which presents a vivid fresco of society, events, and places in Wallachia during the first half of the 19th century.

620 **Burial of the vine.**
Petru Popescu, translated from the Romanian by Carol Telford,
Peter Jay, Petru Popescu. London: Barrie & Jenkins, 1975. 182p.

Petru Popescu (1944-) is one of the most original Romanian post-war novelists whose eight novels and collections of short stories, written before his emigration to the West, enjoyed great critical and public success. *Burial of the vine*, while chronicling the affair of a young Romanian, dismissed from the Party, with the wife of a painter, offers a critique of the new Left establishment of the 1950s.

621 **The Morometes.**
Marin Preda, translated from the Rumanian by N. Mişu.
Bucharest: Foreign Languages Publishing House, 1957. 655p.

A memorable novel by an outstanding post-war novelist who died on 16 May 1980. *The Morometes*, the first volume of which appeared in 1955 (volume 2, 1967), chronicles the problems faced by the eponymous family of peasants during the transition from a pre-war to a post-war society under communism. Ilie Moromete, the philosopher-peasant hero, is one of the most vivid creations of the Romanian post-war novel.

622 **Ion.**
Liviu Rebreanu, translated by A. Hillard. London: Peter Owen, 1965. 411p.

Ion, the son of an impoverished peasant family in a Romanian village in Transylvania at the beginning of this century, is determined to escape from poverty and, to this end, compromises the daughter of a well-to-do peasant, thus abandoning the girl that he has promised to marry. His obsessive greed for land, unsatisfied by his marriage to the hapless daughter, brings his own violent downfall. Although the character of Ion dominates the novel, the author presents at the same time a picture of village life in all its facets.

623 **The uprising.**
Liviu Rebreanu, translated by P. Grandjean, S. Hartauer.
London: Peter Owen, 1964. 385p.

Rebreanu's *Răscoala* weaves a tapestry of life in Bucharest and rural Wallachia at the time of peasant agitation against landlord abuses in 1907. The author shows how certain groups in Romanian society are caught up in the tension of unrest and violence on the large country estates, and how this turmoil erupted into a peasant revolt in eastern Wallachia which was brutally suppressed by the army.

624 **The forest of the hanged.**
Liviu Rebreanu, translated from the Rumanian by A. V.
Wise. London: Peter Owen, 1967. 350p.

Pădurea spînzuraţilor derives its name from a forest where, during the First World War, the Austro-Hungarian army hanged deserters. To this forest comes Apostol Bologa, a young Romanian officer from Transylvania, which was then under Hungarian rule, who had joined the Austro-Hungarian army. When Romania entered the war Bologa found himself fighting his fellow Romanians.

His consequent conflict between opposing loyalties, his desertion, and his execution by hanging are the subjects of this tense novel which is based in part on the experience of the author's brother.

625 **Creanga de aur. The golden bough.**
Mihail Sadoveanu, translated by Eugenia Farca. Bucharest: Minerva Publishing House, 1981. 397p.

Only the title of this novel owes its inspiration to Frazer's *Golden bough* for it is both a historical novel, set in Egypt and Byzantium between 780 and 794 AD, and a philosophical work. The original Romanian text is accompanied by a parallel English translation.

626 **The hatchet.**
Mihail Sadoveanu, translated from the Rumanian by Eugenia Farca. London: Allen & Unwin, 1965. 163p.

This translation of *Baltagul* occasionally omits passages from the original but, nevertheless, conveys the starkness of pastoral life amongst a community of shepherds in northern Romania which provides the background for this 'detective' novel. The subject is the heroine's search for her missing husband, murdered by two of his fellows who coveted his flocks. The narrative thread is tightly drawn and leads the reader along the trail followed by his wife from the sheltered valleys up to mountain peaks. This translation was republished in Romania by Minerva Publishing House (Bucharest, 1983, 143p.).

627 **Mitrea Cocor.**
Mihail Sadoveanu. London: Fore Publications, 1953. 178p.

The picaresque adventures of the eponymous hero of this novel and the realization of his ambitions after the Soviet occupation of Romania in 1944 form the subject of this 'socialist realist' work. Its publication in 1949 marked a new departure for the author.

628 **The still unborn about the dead.**
Nichita Stănescu, translated by Petru Popescu, Peter Jay. London: Anvil Press Poetry associated with Routledge & Kegan Paul, 1975. 94p.

A representative selection of poems by one of Romania's foremost contemporary poets (1933-1983), the first to appear in English translation outside Romania. The translations include Stănescu's major sequence of *Eleven elegies*, together with a wider selection of his shorter poems.

629 **Gates of the moment. Porţile clipei.**
Ion Stoica, translated by Brenda Walker, Andrea Deletant. London; Boston: Forest Books, 1984. 115p.

Stoica (1936-) published his first volume *Casa de vînt* in 1981 and *Porţile clipei* followed a year later. The image of man and the universe recurs in several of his poems, some of which are reminiscent of Blaga. His blend of vision and feeling, punctuated occasionally by a flash of humour, is faithfully conveyed in these sensitive translations.

630 **Ultimele sonete închipuite ale lui Shakespeare în traducere imaginară. Shakespeare's last sonnets as fancied in an imaginary Romanian translation.**
Vasile Voiculescu, selection, English version and illustrations by Margareta Sterian. Bucharest: Editura Eminescu, 1982. 71p.
A more apposite translation of the title of this cycle of poems would be 'simulated translations of an imaginary last sonnet sequence by Shakespeare'. The composition of this cycle of poems, begun in 1954 by Voiculescu (1884-1963), came to an abrupt end with his arrest in the late summer of 1958 after being denounced for reading poems of religious inspiration to a circle of friends. Released a few months before his death, Voiculescu never saw any of his major post-war works published. These poems and his extraordinary novel *Zahei Orbul* (The blind man Zahei) only appeared in 1964 and 1970 respectively. Voiculescu's pre-war verse expresses a mysticism in a language that is occasionally discordant, owing to his use of dialectal vocabulary and disrupted metre.

631 **Duiliu Zamfirescu.**
Sanda Stolojan, translated by Eric D. Tappe. New York: Twayne, 1980. 156p. bibliog. (Twayne's World Authors Series, no. 551).
A sympathetic biographical monograph of Duiliu Zamfirescu (1855-1922) by his granddaughter. Although he completed eight novels, six plays, several volumes of poetry, and a number of short stories, it is for one particular novel, *Viaţa la ţară* (1894-95), that he is chiefly remembered. The fine characterization of its principal figures, the sincerity of detail, and the art of its language are given a stimulating appreciation by Mme Stolojan.

632 **Sasha.**
Duiliu Zamfirescu, translated from the Roumanian by Lucy Byng. London: A. M. Philpot, 1926. 246p.
A translation of *Viaţa la ţară* (Life in the countryside) by Zamfirescu, a novel depicting the patriarchal world in which country gentry and peasants lived at ease alongside each other in Romania of the 1860s.

The Arts

Cultural policy

633 **La République populaire roumaine contre la culture française**
(The Romanian people's republic against French culture.)
Marcel Fontaine.   Paris: Fundaţia regală universitară Carol I,
1962. 256p.

For over a century French culture was virtually worshipped in 'polite society' in
Romania. The measures taken by the communist authorities in the country
against the study of French and the dissemination of French culture are
epitomized by the official pronouncement: 'do not forget that in France
everything is rotten and that all consciences are for sale there'. This unique book
chronicles the Soviet-inspired steps taken to eliminate the study of French,
beginning with the closing of the Instituts français in 1948 and the reform of the
Romanian educational system a year later. De Gaulle was identified with Hitler in
official propaganda and everything French was denigrated. By substituting
English for French in this book, the reader will form a clear idea of the parallel
campaign waged against the culture of English-speaking peoples. After 1964 there
was a relaxation in the official attitude towards non-Russian culture. Today, the
cultivation of French both privately and officially as the principal foreign
language is on the wane, its place being taken by English.

634 **Romania and her cultural policy.**
Mihnea Gheorghiu, George Ciucu, Robert Deutsch, Aurel Martin,
Vasile Tomescu, Radu Popescu, Ion Frunzetti, Mihai Pop,
Ecaterina Oproiu, Valentin Lipatti.   Bucharest: Meridiane
Publishing House, 1973. 196p.

A collection of articles by Romanian scholars on what they regard as the features
of Romanian culture since the 1950s. Literature, music, the fine arts, folklore and
film are represented.

154

Visual arts

635 Byzantine art in Roumania.
Marcu Beza. London: B. T. Batsford, 1940. 104p.

The Byzantine legacy of icons, caskets and service books is illustrated by over forty black-and-white plates. Many of the objects presented by the author, although originating from Moldavia and Wallachia, are located on Mount Athos and in Orthodox churches and monasteries in the Holy Land.

636 Romanian culture abroad.
Virgil Cândea, Constantin Simionescu. Bucharest: Editura Sport-Turism, 1982. 132p.

Following in the pre-war footsteps of Marcu Beza, the authors have compiled a richly illustrated record of the generosity of the princes of Moldavia and Wallachia towards the monasteries in the Eastern Mediterranean. Illustrated manuscripts, goldsmiths' work, and embroideries preserved in Orthodox churches and museums in Istanbul, Jerusalem, Paros, Patmos, Sinai, and Aleppo are described and photographed.

637 Romanian folk painting on glass.
Juliana Dancu, Dumitru Dancu, translated into English by Andreea Gheorghiţoiu. Bucharest: Meridiane Publishing House, 1979. 220p. 150 plates.

Painting on glass is not unique to Romania. The technique seems to have originated in Silesia and the Bavarian forest about 1740 and gradually spread to Bohemia, Moravia, Slovakia, Hungary, Transylvania, and Yugoslavia. The similarity between the composition of a number of icons produced in the Transylvanian centre of Nicula and that of icons from Sandl in Austria, and from Bohemia and Slovakia, indicates that the icon painters in northern Transylvania adopted the technique from these sources. Transylvania marks the Southeastern extremity of the practice; across the Carpathians in Moldavia and Wallachia we find only rare examples of this craft. This splendidly illustrated volume provides the most vivid catalogue of Romanian achievements in this art.

638 Folk glass-painting in Romania.
Juliana Dancu, Dumitru Dancu. Bucharest: Meridiane Publishing House, 1982. 179p. bibliog.

An excellent survey of this art illustrated by a number of coloured plates.

639 Humor.
Vasile Drăguţ, translated from the Romanian by Caterina Augusta Grundbock. Bucharest: Meridiane Publishing House, 1973. 43p. 78 plates.

A lavishly illustrated volume presenting one of the Moldavian painted monastery churches. Humor, completed in 1530 and decorated five years later, is notable for its external frescoes by a team of artists led by Toma of Suceava.

155

640 **Colloque sur la conservation et la restauration des peintures murales.** (Colloquium on the conservation and restoration of frescoes.)
Edited by Vasile Drăguţ, Tereza Sinigalia, Ioan Opriş. Suceava, Romania. 1977. 131p.

A selection of papers given at a colloquium held at Suceava in July 1977 in the proximity of the Moldavian painted monasteries. This volume is illustrated with photographs and drawings to explain the points raised in each paper, and provides a fascinating insight into the genesis of the Moldavian frescoes.

641 **Moldavian murals from the 15th to the 16th century.**
Vasile Drăguţ, selection of illustrations and captions by Petre Lupan, translated from the Romanian by Andreea Gheorghiţoiu.
Bucharest: Meridiane Publishing House, 1982. 48p. 235 plates. bibliog.

The painted churches of northern Moldavia are jewels in Romania's artistic heritage. Their splendour is conveyed by the colour plates in this volume which include, alongside the famous monastery churches of Voroneţ, Moldoviţa, Suceviţa, Arbore and Humor, lesser known churches at Pătrăuţi, Rîşca, Coşula and Dorohoi.

642 **Artistic handicrafts in Romania.**
Olga Horşia, Paul Petrescu, translated from the Romanian by Sorana Chivu. Bucharest: UCECOM, 1972. 298p. bibliog.

A richly illustrated guide to the Romanian handicraft heritage which presents examples of architecture, furniture, wooden tools and vessels, pottery, metal-work, textiles, costumes, painting, embroidery, knotted carpets, rugs, lace work, ceramics, basketry, leather work, and dolls.

643 **Curtişoara.**
Ion Miclea, English version by Sergiu Celac. Sibiu, Romania: Transylvania Monthly, 1981. 70p.

A sensitive portrayal with many photographs of the houses and costumes of one of Romania's more picturesque villages, situated in the south-west of the country.

644 **Voroneţ.**
Maria Ana Musicescu, Sorin Ulea. Bucharest: Meridiane Publishing House, 1969. 24p. 60 plates.

One of a series of pictorial presentations devoted to the external frescoes on the Moldavian monastery churches. Each volume is lavishly illustrated and preceded by an essay in English on the history of the church and on the symbolism of its decoration. Voroneţ is architecturally and iconographically one of the most striking of these churches. It was built in 1488 and decorated in 1547.

645 **L'art roumain.** (Romanian art.)
Louis Réau. Paris: Librairie Larousse, 1946. 105p. bibliog.

A brief but excellent introduction to Romanian architecture, folk art, painting and sculpture which highlights significant features and draws parallels and contrasts with artistic expression in Western Europe.

646 **Romanian folkart. Historical and descriptive notes and a catalogue for an exhibition from the Romanian people's republic.**
London: British-Romanian Friendship Association, 1954. 30p.

A short but precise description of Romanian costumes from the various regions, of house types, woodcrafts, textiles and embroidery, tapestries, carpets, musical instruments, and ceramics.

647 **L'évolution de la peinture religieuse en Bukovine et en Moldavie depuis les origines jusqu'au 19ème siècle.** (The evolution of religious painting in Bukovina and Moldavia from its origins to the 19th century.)
I. D. Ştefănescu. Paris: Geuthner, 1928. 2 vols. plates. bibliog.

The complete external decoration of the monastery churches of Humor (1535), Moldoviţa (1537), Arbore (1541), Voroneţ (1547), and Suceviţa (1595-96) with frescoes provides Romania with one of its artistic treasures. This detailed study of the iconography of these frescoes is largely unsurpassed and discusses the evident Byzantine, and more controversial local influences reflected in the frescoes.

648 **La peinture religieuse en Valachie et en Transylvanie depuis les origines jusq'au 19ème siècle.** (Religious painting in Wallachia and Transylvania from its origins to the 19th century.)
I. D. Ştefănescu. Paris: Geuthner, 1932. 439p. plates. bibliog.

A companion volume to item 647. Romanian art and architecture in Wallachia were greatly indebted to Byzantium whose influence can be seen in the two outstanding Wallachian churches of the 14th century, the St Nicholas church at Curtea de Argeş, and the church of Cozia monastery. The former contains a series of Palaeologan frescoes that is unique in the Romanian pcinipalities while the latter, built in the style of the north Serbian churches of the period, presents examples of Byzantine painting in its narthex.

649 **Iconografia artei bizantine şi a picturii feudale româneşti.** (The iconography of Byzantine art and of Romanian feudal painting.)
I. D. Ştefănescu. Bucharest: Editura Meridiane, 1973. 269p. plates. bibliog.

An abridged synthesis of the author's studies of the frescoes and icons in Romanian churches. Contains an excellent bibliography.

650 **The handicraft co-operative system in Romania.**
Eugen Tomescu.   Bucharest: The Central Union of Handicraft
Co-operatives in Romania, 1972. 111p.

A guide to the handicraft co-operative system which opens with an account of its establishment in 1949. The chapters cover the economic activity of the co-operatives, the system of payment, the training of new members, and the social security system.

651 **Wall painting in northern Moldavia.**
Virgil Vătăşianu, translated from the Romanian by Caterina
Augusta Grundbock.   Bucharest: Meridiane Publishing House,
1974. 43p. 110 plates. bibliog.

The external and internal frescoes of the churches at Neamţu, Suceava, Pătrăuţi, Voroneţ, Bălineşti, Humor, Moldoviţa, Arbore, Rişca, and Suceviţa are well represented in the colour reproductions in this volume. The excellent introduction contains a brief history of religious architecture in Moldavia from the middle of the 14th century to the middle of the 16th century, and provides an appreciation of the wall paintings in the northern Moldavian churches.

652 **Folk art in Rumania.**
B. Zderciuc, P. Petraşcu, I. Bănăţeanu.   Bucharest: Meridiane
Publishing House, 1964. 60p.

An introduction to Romanian folk art with illustrations of ceramics, earthenware, embroidery, painting on glass, and village architecture.

Individual artists

653 **Art journey.**
C. Calafeteanu.   Bucharest: Editura Sport-Turism, 1982. 14p. 80
plates.

A representative album of the work of one of Romania's most successful contemporary artists whose predilection is for landscapes. The introduction and biographical notes are in English.

654 **Constantin Brâncuşi.**
Mircea Deac.   Bucharest: Editura Meridiane, 1966. 199p. plates.
bibliog.

Brâncuşi (1876-1957) was born near Tîrgu Jiu in southern Romania and settled in Paris in 1904. His simple, near abstract sculptures have had a profound influence on the development of plastic art and reflect a love and respect for his materials – marble, wood, and metal. He lived in seclusion with his forms which sometimes remained incomplete for years. This is a biographical essay in Romanian illustrated by a great many photographs.

655 **Brancusi: the sculpture and drawings.**
Sidney Geist. New York: H. N. Abrams, 1975. 200p. illus.
bibliog.

A lavishly illustrated album of Brâncuşi's work, including several colour photographs that constitutes the most complete published record of his achievements. The quality of the photographs surpasses that of other albums and enables the viewer to appreciate the sculptor's reverence for his materials.

656 **Constantin Brancusi 1876-1957: a retrospective exhibition.**
Sidney Geist. New York: S. R. Guggenheim Museum, 1969.
157p. illus.

An illustrated catalogue of an impressive exhibition of the sculptor's work that was mounted at the Solomon R. Guggenheim museum.

657 **Brancusi: a study of the sculpture.**
Sidney Geist. New York: Grossman, 1968. 247p.

An excellent album of Brâncuşi's sculpture.

658 **Constantin Brancusi.**
David Lewis. London: Academy Editions; New York: St Martins
Press, 1974. 80p. illus. bibliog.

A fine introduction to the sculptor's work that allows us to sense his artistry and craftsmanship.

659 **N. Grigorescu.**
George Oprescu. Bucharest: Meridiane, 1961. 181p.

Nicolae Grigorescu (1838-1907) has the greatest claim to be Romania's national artist. His scenes from Romanian peasant life, his portraits of Jews, his landscapes and his depiction of episodes in the War of Independence in 1878, were brought to international attention by his one-man exhibition at the Galleries Martinet in Paris during the winter of 1886-87. Fifty-six of these canvases are illustrated in this volume. Born into a family of icon-painters, Grigorescu spent his youth painting iconostases and church interiors. A visit to Paris in 1861, and a period spent at Barbizon, led him to adopt the techniques of the impressionists, using the palette knife in combination with the brush. A major change in the style of many Romanian artists can be attributed to Grigorescu's influence following his return to Wallachia in 1873.

660 **The merry cemetery.**
Pop Simion, translated from the Romanian by Mary Lăzărescu,
Leon Leviţchi. Bucharest: Publishing House of Tourism, 1972.
40p. 116 plates.

A splendid album devoted to the cemetery at Săpînţa in Maramureş where the headpieces of the graves have been carved from wood and painted by Ion Stan Pătraş. The plates consist of 116 photographs taken by Ion Miclea-Mihale.

661 **Ion Ţuculescu.**
Ion Vlasiu. Bucharest: Meridiane Publishing House, 1966. 149p.

The eighty-six colour plates in this volume offer an introduction to the paintings of one of Romania's most original 20th century artists. Dolls, birds, gigantic flowers, and trees are the motifs expressed in novel chromatic harmonies and in a rhythmic geometry by Ţuculescu (1910-62). His influence on contemporary Romanian art has been most profound.

Architecture

662 **Traditional house decoration in Romania: survey and bibliography.**
Jan Harold Brunvand. *East European Quarterly*, vol. 14, no. 3 (autumn 1980), p. 255-301.

Whereas most traditional arts in Romania still reflect old skills and designs, house decoration is strongly influenced by contemporary life and individual tastes. This article compares the traditional and modern aspects of Romanian peasant houses, including details of their construction and decoration. It is supplemented by a bibliography of over 175 titles on folk architecture in Romania, arranged alphabetically by author.

663 **Romanian house decoration in stucco.**
Jan Harold Brunvand. *Mioriţa: a Journal of Romanian Studies*, vol. 3, no. 1 (1976), p. 2-11.

A brief account of construction techniques and patterns of design used in houses in stucco.

664 **Wooden churches in Eastern Europe.**
David Buxton. In: *Architectural conservation in Europe*. Edited by Sherban Cantacuzino. New York: Watson-Guptill, 1975. p. 107-20.

A succinct survey of a number of the wooden churches in Romania with illustrations.

665 **Romanian folk architecture: the wood tradition.**
Joby Patterson. In: *Festschrift (in honor of Marian Dean Ross): a collection of essays on architectural history*. Salem, Oregon: North Pacific Coast Chapter Society of Architectural Historians, 1978. p. 21-28.

An outline of the traditional use of wood in the construction of peasant houses.

Music and Dance

Music

666 Music in Rumania.
Leonard Cassini.   London: Fore Publications, 1954. 72p.
A finely written but highly subjective account of the opportunities afforded Romanian citizens to study, practise, and enjoy classical music in Romania of the early 1950s. The author's observations are based on three visits made to the country in the period 1951-53. Includes a unique index in English of contemporary Romanian composers with biographical details.

667 Historical atlas of music.
Paul Collaer, Albert Vander Linden.   London: Harrap, 1968.
176p.
A concise study of the world's music that includes a short account of Romanian music.

668 George Enescu.
Viorel Cosma, John Waterhouse. In: *The new grove dictionary of music and musicians, vol. 6.* Edited by Stanley Sadie.   London: Macmillan, 1980. p. 163-66.
George Enescu (1881-1955), known outside Romania under the form of his name that he adopted while resident in France, Georges Enesco, is considered to be Romania's most accomplished musician and composer. This biographical entry provides details of his career as a violinist and teacher in Paris, and of the character of his compositions. It is supplemented by a list of his works and a bibliography of studies about him.

669 **Georges Enesco dans la conscience du présent.** (George Enescu in the consciousness of the present.)
Cornel Țăranu. Bucharest: Editura științifică și enciclopedică, 1981. 127p.

An excellent introduction to the life and work of Enescu, which is particularly informative on the influences that shaped his compositions. This book was published to mark the centenary of his birth at Liveni-Vîrnav in the county of Dorohoi.

Dance

670 **The fairies and the călușari.**
Mircea Eliade. *International Journal of Rumanian Studies*, vol. 2, nos. 3-4 (1980), p. 5-12.

An investigation into the origin and function of the *călușari*, performers of a ritual dance called the *căluș* which derives from the Romanian word for 'horse', *cal* (from Latin caballus). A wooden horsehead, partially or wholly covered, is carried by one of the dancers. The principal attribute of the *călușari* is their ability to resemble the leaping and jumping of a horse. 'Whatever its origin', writes Eliade, 'the *căluș*, in the forms known in the last centuries, is found only in Rumania and can be considered a creation of Rumanian folk culture'.

671 **Căluș. Symbolic transformation in Romanian ritual.**
Gail Kligman. Chicago; London: University of Chicago Press, 1981. XVIII+ 210p.

The most detailed study in English of the significance of the ritual dance *căluș*. Based on information gathered from thirty villages in Wallachia where the dance is still performed, the writer's fieldwork enables her to compare the characteristics of the ritual village by village.

672 **On rhythm in Rumanian folk dance.**
V. Proca-Ciortea. *Yearbook of the International Folk Music Council*, Urbana, Illinois, 1969. p. 176-99.

673 **Some werewolf legends and the *Călușari* ritual in Romania.**
Harry A. Senn. *East European Quarterly*, vol. 11, no. 1 (spring 1977), p. 1-14.

A brief analysis of the werewolf and vampire myths that circulate in the region of Bihor in Transylvania, and their relationship to the ritual of the *căluș* that begins on Pentecost and lasts from three to seven days. The author reproduces fourteen accounts of werewolf legends, which were related to him by Romanian villagers.

Theatre and Film

Theatre

674 **100 de ani de teatru evreiesc în România.** (One hundred years of
Jewish theatre in Romania.)
Israil Bercovici.   Bucharest: Kriterion, 1976. 312p.

A unique account of the evolution of Jewish theatre from its beginnings in the
Romanian principalities during the second half of the 19th century down to its
activity in the Socialist Republic of the 1970s.

675 **Romanian theatre and drama: turning point '74.**
E. J. Czerwinski.   *Books Abroad: An International Literary
Quarterly*, vol. 48, no. 1 (winter 1974), p. 52-58.

A survey of activity in the contemporary Romanian theatre that encapsulates the
author's impressions gained during a visit to the country in 1973. The works of the
most acclaimed playwrights are briefly presented, and the content of the leading
Romanian journal of the theatre, *Teatrul*, is discussed. Why the year 1974 is
considered a 'turning point' is not explained.

676 **A concise history of theatre in Romania.**
Medeea Ionescu.   Bucharest: Editura ştiinţifică şi enciclopedică,
1981. 69p.

A historical sketch of the theatrical art amongst the Romanians. Folk dance and
theatre are described in the opening pages from which the author moves directly
to the professional theatre in the Romanian principalities during the 19th century.
No mention is made of the itinerant French and Italian companies from whose
repertoire of farces the Romanian playwrights took their inspiration. The first
Romanian company was formed in 1834 and by the middle of the century the
nucleus of a repertoire in the native language had been established. The

163

developments in drama and the careers of notable actors and actresses down to the 1970s are ably chronicled.

677 **Teatrul românesc: privire istorică.** (The Romanian theatre: an historical view.)
I. Massoff. Bucharest: Editura Pentru Literatură; Editura Minerva, 1961-78. 7 vols.

The standard work on the history of the Romanian theatre that, with volume 7, reaches the year 1940. The performance of plays in the Romanian principalities was an initiative taken in 1818 by Greeks established in Bucharest. Their example prompted young Romanians to translate plays from French, German and Classical Greek which were staged by the pupils of St Sava, the first institute of higher education in Romanian, in the 1820s. The creation of a theatrical repertoire in Romanian was the work of Vasile Alecsandri (1821-90), but it was with the more enduring farces and dramas of I. L. Caragiale (1852-1912) that the Romanian theatre came of age.

Film

678 **Filmul documentar românesc.** (The Romanian documentary.)
Călin Căliman. Bucharest: Meridiane, 1967. 119p.

The earliest Romanian films date from 1897 and this survey examines the development of the Romanian documentary from that date to 1967. It contains a list of Romanian documentaries which won awards at international festivals.

679 **Momente din trecutul filmului românesc.** (Landmarks in the history of the Romanian film.)
Ion Cantacuzino. Bucharest: Editura Meridiane, 1966. 91p. bibliog.

A laudable survey of the development of Romanian film-making from its inception in 1891 to the arrival of sound and the production of full-length features. Since the publication of this book Romanian film production has developed considerably in the fields of feature films and documentaries.

680 **Film Roumain. Romanian Film.**
Bucharest: Cinema magazine, 1966-. irregular.

An illustrated magazine in English and French with features on Romanian films of which there are often extensive reviews.

681   **Eastern Europe: an illustrated guide.**
      Nina Hibbin.   New York: A. S. Barnes; London: Zwemmer,
      1969. 239p. (Screen Series).

'This guide has been designed to help filmgoers and televiewers to get to know more about the films they have enjoyed and the film-makers they admire, and at the same time to provide students of cinema with a compact source of information, most of which has not been previously collated in English, about filming in Eastern Europe'. This is a brief 'Who's Who' of the cinema in Eastern Europe with an index of the films mentioned. Romania is covered on p. 116-31.

Sports

682 Romanian game.
A. M. Comşia.   Bucharest: Meridiane Publishing House, 1968.
36p.

Red deer, roe deer, chamois, hogs, bears, wolves, lynxs, bustards, and, surprisingly, pelicans constitute the subject matter of this rather pretentiously titled volume. Much of it is devoted to a presentation with photographs of trophies such as antlers, horns, wild boar tusks, and bear rugs.

683 L'éducation physique et le sport dans la République Socialiste de Roumanie. (Physical education and sport in the Socialist Republic of Romania.)
Bucharest: Conseil National pour l'Education Physique et le Sport. Comité Olympique Roumain, 1973. 80p.

A brief compendium of information about the organization and practice of sport in Romania. Contains details of the principal sporting journals, clubs, stadia, outstanding Olympic performances, and the various sporting federations such as basketball, boxing, ice-hockey, football and rugby.

684 The magic square of Romania.
Paul Ochialbi, Petre Heutz.   Bucharest: Stadion, 1975. 74p. photos.

Romanian boxing enjoys great prestige internationally and this excellent history presents the careers of outstanding Romanian exponents of 'the noble art', significant events in the history of Romanian boxing, and tables of Romania's international successes. It is complemented by fine photographs of Romanian boxers in action.

685 **Handball in Rumänien. Wann? Wer? Romanian handball. When? Who?**

Bucharest: Romanian Olympic Committee, 1972. 34p.

Parallel texts in German and English present the history of this popular sport in Romania and the domestic and international achievements of Romanian teams.

686 **Sports in Romania.**

Bucharest: The Romanian Olympic Committee, 1958-. quarterly.

An illustrated magazine in English devoted to Romanian participation in major international sporting events and, in particular, in the Olympics.

687 **Der Rumänische magische Ring – the magic Romanian ring.**

Bucharest: Romanian Olympic Committee, 1972. 36p.

Parallel German and English texts give a brief introduction to the history of Romanian boxing and present the careers of several Romanian boxers.

688 **Die Rumänischen Meister der Wasserbahnen – Romanian champions of waterways.**

Bucharest: Romanian Olympic Committee, 1972. 48p.

An interesting account in parallel German and English texts of Romanian successes in rowing and canoeing at international level. Well illustrated with photographs and tables of championship titles and medals.

Printing and
Publishing

689 Romanian Books.
Bucharest: 1964-. quarterly.

A bulletin in English containing articles on Romanian books, book publishing, and related topics with a selective bibliography of books published in Romania during the preceding three months.

690 Rumanian presses and printing in the seventeenth century.
Dennis Deletant. *Slavonic and East European Review*, vol. 60, no. 4 (Oct. 1982), p. 481-99; vol. 61, no. 4 (Oct. 1983), p. 481-511.

An examination of the activity of the presses in Wallachia, Moldavia, and Transylvania that served the spiritual and cultural needs of educated Romanians and the Orthodox clergy during the seventeenth century. In the case of Wallachia the survey is extended to 1715. Part 2 presents a table of books printed in Romanian, Church Slavonic, and Greek throughout the seventeenth century.

691 A survey of Rumanian presses and printing in the sixteenth century.
Dennis Deletant. *Slavonic and East European Review*, vol. 53, no. 131 (April 1975), p. 161-74.

A descriptive account of the history of the printed book in Transylvania, Moldavia and Wallachia covering the presses that produced books in Romanian and Church Slavonic in the period.

692 La typographie cyrillique de Sibiu au milieu du XVIe siècle. (The cyrillic printing-press of Sibiu in the middle of the 16th century.)
Ludovic Demény. *Romanian Studies*, vol. 2 (1971-72), p. 30-47.

The Lutheran reform played a crucial part in the printing of the first books in Romanian and thus fostered a Romanian Catechism, printed in 1544 at Sibiu in

Transylvania. This is an excellent survey of the activity of the printer Filip Moldoveanu (Philippus Pictor) in Sibiu (Hermannstadt) and of the influence of the reform in his books.

Mass Media

General

693 How the communist press works.
Anthony Busek. New York: Praeger, 1964. 287p. bibliog.
(Praeger Publications in Russian History and World Communism,
no. 147).

As a description of the operation of the press in communist countries this book
includes much material, albeit scattered, on the press in Romania.

**694 Newspapers of east central and south eastern Europe in the Library
of Congress.**
Edited by Robert G. Carlton. Washington, DC: Slavic and
Central European Division, Reference Department, Library of
Congress, 1965. 204p.

This publication embraces newspapers issued during the period from 1918 to 1964
within the present boundaries of Albania, Bulgaria, Czechoslovakia, Hungary,
Poland, Romania, and Yugoslavia as far as they are represented in the Library of
Congress. Ninety-three Romanian newspapers are listed.

695 The press of Rumania.
Kenneth E. Olson. In: *The history makers. The press of Europe
from its beginnings through 1965.* Baton Rouge, Louisiana:
Louisiana State University Press, 1966. p. 400-13.

A summary of the history of the press in Romania up to the mid-1960s.

170

Newspapers

696 **Acţiunea românească.** (Romanian Action.)
New York: 1970-. quarterly.
Romanian language newspaper, organ of the Romanian national council, an exile body, founded in New York in 1970.

697 **Curierul.** (The Courrier.)
Santa Clara, California: 1981-. monthly.
Romanian language newspaper, organ of the Romanian-American national congress. The journal is anti-communist in tenor.

698 **Cuvântul Românesc. The Romanian Voice.**
Hamilton, Ontario: 1976-. monthly.
The Romanian newspaper with the widest circulation outside Romania. It carries political, economic, and cultural commentaries that reflect anti-communist views. A useful source of information on books published in Romanian outside the Socialist Republic.

699 **Drapelul Roşu.** (The Red Flag.)
Timişoara, Romania: 1944-. daily.
Organ of the regional committee of the Romanian Communist Party and of the regional people's council.

700 **Făclia.** (The Torch.)
Cluj-Napoca, Romania: 1945-. daily.
Mouthpiece of the regional committee of the Romanian Communist Party and of the regional people's council.

701 **Flacara Iaşului.** (The Iaşi Flame.)
Iaşi, Romania: 1946-. daily.
The official paper of the regional committee of the Romanian Communist Party and of the regional people's council.

702 **Free Romanian Press.**
London: 1956-. fortnightly.
A news-sheet founded by Ion Raţiu which provides a summary in English of current significant political developments in Romania.

703 **Informaţia Bucureştiului.** (Bucharest Information.)
Bucharest: 1953-. daily.
The official afternoon daily of the Bucharest people's council.

Mass Media. Magazines

704 **Lupta. The Fight.**
Providence, Rhode Island: 1983-. fortnightly.
A bilingual Romanian-English journal with informed comment on events in Romania and with details of the cultural activity of Romanians abroad.

705 **Micromagazin.**
New York: 1974-. trimonthly.
Romanian language newspaper with an emphasis on report and comment about political and economic developments in Romania. Markedly anti-régime in tenor, it includes contributions by the staff of the Romanian section of Radio Free Europe.

706 **Munca.** (Labour.)
Bucharest: 1953-. daily.
Official paper of the Central Council of Trade Unions of the Socialist Republic of Romania.

707 **România liberă.** (Free Romania.)
Bucharest: 1943-. daily.
National paper of the people's councils of the Socialist Republic of Romania.

708 **Scînteia.** (The Spark.)
Bucharest: 1931-. daily.
National party newspaper of the Central Committee of the Romanian Communist Party.

709 **Siebenbürgische Zeitung.** (Transylvanian Newspaper.)
Munich: Landmannschaft der Siebenbürger Sachsen, 1951-. fortnightly.
A German-language newspaper for members of the Transylvanian Saxon and Swabian communities in Romania that have emigrated to the West, principally to West Germany. It provides excellent coverage of political and cultural developments in Romania that affect the German community living there.

Magazines

710 **Lumea.** (The World.)
Bucharest: 1976-. weekly.
An English-language version of an informative Romanian weekly of current international affairs which also includes topical items of light-hearted news from around the globe.

711 **News of the Day.**
Bucharest: Romanian News Agency Agerpres, 1973-. daily.
Major news items focusing on Romania's relations with other countries are presented in this journal.

712 **News from Romania.**
Bucharest: Romanian News Agency Agerpres, 1973-. fortnightly.
A résumé of political, economic, and cultural news.

713 **Radio Free Europe Research.**
Research and analysis department of Radio Free Europe. New York; Munich: Radio Free Europe/Radio Liberty, n.d. weekly.
Expert analysis of current political, economic, and cultural developments in Romania and in the other countries of the Eastern bloc. This weekly digest of significant news from these countries is supplemented regularly by situation reports on Romania which offer a critical appreciation of recent economic and political trends.

714 **Romania: Articles, Features, Information.**
Bucharest: Romanian News Agency Agerpres, 1973-. monthly.
Reports and information in English relating to Romania's domestic and foreign policy.

715 **Romanian Bulletin.**
Romanian library, New York: 1964-. monthly.
A Romanian government sponsored publication with material on life in Romania for US residents with Romanian interests.

716 **Romania: Documents-events.**
Bucharest: Romanian News Agency Agerpres, 1950-. weekly.
Contains speeches, communiqués, and documents in English translation released by the Romanian Communist Party. Between 1950 and 1970 it was published fortnightly as *Documents, articles and information on Romania*, and from 1971 to 1974 as *Romania: articles, features, information*.

717 **Romanian Press Review.**
Bucharest: British and US missions, 1946-. irregular, now defunct.
Published jointly by the US and British diplomatic missions in Romania and issued originally on a daily basis.

718 **Romania Today.**
Bucharest: 1955-. monthly.
A pictorial magazine in English which presents aspects of life in Romania.

173

719 **Summary of world broadcasts. Part 2. Eastern Europe.**
Reading, England: British Broadcasting Corporation Monitoring
Service, 1948-. daily.

International and domestic news as presented by the broadcasting services of the
East European countries. Romania is represented by translations of transcribed
broadcasts from Bucharest. Unfortunately, there is no index of items.

720 **Talking to Eastern Europe. A collection of the best reading from the
broadcasts and background papers of Radio Free Europe.**
Edited and introduced by G. R. Urban.   London: Eyre &
Spottiswoode, 1964. 303p.

A book of essays dealing with the impact of communism on history, literature,
and politics. Originally written as broadcasts for Radio Free Europe, they are of
equal value to the western reader. A Romanian experience of censorship is
provided (p. 121-27) by Petru Dumitriu, former director of the State Publishing
House in Bucharest.

Professional
Periodicals

721 **Balkan Studies.**
Thessaloniki, Greece: Institute for Balkan Studies, 1960-. annual.
This scholarly journal includes articles and book reviews on Romanian history and culture by Greek scholars in English, French, and German.

722 **Dacoromania: Jahrbuch für Östliche Latinität.** (Yearbook for
Eastern Latinity.)
Edited by Paul Miron. Freiburg, GDR; Munich: Karl Alber
Verlag, 1973-. irregular.
As the subtitle suggests, this annual stresses the Latin origins and features of·
Romanian culture with scholarly contributions from Romania and elsewhere.

723 **Destin.** (Destiny.)
Madrid: 1950-71 annual, 1971-. irregular.
A Romanian literary review edited by George Uscătescu with articles and original contributions in prose and verse exclusively by Romanian writers in exile. The critical essays, some of which are in French, are refreshingly original and objective in their appraisal of the major talents of modern Romanian culture.

724 **Dialogue: Revue d'études Roumaines.** (Dialogue: Review of
Romanian Studies.)
Montpellier, France: Université Paul Valéry, 1978-. annual.
The emphasis in this excellent review has been on thematic issues dedicated to Romanian writers and trends. Among those thus covered have been Rebreanu, Blaga, and the literature of the avant-garde.

175

Professional Periodicals

725 **East Europe: a Monthly Review of East European Affairs.**
New York: 1952-. monthly.
A lively journal of information on economic, social, and intellectual trends in Eastern Europe including Romania.

726 **East Europe Quarterly.**
Boulder, Colorado: University of Colorado, 1967-. quarterly.
There are frequent contributions on Romania in this fine academic journal devoted mainly to the social sciences and edited by Stephen Fischer-Galaţi.

727 **Ethos.**
Edited by Ioan Cuşa, Virgil Ierunca. Paris: 1973-. irregular.
Only two volumes of this journal have appeared to date. It presents articles by distinguished Romanian exiles on Romanian literature and history. Vol. 1 contains a unique selected bibliography of publications by Romanians in exile since 1965.

728 **International Journal of Romanian Studies.**
Tübingen, GFR: Gunter Narr Verlag, 1976-. irregular.
Published under the auspices of the International Association for Romanian Studies, this journal is the brain child of Sorin Alexandrescu, professor at the Institute of Romance Studies of the University of Amsterdam, who is also the editor. Its contributions have been in the main European languages and have been devoted to aspects of Romanian literature, language, and folklore.

729 **Limite.** (Limits.)
Paris: 1970-. irregular.
Virgil Ierunca and N. Petra, the editors of this Romanian language literary review, have maintained a consistently high standard in their publication of comment on the Romanian literary scene. Poetry and prose by Romanian writers living outside the republic are presented.

730 **Mioriţa: A Journal of Romanian Studies.**
Hamilton, New Zealand; Rochester, New York: New Zealand Romanian Cultural Association and the Department for Foreign Languages, Literatures, and Linguistics, University of Rochester, 1974-. biannual/annual.
A scholarly journal with articles in English on Romanian language, literature, folklore, and history, and book reviews. Produced initially by Norman Simms at the University of Waikato in Hamilton, New Zealand, and now jointly by the latter in association with Charles Carlton of the University of Rochester.

731 **Revista Scriitorilor Români.** (The Romanian Writers' Journal.)
Munich: Societatea Academică Română, 1957-. annual.
A journal devoted to the publication of original works of prose and poetry by Romanian writers in exile which is now edited by Constantin Sporea. Societatea

Academică Română (The Romanian Academic Society) is based in Munich and has also sponsored the publication of a number of scholarly works on Romania in Romanian, French, English, and Italian. Details of these can be obtained from the society at Fritz-Meyer-Weg 47/1, Munich 81, West Germany.

732 **Revue Roumaine des Sciences Sociales. Série de Sciences Économiques.** (Romanian Review of Social Sciences. Economic Science Series.)
Bucharest: Éditions de l'Academie de la République Socialiste Roumaine, 1956-. bi-annual.
Articles in English, French, and occasionally Russian, on aspects of the Romanian economy.

733 **Revue des Études Roumaines.** (Revue of Romanian Studies.)
Paris: Fundaţia Regală Universitară Carol I, 1953-. irregular.
Edited by Emil Turdeanu, this journal of excellence reached its sixteenth volume in 1982. The learned contributions, from scholars established outside Romania, cover aspects of Romanian language, literature, history, and folklore.

734 **Romanian Review.**
Bucharest: 1946-. monthly.
A fine English-language review of developments in Romanian literature, theatre, and art that includes translations of extracts from recently published Romanian works.

735 **Romanian Scientific Abstracts: Social Sciences.**
Bucharest: Scientific Documentation Service, 1964-. every two months.
English-language abstracts of articles published in Romanian journals in the social sciences including history, economics, philosophy, sociology, psychology, and ethnography.

736 **Romanian Sources.**
Pittsburgh, Pennsylvania: University of Pittsburgh Libraries and the American Romanian Institute for Research Inc., 1975-. bi-annual.
A journal of Romanian culture edited by John Halmaghi with contributions in English on history, language, literature, and folklore.

737 **Rumanian Studies: an International Annual of the Humanities and Social Sciences.**
Leiden, Netherlands: Brill, 1970-. irregular.
Edited by Keith Hitchins, this academic yearbook has now reached its fourth volume (1976-79) and has established a reputation as one of the foremost English-

language publications in the realm of Romanian studies. The principal emphasis of its contributions is upon history although literature is occasionally represented.

738 **Secolul 20.** (The 20th Century.)
Bucharest: Uniunea Scriitorilor din Republica Socialistă România, 1964-. irregular.

Regrettably the frequency of publication of this one-time monthly review has been drastically reduced in recent years. This is without doubt the most respected Romanian literary journal both inside and outside Romania, and is notable for the quality of its articles and translations from foreign literature.

739 **Slavic and East European Journal.**
American Association of Teachers of Slavic and East European Languages.   Dekalb, Illinois: Northern Illinois University, 1943-. quarterly.

A scholarly journal with emphasis on studies of the languages and literatures of Eastern Europe.

740 **Slavic Review.**
American Association for the Advancement of Slavic Studies.
Columbus, Ohio: Ohio State University, 1941-. quarterly.

The main focus in this academic journal is upon Russian, Soviet, and East European history, politics, and literature.

741 **Slavonic and East European Review.**
London: Published by The Modern Humanities Research Association for The School of Slavonic and East European Studies, 1922-. quarterly.

The oldest academic English-language journal devoted to the USSR and Eastern Europe which includes a significant number of scholarly articles on Romanian language, literature, history, and folklore by specialists at the School of Slavonic and East European Studies of the University of London and by distinguished foreign scholars.

742 **Southeastern Europe: L'Europe du Sud-est.**
Arizona: Arizona State University, 1974-. bi-annual.

A journal devoted to scholarship in the realm of language, literature, and history. Under its editor Charles Schlacks Jr. particular attention has been paid to Romania, with a special issue on Romanian linguistics and literature (vol. 7, part 1).

178

743 **Yearbook of Romanian Studies.**
Salinas, California: Romanian Studies Association of America,
1976-. annual.

An annual devoted largely to articles on Romanian language and literature. A useful means of keeping abreast of cultural developments amongst the Romanian community in North America.

Encyclopaedias and Directories

744 **Dicţionar enciclopedic romîn.** (Romanian encyclopaedic
dictionary.)
Bucharest: Editura Politică, 1962-66. 4 vols. maps. illus.

Edited by a committee of specialists headed by Athanasie Joja, this was the first
encyclopaedia to be published in Romania after the Second World War. Although
useful for information about contemporary Romania, it suffers from a lack of
bibliographical information. As an encyclopaedia of Romania it pales by
comparison with its predecessor, *Enciclopedia României*. (The encyclopaedia of
Romania.) q.v.

745 **Directory of officials of the socialist republic of Romania.**
National Foreign Assessment Centre. Washington, DC: Central
Intelligence Agency, 1980. 185p.

A reference guide to officials of the Romanian government, Communist Party,
prominent public organizations, and cultural, professional and religious bodies.
An alphabetical table of contents and an alphabetical name index to locate the
2,500 persons listed makes this guide rapid and simple to use. It was prepared
from information received up to 1 August 1980.

746 **Directory of selected research institutions in Eastern Europe.**
Arthur D. Little. New York: Columbia University Press, 1967.
445p.

Lists all major research institutes in Romania established before 1966.

747 **Enciclopedia României.** (The encyclopaedia of Romania.)
Bucharest: Imprimeria Naţională, 1936-43. 4 vols. illus. maps.

The standard encyclopaedia of Romania up to the Second World War. It is
arranged by subject as follows: vol. 1: the State; vol. 2: the Land; vols 3 and 4:

180

the Economy. The projected publication of vols 5 and 6, which were to have covered Romanian culture, was abandoned. Each volume is indexed by author and subject.

748 **Organizaţii şi instituţii din Republica Socialistă România.**
(Organizations and institutions in the Socialist Republic of Romania.)
Bucharest: Agerpres, 1980-. annual.

A fairly comprehensive list of state organizations in Romania which provides their addresses.

749 **Romanian.**
Centre for Information on Language Teaching and Research.
London: CILT, 1982. 42p.

A valuable guide, prepared largely by Professor Glanville Price of the University of Aberystwyth, to the provision and use of resources for learning Romanian in the United Kingdom. Contains sections on organizations and centres, teaching, learning, special collections, radio broadcasts, specialist booksellers, film distributors, opportunities for learning Romanian, and examinations.

750 **Who's who in the socialist countries.**
Edited by Borys Letwytzkyj, Juliusz Stroynowski. New York; Munich: K. G. Saur Publishing Inc., 1978. 736p.

A biographical encyclopaedia of 10,000 personalities in sixteen communist countries. Entries are arranged alphabetically but not, unfortunately, country by country, an irritant that is compounded by the absence of an index.

Libraries and Collections

751　**La bibliothèque de l'Académie de la République Socialiste de Roumanie.** (The library of the Academy of the Socialist Republic of Romania.)
Bucharest: Éditions de l'Académie de la République Socialiste de Roumanie, 1968. 144p.

An illustrated presentation of one of Romania's principal libraries with descriptions of its manuscript and rare book holdings, its prints, it maps, its music, and numismatic collections.

752　**Catalogul incunabulelor.** (Catalogue of incunabula.)
Livia Bacâru.　Bucharest: Biblioteca Academiei Republicii Socialiste România, 1970. 72p. 15 plates.

A catalogue of seventy-four incunabula in the library of the Romanian Academy in Bucharest. Each item is accompanied by a brief description in Romanian. The catalogue presents a chronological index by place of printing and printer, and an alphabetical index of printers.

753　**Catalogul incunabulelor.** (Catalogue of incunabula.)
Biblioteca Centrală Universitară, Cluj-Napoca.　Cluj-Napoca, Romania: Editura Dacia, 1979. 122p. bibliog.

This catalogue of incunabula in the Central University Library in Cluj was compiled by Elena Mosora and Doina Hanga, and lists eighty-four items with brief descriptions in Romanian. It includes a chronological index of the books, an index by place of printing and printer, and an alphabetical index of printers.

754 **Newspapers of East Central and Southeastern Europe in the Library of Congress.**
Edited by Robert G. Carlton. Washington, DC: Library of Congress. Slavic and Central European Division, 1965. 204p.

Lists holdings in the Library of Congress of ninety-four post First World War newspapers published in Romania, including titles in current receipt.

755 **A survey of the Gaster books in the School of Slavonic and East European Studies Library.**
Dennis Deletant. *Solanus*, no. 10 (June 1975), p. 14-23.

The library of SSEES in the University of London purchased some 3,500 Romanian titles from the Gaster collection of printed books and manuscripts in 1952 and this article describes the most valuable items. They include a collection of homilies printed at Iaşi in 1643, a code of Byzantine law from 1652, and a copy of the first complete Bible in Romanian, printed at Bucharest in 1688.

756 **East Central and Southeast Europe: a handbook of library and archival resources in North America.**
Edited by Paul L. Horecky, David H. Kraus. Santa Barbara, California; Oxford, England: Clio Press, 1976. 467p.

Significant Romanian collections are to be found in the University of California at Berkeley, in UCLA, in the University of Chicago, in Columbia University, in Harvard, in the Hoover Institution on War, Revolution and Peace at Stanford, in the University of Illinois, in Indiana University, and in the Library of Congress.

757 **Catalogul colecţiei de incunabule.** (Catalogue of the collection of incunabula.)
Veturia Jugăreanu. Sibiu, Romania: Biblioteca Muzeului Brukenthal, 1969. 217p.

A finely produced catalogue of incunabula in the library of the Brukenthal Museum in Sibiu (Hermannstadt). It lists 382 items with descriptions in Romanian of each book, and gives indices by year of the items listed, of the place of printing, of the printer, and of the provenance of each book in the collection.

758 **Historial research materials in Rumania.**
Frederick Kellogg. *Journal of Central European Affairs*, vol. 23, no. 4 (Jan. 1964), p. 485-94.

An outline guide to the nature and wealth of historical materials in Romania that are available for consultation. It contains a brief description of the holdings of the Academy library, of the State archives in Bucharest, as well as of regional archives in Cluj, Iaşi, Braşov, Sibiu, and Timişoara.

759 **Eastern Europe and Russia/Soviet Union: a handbook of West European archival and library resources.**
Richard C. Lewanski. New York, London: K. G. Saur, 1980. 317p.

A companion volume to item 756 that locates and describes printed and manuscript records on Eastern Europe, including Romania, preserved in libraries, archives, and in other centres of research in European countries outside the East European bloc (with the exception of the German Democratic Republic).

760 **Unfamiliar libraries XIV. The Batthyaneum, Alba Iulia.**
Iacob Mârza. *The Book Collector*, vol. 24, no. 4 (winter 1975), p. 558-64. 5 plates.

A fascinating survey of the manuscript and book collections in the library of Ignaz Batthyány (1741-98), Roman Catholic Bishop of Transylvania. The library is accomodated in a building dating from 1719 which originally housed the library of the Trinitarian monastery in Alba Iulia.

761 **Ghidul bibliotecilor din România.** (A guide to libraries in Romania.)
Valeriu Moldoveanu, Gheorghe Popescu, Mircea Tomescu. Bucharest: Editura Enciclopedică Română, 1970. 477p.

An exhaustive catalogue of general and specialist libraries in Romania arranged by town in alphabetical order. There is a brief description of each of the 1,078 libraries listed, together with its address, and an alphabetical index by name of the libraries.

762 **Incunabula in Rumania.**
Dan Simonescu. *The Book Collector*, vol. 25, no. 3 (autumn 1976), p. 332-44.

No books are known to have been printed in what is now Romania until 1508, the date of a Missal printed near Tîrgovişte in Wallachia. This informative article gives a selective list of incunabula housed in Romanian libraries, the richest collections being in Transylvanian libraries such as the Brukenthal Museum in Sibiu (Hermannstadt), the Teleki-Bolyai library at Tîrgu-Mureş (Marosvásárhely), and the Batthyaneum in Alba Iulia (Gyulaféhervár).

763 **Directory of libraries and special collections on Eastern Europe and the USSR.**
Edited by Gregory Walker in collaboration with T. H. Bowyer, P. A. Crowther, J. E. Wall. London: Crosby, Lockwood & Son; Hamden, Connecticut: Archon Books, 1971. 159p.

An aid to exploiting the considerable resources in Britain for the study of Eastern Europe and the USSR, with a brief description of the holdings of each library listed.

764 **Resources for Soviet, East European and Slavonic studies in British libraries.**
Edited by Gregory Walker, with the assistance of Jenny Brine.
Birmingham, England: University of Birmingham, Centre for
Russian and East European Studies, 1981. 240p.

An admirably clear record of library collections in the UK that are likely to be of
use for advanced study or research in the field of Slavonic and East European
(including Romanian) affairs. The index is by discipline and country and therefore
facilitates location of relevant collections.

Bibliographies

General

765 **The American bibliography of Slavic and East European studies.**
American Association for the Advancement of Slavic Studies.
Columbus, Ohio: The Centre for Slavic and East European
Studies, The Ohio State University, 1974-. annual.

This bibliography now has an established home after being produced prior to 1974
at different US universities. It gives an annual list of articles and books on
Slavonic and East European studies published in the US and Canada, and of
works published in English elsewhere. It is arranged under thematic headings,
including history, international relations, economics, linguistics, and literature.

766 **Bibliografia analitică a periodicelor românești, 1790-1850.**
(Analytical bibliography of Romanian periodicals, 1790-1850.)
Biblioteca Academiei Republicii Socialiste România, Institutul de
istorie 'N. Iorga' al Academiei Republicii Socialiste România.
Bucharest: Editura Academiei Republicii Socialiste România,
1966-. in progress.

Volume I, published in three parts (1966-67) covers all articles, reports, and items
of information that appeared on any subject in newspapers and periodicals
published in Moldavia, Wallachia, and Transylvania in Romanian during the
period 1790-1850. Arranged according to the universal decimal system of
classification (UDC), each volume contains an index of authors, translators,
pseudonyms, personalities, institutions, and place-names. Volume 2, also
published in three parts (1970-72), covers the period 1851-58.

767   **Bibliografia periodicelor din Republica Socialistă România.**
(Bibliography of periodicals in the Socialist Republic of
Romania.)
Bucharest: Biblioteca Centrală de Stat, 1953-. fortnightly/monthly.
A guide to the contents of Romanian periodicals. Lacks a cumulative index. Until
1957 it appeared as *Buletinul bibliografic. Seria B. Articole şi recenzii din presă*
(Bibliographical bulletin. Series B. Articles and reviews in the press.)

768   **Bibliografia Republicii Socialiste România; cărţi, albume, hărţi,
note muzicale.** (The bibliography of the Socialist Republic of
Romania; books, albums, maps, music scores.)
Bucharest: Biblioteca Centrală de Stat, 1951-. fortnightly.
The Romanian national bibliography. Although each issue contains an index of
names, there is no cumulative index. Known previously as *Buletinul bibliografic al
cărţii* (Bibliographical bulletin of books) (1951-54), *Buletinul bibliografic. Seria A*
(Bibliographical bulletin. Series A) (1954-57), and *Bibliografia Republicii
Populare Romîne; cărţi, albume, hărţi, note muzicale* (Bibliography of the
Romanian People's Republic; books, albums, maps, music scores) (1958-65).

769   **Bibliographic guide to Soviet and East European studies, 1979.**
The New York Public Library, The Library of Congress. Boston,
Massachusetts: G. K. Hall, 1980. 2 vols.
An annual subject bibliography of publications catalogued by the research
libraries of the New York Public Library and the Library of Congress. This guide
provides comprehensive coverage of published information on and from Eastern
Europe, including Romania, and the Soviet Union. The criteria for the selection
of titles are: Firstly, all titles published in Romania; Secondly, all titles written in
Romanian; And thirdly, all titles dealing with Romania, regardless of language or
country of imprint.

770   **Romanian books. A quarterly bulletin.**
Bucharest: Central Office of the Romanian Publishing Houses and
Bookselling, 1955-. quarterly.
A bulletin listing new books published in Romania in all languages. English
translations of non-English titles are given.

771   **Romanian scientific abstracts Social sciences.**
Bucharest, 1964-. monthly.
Abstracts of Romanian articles in journals embracing not only the social sciences
but also law and the humanities.

772 **Rumania. A bibliographic guide.**
Stephen A. Fischer-Galati. Washington, DC: Slavic and Central European Division, Reference Department, Library of Congress, 1963. 75p.

This guide is in two parts, the first covering in eleven sections such areas as the land, social conditions, history, politics, and religion, and the second offering an index, alphabetically arranged and consecutively numbered, of the items listed. The majority of these, however, are Romanian titles.

773 **ABSEES: Soviet and East European abstract series.**
Glasgow: Glasgow University, Institute of Soviet and East European Studies for the National Association of Soviet and East European Studies, 1970-76; Oxford, England: Oxford Microform Publications for NASEES, 1977-. triannually.

Romania receives its own section in each issue of this abstracting service which provides summaries in English of recent books and periodical articles in the social sciences published in Romania. Annual indices and an annual supplement listing relevant material on Romania published in Britain increase the reference value of this publication.

774 **Russia, the USSR, and Eastern Europe. A bibliographic guide to English language publications, 1964-1974.**
Compiled by Stephen M. Horak. Littleton, Colorado: Libraries Unlimited, 1978. 488p.

Items 1526-1550 comprise this extremely selective survey of books published about Romania. They include works on economics, government and politics, history, language, and literature.

775 **Southeastern Europe. A guide to basic publications.**
Edited by Paul L. Horecky. Chicago: University of Chicago Press, 1969. 755p.

This volume records basic books, periodicals, and articles of special relevance on the lands and peoples of Albania, Bulgaria, Greece, Romania, and Yugoslavia. The subject coverage in the Romanian section (p. 331-448) focuses on the political, socio-economic, and intellectual life in the countries listed. The bibliography includes works in Romanian and in the major West European languages with the emphasis being placed on English-language publications.

776 **The USSR and Eastern Europe: periodicals in Western languages.**
Paul L. Horecky, Robert G. Carlton. Washington, DC: US Government Printing Office, 1967. 89p.

A list of Western-language periodicals that offer specialist coverage of Eastern Europe, including Romania.

777 **European bibliography of Soviet, East European and Slavonic
studies.**
International Committee for Soviet and East European Studies,
Main library and Centre for Russian and East European Studies,
University of Birmingham, Centre d'Études sur l'URSS et
l'Europe orientale, École des Hautes Études en Sciences Sociales,
Paris. Birmingham, England: University of Birmingham, 1977-.
annual.

This bibliography incorporates two former national bibliographies of Soviet
Studies, *Travaux et publications parus en français en . . . sur la Russie et l'URSS*,
published in Cahiers du monde russe et soviétique for the years 1963-74, and
Soviet, East European and Slavonic Studies in Britain, published as a supplement
to ABSEES between 1971-74. The subject area is the USSR and the eight
communist countries of Eastern Europe, with emphasis on the social sciences and
arts. In each volume there are items originating from Britain, France, West
Germany, Belgium, Switzerland, and Austria.

778 **East Europe: bibliography index to US JPRS research translations.**
Compiled by Theodore E. Kyriak. Washington, DC: Research
Microfilms. monthly.

A unique guide to the US Joint Publications Research Service social science
publications and reports in which Romania is featured.

779 **The year's work in modern language studies.**
London: Modern Humanities Research Association, 1931-. annual.

The section on Romania in each volume provides an annual critical review of
selected books and articles published during the previous year on aspects of
Romanian language and literature.

780 **Periodicals on the socialist countries and on Marxism. A new
annotated index of English-language publications.**
Harry G. Shaffer. New York, London: Praeger, 1977. 135p.

A useful list of English-language periodicals published in sixteen communist
countries, including Romania.

781 **Bibliography for the study of the communist world.**
Michael Shafir, Galia Golan. Jerusalem: Akademon, 1971. 249p.

Compiled primarily for students of comparative communism and related topics
such as Soviet and East European foreign policy. It includes books and
periodicals in the libraries of the Hebrew University of Jerusalem in West
European languages.

782 **Bibliography of articles on East European and Russian history selected from English-language periodicals, 1850-1938.**
Manfred Späth, edited by Werner Philipp. Wiesbaden, GFR: Otto Harrassowitz for the Osteuropa-Institut, West Berlin, 1981. 98p. (Bibliographische Mitteilungen des Osteuropa-Instituts an der Freien Universität Berlin, vol. 20).

A small number of items on Romanian history are included in this list which contains an author index.

783 **Südosteuropa-Bibliographie.**
Südost-Institut, Munich. Munich: R. Oldenbourg Verlag. 1956. 5 vols. in progress.

This invaluable selective bibliography on publications in and on Southeastern Europe includes significant sections on Romania. Volume 1, covering the years 1945-50, lists 515 Romanian items, volume 2, part 2 (1951-55) contains 1,319 Romanian entries, volume 3, part 1 (1956-60), has 3,035 Romanian works, volume 4, part 1 (1961-65) 3136 entries, volume 5, part 1 (1966-70) 3648 entries. There are no annotations of items listed.

784 **East European languages and literatures, II.**
Garth M. Terry. Nottingham, England: Astra Press, 1982. xxviii + 214p.

The subtitle of this bibliography is 'A Subject and Name index to articles in Festschriften, Conference Proceedings, and Collected Papers in the English language, 1978-1981, and including articles in journals, 1978-1981'. The total number of entries is 4,619 and many relate to Romanian language and literature. English-language periodicals in Romania are excluded, thus articles by non-Romanian scholars published in such journals are not listed.

785 **Books on communism and the communist countries.**
Edited by P. H. Vigor. London: Ampersand, 1971. 444p.

A selected and annotated bibliography of studies in English, principally on the USSR. The section on Romania lists only fourteen titles.

786 **Official publications of the Soviet Union and Eastern Europe, 1945-1980. A select annotated bibliography.**
Edited by Gregory Walker. London: Mansell, 1982. 620p.

A work that provides the first extensive and annotated guide to those documents of State that regulate life in the countries of Eastern Europe, and publicize and justify the views and policies of their leaders. The section on Romania (p. 221-62), compiled by Brian Hunter, is preceded by a brief historical introduction and contains some 270 entries on constitutional documents, law codes, statistics, economic planning, and international relations, many of which are in English.

Specialized

787 **Hungarians in Rumania and Transylvania: a bibliographical list of publications in Hungarian and West European languages compiled from the holdings of the Library of Congress.**
Elemer Baka, William Sólyom-Fekete. Washington, DC: Library of Congress, 1969. 192p.

An extremely useful list of materials relating to the Hungarians in Transylvania, a province which has been part of Romania since 1920. It includes many items in English on this significant minority.

788 **Bibliographie zur Landeskunde der Bukowina. Literatur bis zum Jahre 1965.** (Bibliography of the Bukovina province. Publications to 1965.)
Erich Beck. Munich: Verlag des Südostdeutschen Kulturwerks, 1966. 378p. (Veröffentlichungen des Südostdeutschen Kulturwerks. Reihe B. 19).

A list of 7,371 items, chiefly in German, relating to the history, geography, literature, and other aspects of this region.

789 **Bibliografia românească veche, 1508-1830.** (Early Romanian bibliography, 1508-1830.)
Ioan Bianu, Nerva Hodoş, Dan Simonescu. Bucharest: Academia română, 1903-44. 4 vols.

The standard reference work on the early printed book in Romania. It includes bibliographic descriptions, facsimiles of title-pages, prefaces, dedications, colophons, and engravings.

790 **Bibliografia generală a etnografiei şi folclorului românesc. Vol. 1. 1800-1891.** (A general bibliography of Romanian ethnography and folklore. Vol. 1, 1800-1891.)
Institutul de etnografie şi folclor al Academiei Republicii Socialiste România. Bucharest: Editura pentru literatură, 1968. 739p.

A comprehensive bibliography of literature on folklore and ethnography published in Moldavia, Wallachia, and Transylvania during the period indicated. The entries are arranged by author under the headings: general, ethnography, demography and anthropology, folk art, folklore, performances and performers of folklore, and foreign folklore. Volume 2 is still awaited.

191

791 **Bibliografia militară românească.** (Romanian military bibliography.)

Bucharest: Biblioteca centrală a ministerului apărării naţionale. 3 vols. 1975.

A selective bibliography listing, by author or title, books, periodicals, regulations, and laws relating to the Romanian armed forces from 1831 to 1973. Volume 1 presents an alphabetical list of 1,842 items published between 1831 and 1913, volume 2 covers 1914 to 1944 with 3,688 items, and volume 3 lists 1,322 books from the years 1944 to 1973, and 228 periodicals from the period 1859 to 1973. Each volume contains a thematic, author, and chronological index.

792 **Tratat de bibliografie.** (Treatise on bibliography.)

Gheorghe Cardaş. Bucharest: Tipografia Bucovina, 1931. 380p.

In spite of its age, the list of Romanian bibliographies contained in the section Bibliografia bibliografiilor româneşti (Bibliography of Romanian bibliographies) is invaluable to the scholar since it contains descriptions of 506 general and specialist bibliographies, several of which have been overlooked by more modern compilations.

793 **The independence of Romania: selected bibliography.**

Bucharest: Editura Academiei Republicii Socialiste România, 1980. 130p.

An annotated list of 701 international publications relating to the Russo-Turkish War of 1877-78, better known in Romania as 'the war of independence' because, during its course, the Romanian parliament proclaimed the independence of the country (May 1877). The Russo-Romanian victory over the Turks at Plevna sealed this independence.

794 **Anglo-Roumanian and Roumanian-English bibliography.**

Octav Păduraru. Bucharest: Monitorul Oficial şi Imprimeriile Statului, 1946. 244p.

A unique list of over 9,000 items, many of which are not in English, nor by British or American scholars. It includes articles from journals, most of which are not available in Western libraries.

795 **East European peasantries: social relations. An annotated bibliography of periodical articles.**

Compiled by I. T. Sanders, R. Whitaker, W. C. Bisselle. Boston, Massachusetts: G. K. Hall, 1976. 179p.

A bibliography of a 30 volume collection of periodical articles at the Mugar library in Boston University. Articles relating to Romania are presented on p. 105-23.

796 **Some recent literature on Romania's role in the First World War.**
Glenn Torrey. *East European Quarterly*, vol. 14, no. 2 (summer
1980), p. 189-206.

A bibliographical essay listing over 100 titles which treat aspects of Romania's
history during the First World War. The emphasis is on works in Romanian
although a number of significant contributions in other languages are mentioned.

797 **Bibliografia română-ungară.** (Romanian-Hungarian bibliography.)
Andrei (Endre) Veress. Bucharest: Cartea Românească, 1931-35.
3 vols.

The standard bibliography of literature on the Romanian presence in Hungarian
culture and vice versa. It is divided chronologically as follows: volume 1, 1473-
1780; volume 2, 1781-1838, and volume 3, 1839-1878. It includes a number of
items in German and English and is indexed by author, publisher, and printer.

Index

The index is a single alphabetical sequence of authors (personal and corporate), titles of publications and subjects. Index entries refer both to main items and to other works mentioned in the notes to each item. Title entries are in italics. Numeration refers to the items as numbered.

196

198

201

202

203

205

216

222

226

229

Map of Romania

This map shows the more important towns and other features.

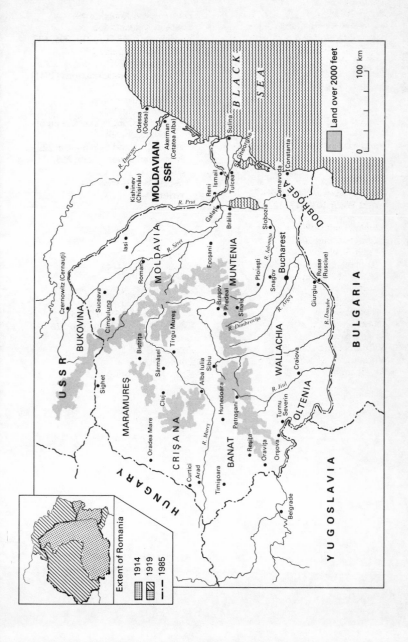